POSITIVE DISCIPLINE

THE FIRST THREE YEARS

POSITIVE DISCIPLINE

THE FIRST THREE YEARS

Revised and Updated Edition

JANE NELSEN, ED.D., CHERYL ERWIN, M.A., AND ROSLYN ANN DUFFY

HARMONY
BOOKS · NEW YORK

Published in the United States by Harmony Books, an imprint of the Crown
Publishing Group, a division of Random House LLC, a Penguin Random House
Company, New York.

www.crownpublishing.com

Harmony Books is a registered trademark, and the Circle colophon is a
trademark of Random House LLC.

Originally published in hardcover in the United States by Prima Publishing, Rocklin,
CA, in 1998. Subsequent edition published by Harmony Books, an imprint of the
Crown Publishing Group, a division of Random House LLC, New York, in 2007.

Library of Congress Cataloging-in-Publication Data
Nelsen, Jane.
  Positive discipline : the first three years / by Jane Nelsen, Cheryl Erwin, and Roslyn
    Ann Duffy.
      pages   cm
  Revised edition of the authors' Positive discipline : the first three years : from
    infant to toddler—laying the foundation for raising a capable, confident child.
  Includes bibliographical references.
  1. Discipline of children. 2. Toddlers—Discipline. 3. Parenting. 4. Child
    rearing. I. Erwin, Cheryl. II. Duffy, Roslyn. III. Title.
  HQ770.4.N437 2014
  649'.122—dc23   2014045390

ISBN 978-0-8041-4118-5
eBook ISBN 978-0-8041-4119-2

Printed in the United States of America

Illustrations by Paula Gray
Jacket design by Nupoor Gordon
Jacket photographs: (left to right) Rubberball/Getty Images; Gelpi JM/Shutterstock;
Joakim Leroy/E+/Getty Images

10 9

Revised Edition

CONTENTS

CONTENTS

INTRODUCTION

PARENTS HAVE BEEN raising children since the dawn of time. You might wonder what could have changed in the sixteen years since *Positive Discipline: The First Three Years* was originally published. The basic Positive Discipline concepts remain the same. Still, we discovered through our own studies and work with families that much of what we know and understand about young children has indeed grown and shifted in recent years. There is now more and more brain research that validates what we teach, and the world we live in has changed, too—9/11 and technology being two examples.

Many things will never change: young children will always need unconditional love, encouragement, skills, supervision—and lots of patience. In other areas, however, we are still learning. Technology has become more sophisticated—and more invasive—and we do not yet fully understand its impact on young children and their families. Parents have shared new stories with us—and we are happy to share them with you. We are grateful to have the opportunity to update and revise this book so it can be even more useful to parents just setting out on the amazing and sometimes challenging journey of parenting.

Some parents have commented over the years on the title of this book. "How," they ask, "can you even talk about discipline in the first years of life? Why would parents need to punish infants and toddlers?" As you read, you will discover that we do not advocate punishment at all, for any age. Instead, we believe in discipline that teaches young children in a kind, respectful, and gentle manner; discipline that imparts valuable social and life skills as a foundation for success in relationships and in life itself. Punishment is designed to make kids "pay" for their mistakes (even when they are not truly mistakes but come under the heading of "developmentally appropriate behavior"). Positive Discipline is designed to help children *learn* from their mistakes in a loving and supportive atmosphere.

Above all, we believe in loving, connected relationships that form the enduring bond between a parent and his or her child. A new and important theme of Positive Discipline is "connection before correction." The connection you create with your little one is by far your most valuable parenting tool; everything else depends on the quality of the relationship you share together. When we hear parents say, "Well, that Positive Discipline tool didn't work," we have to wonder if these parents are using the tools to win power struggles or if they truly understand the principles behind the tools—the foremost of which is that connection always comes first.

In this edition we place greater emphasis on the beliefs children are forming about themselves based on their perceptions of their daily experiences: these beliefs provide the fuel for their behavior. Children who grow up in an environment of excessive control or an environment of permissiveness will form different beliefs than those who are raised in an environment of kindness and firmness at the same time. Understanding the "belief behind the behavior" is foundational to understanding how to motivate change—and accepting that it might take as long to help children change their beliefs as it took to form those beliefs in the first place. Positive Discipline is not about quick fixes but about creating an environment where children can make healthy decisions that will serve them throughout their lives.

As parents who have raised families and watched their children embark on their own lives and journeys, we can tell you that what remains, after all the tantrums, sleepless nights, mistakes, and worries that come with raising little ones are done, is *love*. When all else fails and you don't know what to do, fall back on love. Love and your own inner wisdom will help you know what to do.

It is our hope that this book will become a valuable friend and guide as you share these busy and exciting years with your child. Don't be afraid to ask questions or to learn new skills and ideas. It takes courage to raise a child; it also takes courage to *be* one. Take time to savor these first three wonderful years; they will pass all too quickly.

PROLOGUE:

By the Children

"I am Serena. I am three months old. I know my mother's voice, I look for her face, and I love to snuggle when she picks me up. I like to drink my milk. I cry when she isn't ready to give me my milk on time. When my mother rocks me to sleep, I like to look around. I like to take my bath but I don't like it when she washes my hair or face. I like it when people talk to me, laugh out loud, and play with me. I want to hold my toys—but I can't yet. I like to go out every day because I want to know what is going on. I watch everything."

"I'm James. I turned two in December. I want to do every-thing myself. I don't want any help. I like to do things my own way, even if it takes longer, and if you try to help we have to start all over. If you try putting on my sock, I have to pull it off and do it myself. That is much more important to me than whether I got it on backward. I keep wishing everybody 'Happy Birthday.' Sometimes I scream. I can't talk too well—I *have a hard time getting everything out. But I've learned one word that's very powerful: No."*

"I am Jose. Next month I will be one year old. I laugh all the time. I like to get my way. I love to eat. Food is my favorite thing—especially big people's food, but I don't like squash. I am learning to walk. I get a lot of bumps and bruises. I like to chase my cat around the house. Maybe I love him too tight, because he bit my hand yesterday. My favorite words are 'ma-ma,' 'da-da,' 'good,' and 'baby.'"

"My name is Bonnie and I am eight months old today. I have two teeth and an older sister. I love to flap my arms when I am happy. I invented a fun game. My mom gives me paper and I eat it up, and she has to fish it out of my mouth. Then I grin. We play this game with lots of things. We play this game all the time with the pebbles at the beach and anything else I can find to put in my mouth. Mommy stays real busy searching my mouth. It is fun."

We are babies and toddlers. This book is all about us. The children you know may be like us in some ways. This book takes a peek into our world—or what the world looks like as we lie on tables getting our diapers changed. It's about what we might be thinking when we grab for the shiny things on store shelves, or why we sometimes refuse to go to sleep at night, eat our peas, or use the potty. Learning to understand our world will give you lots of ideas about how to help us grow and how to encourage and teach us. We're newcomers in this world and we need your help all the time. We are lovable, time-consuming, and often messy. And there is no one like us in the whole world. This book is for those who love us most.

SECTION ONE

LIFE WITH BABY

WELCOMING BABY

What You Need to Know in the First Few Months

The birth of a baby is a momentous occasion, a landmark event never forgotten by those who have experienced it. A new parent may be shocked by the news that a baby is on the way, or thrilled that the days of pregnancy tests and "trying" are finally over. Either way, there is no ignoring this life-changing bit of news. Your life as an independent, spontaneous person will change: Baby is on the way.

Most adults find that adding an infant to the family, no matter how anticipated and dearly loved that infant may be, brings changes that take some getting used to. Adult relationships must flex and adapt, making room for the new addition. Schedules and priorities change, as does Mom's body. Babies can be perplexing little people, operating by rules known only to them—and each comes with his own unique set of rules. Some parents are blessed with an "easy" first baby, and are then

shocked and mystified when their second baby is not so easy. Others begin with a "challenging" baby, and are pleasantly surprised when their second baby is "easier."

The first few months of your new baby's life may be exhausting, exhilarating, and challenging, all at once. It may be hard to believe, but one day you will look back at these demanding days and sleepless nights with nostalgia and realize your child grew up much too fast. But for now, those musings lie far in the future.

SETTING THE STAGE FOR BABY

Close your eyes for just a moment and think back to the first time you saw your newborn's face. She may have been red, bald, and wrinkled, but chances are you felt you'd never seen anything more beautiful, or heard anything sweeter than her first cries. Writers and painters have tried to capture the magic of those first moments of life, but words and pictures are rarely powerful enough to convey what happens between parent and child.

For most parents, the months leading up to that miraculous moment of birth are filled with plans, dreams, and a few worries. In reflective moments, you probably wondered whether you would be a good parent, whether you'd know what to do, whether the baby would be "all right." Expectant parents talk endlessly about the relative merits of cloth and disposable diapers, of nursing and formula feeding, of store-bought and homemade baby food. They discuss names for hours, saying them aloud to see how they fit.

New parents buy and are given impossibly tiny garments and mysterious articles with odd names like "receiving blanket." They wonder if they'll somehow know what to do with them (both the babies and the blankets) when the time comes. They purchase and ponder over the fascinating gadgetry of babyhood: car seats, carriers, cribs, pacifiers, bottles, breast pumps, and monitors. The grandparents "tsk, tsk" as they point out that millions of children were raised without all these fancy gadgets, or they rush out to buy even more dazzling ones. In this age of consumerism, with so many adorable clothes and such tempting equipment available, who can possibly resist? This is a time for endless dreaming, a time for hope and wonder.

FANTASY VERSUS REALITY

Sometimes, though, when you carry that helpless little bundle of humanity home from the hospital, the dreams fade a bit in the harsh light of reality. The baby cries, sometimes for hours, and it's up to you to figure out why. Or the little darling sleeps all day then gurgles happily all night, much to the dismay of his sleep-deprived parents. Babies seem to be born with a detector that lets them know when Mom wants to eat, so they can interrupt with a need of their own. The baby spits up when you're dressed to go out, may have several bowel movements in a single night, and sometimes cries angrily when handed to eager relatives.

From those first moments, parenting young children can become an avalanche of questions, anxieties, and frustrations, as well as an incredible source of love and joy. As that precious baby grows, develops, and changes, life can become a seemingly endless stream of challenging decisions and new ideas to be tested.

As your child grows, people in public places may smile knowingly or talk about the "terrible twos." Many parents feel completely at the mercy of the adorable little tyrant their baby or toddler has become, while others seem confident and at ease handling meltdowns or constant interruptions.

HOW WILL I KNOW WHAT TO DO?

Most of us learn parenting skills from our parents or by trial and error. You may not like the way you were raised and vow to be different from your own parents, or you see others raising children and disagree with their choices. (Judging the parenting choices of others has become an international pastime.) But what should you do instead? You don't want to be too strict, but is permissiveness the only alternative? You don't want to be overly controlling—but how do you create order and consistency? You may worry that your mistakes will have too high a cost.

You have so many questions: Do I spank my child or not? If spanking is okay, how soon should I start? How do I communicate with an infant who doesn't understand words? How do I get my child to listen? How do I handle a defiant toddler? How do I decide what's really important? How can I help my child develop a sense of self-worth, while teaching her responsibility, honesty, and kindness? How do I take care of myself so I can relax and enjoy this experience?

Advice is in plentiful supply—grandparents, uncles, and aunts (and the lady behind you in line at the grocery store) will have lots of it—but whose advice is right? Even the "experts" disagree. Some suggest punishment (even in the poorly disguised form of logical consequences), while others (including the authors and the latest brain research) suggest that punishment is not effective. Some claim rewards are important. Others (including the authors and many researchers) believe rewards teach manipulation and a reduced sense of self-worth instead of valuable social and life skills. It is our hope as authors, and as parents, that you will find answers in this book that will make sense to you, as well as clues to help you use your own wisdom, creativity, and knowledge of your child to go beyond what can be written in words.

This book is designed to be of use to both parents and their frequent partners in child rearing: childcare teachers, nannies, sitters, and relatives. Examples of home and childcare situations will be given throughout this book to show how the principles of Positive Discipline can be applied to all aspects of a young child's life.* Developmental information and research will be included wherever appropriate, along with information about the way babies and young children grow and

---

* If you have specific questions about childcare, find a copy of *Positive Discipline for Childcare Providers* by Jane Nelsen and Cheryl Erwin (New York: Three Rivers Press, 2002).

learn. Because it can be immensely helpful for all the adults who influence a child's life to have the same understanding about how to raise him, you may want to share this book with the staff at your childcare center, your babysitter, or other members of your family.

YOUR FAMILY IS YOUR FAMILY

All families, like all children, are different. Not all babies are born into two-parent families with a home in the suburbs, two cars, and a family dog. Your family may indeed look like that, or it may take a different shape altogether. You may be a single parent, through divorce or death or because you never married; you and your partner may have brought children from previous relationships, and added those you have had together; you may have live-in grandparents or other relatives; or you may share a home with friends and their children. You may be part of the LGBT community, or a particular ethnic group with its own valued traditions. In the end, what matters is the connection you build with your child and your commitment to respectful, effective parenting.

A family, it has been said, is a circle of people who love one another. ***Whatever form your family takes, remember that it will be whatever you have the courage to make it.*** With wisdom, patience, and love, you can create a home where your child feels safe, secure, and free to grow and learn, and where she can become a responsible, respectful, and resourceful person—and where you will find joy in your parenting role.

WHAT DO YOU WANT FOR YOUR CHILD?
THE IMPORTANCE OF LONG-TERM PARENTING

Life with an active toddler can make you feel like you're on a runaway train. The days zoom past, each one filled with new marvels, new discoveries, new crises. Parents often have to scurry to keep up with their young offspring and sometimes have little time available for thoughtful planning. But think for a moment: Wouldn't it be helpful, as you set out on the journey of parenting, to have some idea of your final destination?

Perhaps one of the wisest things you can do right now is to take a moment to ask yourself a very important question: What is it that I really want for my child? When your baby, your toddler, or your preschooler has grown into an adult (as impossible as that may seem now), what qualities and characteristics do you want this adult to have? You may decide that you want your child to develop responsibility, resilience, honesty, compassion, self-reliance, courage, and gratitude—each parent's list will be a little different. What truly matters is this: From your child's earliest moments of life, the decisions you make as a parent will help shape his future. Each and every action you take—whether or not you slap your child's hand as he reaches for a delicate object, how you deal with food thrown across the kitchen, or how you respond to bedtime demands—can nurture or discourage those qualities you want to promote. Your child is constantly making decisions about himself and the world, and how to find belonging and significance in that world. These decisions are based on how he interprets his experiences in life, and they create his "blueprint" for living. Your actions and beliefs will have a strong influence on his decisions.

This idea feels overwhelming to most parents. You may be wondering, "What if I make mistakes? How will I know what to do?" Please, be reassured: *Mistakes are not insurmountable failures, but valuable opportunities to learn.* (Seeing mistakes as opportunities to learn is a fundamental concept of Positive Discipline.) Trying to protect your child from all mistakes is detrimental to learning resilience and developing a sense of capability. Both you and your child will make many mistakes along the way, but they needn't cause irreparable damage if you're willing to learn from them together. The most valuable parenting tools are those you already possess: your love for your child and your own inner wisdom and common sense. Learning to trust these instincts will carry you far along the road to successful parenting.

Remember, too, that children, especially very young children, learn by watching and imitating those around them. Your little one not only will want to push the vacuum or wash the dishes the way Mom, Dad, or Grandma does, but also will imitate the values you live by, such as honesty, kindness, and justice. When you use mistakes as opportunities to learn, your children will absorb this valuable attitude. Let your actions as a parent teach your child that he or she is loved and respected, that choices have consequences (not the kind you impose, but the kind you can help her explore), and that home is a safe and wonderful place to be.

A WORD ABOUT LOVE

Many things are done to children (or withheld from children) in the name of love. "I spank my children because I love them," parents say. Or "I rescue and overprotect my children because I love them." "I love my children, so I don't help them much—they need to learn it's a tough world out there." "I push my children (in toilet training, or early reading, or sports activities, or academic excellence) because I love them." "I work long hours because I love my children and I want them to have everything I never had." "I make decisions for my children because I love them too much to risk letting them make wrong choices." In this book, you will have an opportunity to explore the long-term effects of what you do in the name of love.

Parents often say that they feel overwhelmed by the intensity of their love for their children, and it is tempting to demonstrate that love by allowing children to do, say, and especially *have* whatever they want. Your eighteen-month-old may be cute and adorable *now* when he grabs your smartphone out of your hands to play a game. You may even giggle when he tries out the four-letter word he learned from his older brother. Will it still be cute when he's five and does the same things?

Actually, whether you love your child is not the question. The real issue is whether you can show that love in ways that nurture accountability and a sense of capability, and that encourage your child to blossom into his full potential as a happy, contributing member of society. Eventually, most parents realize that ***genuine love requires that they love their children enough to set wise boundaries, to say no when they must, and to help them learn to live peacefully and respectfully in a world filled with other people.***

FIRM, FLEXIBLE, AND GENTLE

Imagine a tree, its roots anchoring it deep into the ground. Far above, at the tips of its slender branches, rests a bird's nest. In that nest are one or more tiny, fragile eggs. When the wind blows, the tree's branches sway in gentle arcs, but its grip on that small nest remains firm.

This image of gentleness combined with flexibility and firmness translates well to the task of parenting young children, and forms the foundation for many of the principles you will learn throughout this book. You can stand with your feet (or values) firmly rooted while still guiding your child with steady, gentle hands and a kind voice. This is not an easy task; it requires patience, energy, and boundless hope.

REDEFINING "WE" AND "ME": CARE FOR PARENTS

Adding "parent" to your definition of who you are means adding all sorts of new roles and responsibilities. It may also mean rearranging some of the roles you already have. One study found that many cou-

ples who had previously reported being happily married experienced a sharp drop in marital satisfaction after the arrival of a baby. Why?

Parents who are contented, healthy, and relatively well rested (being tired seems to be an unavoidable part of raising young children) will cope best with the challenges of these early months and years. If you are a single parent who must handle it all, there is even more reason to take special care of yourself. If you have a partner, remember that your relationship is the foundation of your family; invest the time and energy it takes to keep it strong.

A couple can easily lose sight of their relationship in the headlong rush to care for their baby. Mom nurses the baby; her partner feels left out or a little jealous—and guilty for having those feelings. One parent wants a little snuggling, while the other is "too tired." One parent is dying for dinner and a movie out; the other doesn't trust the babysitter or spends the evening texting every fifteen minutes to make sure everything is okay. And sex? Baby seems to possess a sixth sense that tells her just when adults are contemplating a little intimacy—and that's precisely when she feels hungry or damp and squalls to alert her frustrated parents.

Taking time to cherish a partner as well as meeting your individual needs isn't selfishness or bad parenting—it's wisdom. If you do not have a partner, connecting with other adults will give you a valuable energy boost. Your child will learn to respect and value the needs and feelings of others by watching the choices you make. Be sure you leave time each week for activities you enjoy and that nurture your physical and emotional health, whether it's laughing with a neighbor over a cup of tea, a "date night" out with your partner, or a morning walk (perhaps with the baby along in a backpack or stroller). Redefining "we" and "me" is an ongoing process rather than an intellectual activity. An older child who feels sad, a partner who feels ignored, and a parent who feels lonely for adult companionship are all responding typically to this change in the family. Sometimes what is most needed is simply time to express painful feelings so that love, joy, and connection can be rekindled. Remember, too, that feelings can serve as useful reminders to take care of yourself and those you love. By honoring your own emotions and those of other family members, you can focus on discovering solutions to the problems you face, enabling you to enjoy life more fully.

PARENTING PARTNERS

If you are a single parent, you can raise a happy, healthy child alone (pick up a copy of *Positive Discipline for Single Parents* to learn more), but if you're lucky enough to be part of a loving parenting team, make the most of it. Raising your young child can be more enjoyable and less frustrating when you make use of the resources and wisdom of those you trust and who share in caring for your child. Grandparents, aunts, and uncles can be invaluable resources. Your child will benefit from what each person has to give, while forming wonderful lifelong memories. If you do not have relatives and friends close by, consider looking for other means of support.*

Parents will rarely agree all the time about how to raise their children. One may favor firmness, while the other prefers kindness—and sometimes, each parent takes his or her view to extremes. One excellent solution is to read and discuss this book, or take parenting classes together, so you can raise your child as a cooperative team, learning to be both kind and firm at the same time.†

Resist the temptation to label caregiving tasks so that one parent feels like an assistant. Have you ever heard someone say, "My husband is watching the kids for me"? Aren't they his children, too? How about: "I don't know how to give her a bath (feed her, change her diaper, and so on). Her mom's the expert on that!" **Remember that practice makes better (not necessarily perfect)—and better is usually plenty good enough.** In generations past, parenting, especially of infants and toddlers, was assumed to be a woman's job. These days, however, research tells us that men are far more involved with all aspects of parenting—and children are the beneficiaries.

Wise parents know that parenting is a partnership and when parents treat it as such, the real winners will be their children. Sure,

---

* Chapter 21 contains suggestions for establishing a support community.

† If your partner does not have time to read a book, he or she may enjoy listening to "Positive Discipline: Birth to Five," a two-hour lecture by Jane Nelsen, available at www.positivediscipline.com.

parents, grandparents, or other care-givers have different styles. The great news is that those differences can be a real plus for your child, who will learn skills for interacting with different kinds of people. Children often learn to change their behavior depending on the different parenting styles they encounter. This is particularly true for the different ways in which men and women tend to handle and interact with children.

Watch a mom greet her child. She may wrap her arms around little Justin or cuddle baby Megan against her chest, showering her soft head with kisses. Then watch Dad greet these same little ones. When Dad says "hi" to Justin, he swoops him into the air, holding him at arm's length as Justin squeals and giggles with delight. His greeting to Megan often begins with blowing raspberries on her round belly and laughing as she squirms with plea-sure. These tendencies toward either active or nurturing interactions provide unique benefits.

Physical stimulation is great for brain development and encourages healthy risk-taking. *(Warning: Never shake or toss a young baby or leave her head unsupported! And keep in mind that tickling may feel like tor-ture to a young child, even though he*

Colic

Some babies seem to fuss, cry, or scream for no apparent reason for long periods at a stretch, particularly around dinnertime. If your baby cries or screams excessively, by all means check with your doctor to be sure there is no medical reason for her behav-ior. Many times, however, the doctor will say, "There is nothing seriously wrong. It's just colic." It is reassuring to know that your child is not in physical danger, but it is still extremely frustrating when you can't seem to comfort your child.

What is colic, anyway? No one seems to know. The Mayo Clinic (www.mayoclinic.com) describes colic as crying for more than three hours a day, three days a week, for more than three weeks, in an otherwise healthy and well-fed infant. Colicky babies can appear inconsolable (and often draw their tiny legs up as though in terrible pain). What can you do? First, remember that it doesn't last for-ever. Also, don't look for blame. Try to remain calm and connected as you rock, burp, walk the floor with, and offer a pacifier to your little one, holding your arms tightly (but not too tightly) around his tummy. Unfortunately, none of these methods is guaranteed to work for long. It helps if you have the luxury of a partner or relative who will take turns trying to help you all through this miserable time.

laughs—until he cries.) Cuddling supports a child's sense of well-being, safety, and security. Also, research has demonstrated that a father's more active style of playing with his baby may actually help her learn self-awareness ("Is this fun?" "Am I getting tired?" "How do I let him know that I want to stop?") and begin communicating her feelings and needs to the adults around her. If you are attuned to your little one and are paying attention to her cues and signals, you will be able to decide how best to offer her that critical sense of belonging and connection, and how to respond appropriately to her needs.

SLEEPING: "SHHHH . . . THE BABY IS ASLEEP!"

One of the first issues new parents face is the challenge of helping their baby create a consistent sleep pattern. Most babies spend more time asleep than awake during the first few months of their lives—though that may seem hard to believe. Power struggles over sleeping can be avoided if you allow your child to learn to fall asleep by herself as early in her life as possible. This means putting her in her crib just *before* she falls asleep. (We know this isn't always possible with tiny babies who doze off after a few sucks on the bottle or breast, but making an effort will promote healthy sleep patterns.)

Some parents find they are afraid to lay down a drowsy or sleeping baby for fear of waking her, but waking up and being allowed to go back to sleep after a little fussing is fine. Adults often try to take responsibility for getting the baby to sleep and then managing the environment to keep him asleep ("Shh! The baby is *asleep!*" they anxiously stage-whisper), then feel guilty, frustrated, or annoyed when they fail to ensure uninterrupted snooze time.

Do your best to establish good sleeping habits as soon as you can—and be aware that an infant's schedule is often unpredictable for the first month or two of her life. (We will talk about sleep in more detail in Chapter 13.)

NURSING

Feeding is also one of the first challenges you will face with your baby. Not all mothers can (or choose to) nurse, and you can build a strong, loving connection with your baby no matter how you feed him. Still, many mothers want to nurse, or believe they should, and find that it's more difficult than they had hoped. Listen to Jane's story about nursing her firstborn:

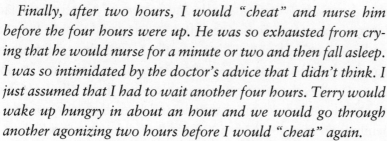

How I wish I'd had more information on nursing from the beginning; I wouldn't have created so much pain for myself and my children as I learned. My first child was born when doctors were advocating a strict feeding schedule of every four hours. I just assumed they must know what they were talking about. Baby Terry would nurse for a short time and fall asleep. Often, during the afternoon, he would wake up after an hour and start crying. I would think, "Oh no! Three more hours before he can nurse." I would walk the floor with him and try to comfort him, but he would just cry until he was screaming. I tried pacifiers and water. They might work for a few minutes but soon he would be screaming again. (It is painful for me to even remember this.)

Finally, after two hours, I would "cheat" and nurse him before the four hours were up. He was so exhausted from crying that he would nurse for a minute or two and then fall asleep. I was so intimidated by the doctor's advice that I didn't think. I just assumed that I had to wait another four hours. Terry would wake up hungry in about an hour and we would go through another agonizing two hours before I would "cheat" again.

Because of my lack of information about nursing, I believed that if my breasts weren't engorged, I didn't have any milk, that my milk must not be rich enough because it wasn't "milky white," and that Terry cried because I didn't have enough milk. The truth was that he cried because he wasn't nursing long enough to get enough nourishment and to build up my milk supply in the process. I gave up in frustration after three weeks and put him (and three succeeding children) on a bottle.

When my fifth child, Lisa, was born, I tried nursing again. I was on my way to failure once more when my sister-in-law told me about La Leche League (www.lalecheleague.org), which has offered support to nursing mothers for many years. She told me there was no such thing as bad mother's milk and that I should throw away all the formula bottles and supplemental foods and just nurse whenever my baby wanted to in order to build up my milk supply. I read the book, threw away the bottles and solid foods, and began a successful nursing experience.

I loved nursing on demand. Sometimes Lisa would nurse as often as every hour—or sometimes every fifteen minutes! By the time she was three and a half months old, she had regulated herself to a three-hour schedule during the day and would sleep through the night, even without cereal to "fill her up."

Most mothers find they occasionally have questions about nursing, feeding, bottles, and their babies' nutritional needs. One of the wisest things mothers can do is to begin right away to build a support and resource network. Many hospitals and maternity centers have lactation specialists; in fact, some even offer websites and twenty-four-hour phone lines to call when you have questions. Churches, childcare centers, and pediatricians may have information on new mothers' support groups, as well as the many online resources out there, all of which can be invaluable in answering questions and boosting your confidence. Remember, no question is ever "stupid." Decide what works best for you and your infant, ask for help when you need it, and have confidence in your own wisdom and growing knowledge of your baby.

GETTING THE HELP YOU NEED

All parents have questions and concerns. Fortunately, parent education and training is finally gaining wide acceptance and credibility. Society has never questioned the need for education and training in occupational fields, be it bricklaying or accounting, but somewhere along the line the notion got planted that parenting should come "naturally" and that attending a parenting class or reading a book on parenting was an admission of inadequacy.

These days, parents are reading books, connecting through social media, and attending parenting workshops—and they testify that what they learn helps them enjoy the important job of parenting as their children learn more self-discipline, responsibility, cooperation, and problem-solving skills. Often, simply knowing that others share your concerns will help you feel less isolated. When you make mistakes, you will know how to correct them, and you will be able to teach your children that mistakes provide wonderful opportunities to learn. (We can't say it often enough!)

PARENTING FROM THE HEART

Parenting groups (and parenting books) are great ways to learn new skills and ideas and to get a little moral support along the way. But when all is said and done, parenting is a matter of the heart and spirit, as well as of training and knowledge. Perhaps the greatest parenting skill of all is the ability to feel an unbreakable bond of love and warmth for your child, and to be able to listen to the voice of love and wisdom even when your patience has been stretched to the breaking point. The next time you tuck your little one in at night, let your gaze rest on that sleeping face; print it firmly in your memory. When you're confronted with a hysterical infant, a defiant toddler, or an angry preschooler (and there will be many such times as the years roll by), close your eyes for just a moment and look in your memory for the face of your sleeping child. Then let that love and tenderness give you the wisdom to deal with the crisis at hand.

The best parenting translates love from words into thoughtful, effective action. There is a popular children's book by Robert Munsch titled *Love You Forever*. In this little gem, a mother watches her infant sleep and croons to him, "I'll love you forever, I'll like you for always. As long as I'm living, my baby you'll be." As that child grows from baby to challenging toddler to awkward adolescent, the mother creeps into her son's room at night to watch him sleep and to croon that same little song.

The day comes at last when the mother lies dying, and the son sits by her bedside to sing the old song to her. When he returns home, he shares the song—and the bond of love—with his newborn baby daughter. That feeling—that indescribable tenderness and warmth that a parent feels for a sleeping child—is the heart of parenting.

There will be ample room in the chapters ahead for information, tips, and techniques, but remember that **it is always the relationship between parent and child that matters most.** If that relationship is based on unconditional love and trust—if your child knows from his earliest days that you love him no matter what—you'll probably do just fine.

QUESTIONS TO PONDER

1. Make a list of the qualities, skills, and character attributes you consider most important for an adult to have. Invite your partner or others involved with caring for your child to make a list, too. Acknowledge the attributes you feel you have. How can you learn and strengthen the qualities you may lack? How will you teach these attributes to your child?

2. Make a list of things that make you laugh, give you joy, or keep you healthy. Resolve to do at least one thing from that list each day to take care of yourself.

3. If you are parenting with a partner, decide together to devote time each week to your relationship. What will you do with your time? How will you learn to parent together while keeping your own love strong? If you are parenting alone, give thought to how you can build a support network for yourself.

2

POSITIVE DISCIPLINE PRINCIPLES FOR YOUR FAMILY

The Philosophy

I n the first weeks and months of a baby's life, discipline is unlikely to be one of your top priorities. Instead, as you've seen, parents are usually focused on welcoming their little one to the family, building a relationship, understanding his cries, and meeting his needs. Before you know it, however, that cuddly infant will become a toddler with a mind of his own. How will you shape and guide his behavior? What does he need from you and his other caregivers to grow into a capable, resourceful, confident young person?

There is a popular cartoon that shows a mother talking to her child. "Honey," she says, "when you're older, I want you to be confident, assertive, and independent. But right now I want you to be compliant, quiet, and obedient." Most parents know the feeling: **The very same qualities that we want for our children** *as adults can make life challenging when they're young.*

Simply put, the word "discipline" means "to teach." Positive Discipline is the most loving kind of teaching. It involves nurturing trust and connection, sharing skills, and creating an environment where your child can develop feelings of capability and confidence. This sort of discipline begins from your child's earliest moments and becomes increasingly important as he journeys toward autonomy and initiative. A toddler's behavior may not always look (or sound) particularly attractive, and can mystify and astonish even the most devoted parent.

Even if you understand and accept that some of this behavior is "developmentally appropriate," what should you do if it's not *acceptable* behavior? It is helpful to know that Positive Discipline will provide you with effective, nonpunitive tools and skills to guide your child's behavior as he grows.

ADLER AND DREIKURS: PIONEERS IN PARENTING

Positive Discipline is based on the work of Alfred Adler and one of his colleagues, Rudolf Dreikurs. Adler was a Viennese psychiatrist and a contemporary of Sigmund Freud—but Adler and Freud disagreed about almost everything. Adler believed that human behavior is motivated by a desire for belonging (connection) and worth, a desire that is influenced by our early decisions about ourselves, others, and the world around us. He believed that one's desire to contribute (*gemeinschaftsgefühl*) is a measure of mental health—a great reason to encourage your budding helper.

Research tells us that children are "hardwired" from birth to seek connection with others, and that children who feel a sense of connection to their families, schools, and communities are less likely to misbehave. All Positive Discipline methods help children achieve that sense of connection, capability, and contribution.

Dreikurs was also a Viennese psychiatrist; he immigrated to the United States before World War II and continued to spread the work of Adler after Adler's death in 1937. Adler and Dreikurs were passionate advocates of the need for dignity and mutual respect in *all* relationships, and wrote books about teaching and parenting that are still widely read, including the classic *Children: The Challenge.** Dreikurs died in 1972. We are honored to continue the work of Adler and Dreikurs through the Positive Discipline series.

WHAT IS DISCIPLINE?

Many have wondered what "discipline" could possibly mean for infants and very young children. Not so long ago (and quite often today), when people talked about "discipline" they really meant "punishment," usually because they believed the two are one and the same. Real discipline, however, involves *teaching.* In fact, the word itself comes from the Latin root *disciplina,* which means "teaching or learning." Positive Discipline is built on teaching, understanding, encouraging, and communicating—not on punishing. Punishment is intended to make children "pay" for what they have done. Discipline is designed to help children learn from what they have done.

As you will learn, much of what your child does in these early years has more to do with emotional, physical, and cognitive development and age-appropriate behavior than it does with "misbehavior." Babies and toddlers need nonpunitive discipline (teaching and guidance) that enhances their development and sense of connection—not blame, shame, or pain.

Discipline with young children is mostly about deciding what *you* will do (and kindly and firmly following through) than with what you expect your *child* to do. And it's never too early to lay a foundation

---

* By Rudolf Dreikurs and Vicki Soltz (New York: Plume Books, 1991).

for respectful, effective parenting. The principles of Positive Discipline will help you build a relationship of love and respect with your child, and will help you live and solve problems together for many years to come.

WHY SOME PARENTS DON'T ACCEPT NONPUNITIVE METHODS

Most of us absorbed our ideas about discipline from our own parents, our society and culture, and years of tradition and assumptions. Many believe that children must suffer (at least a little) or they won't learn anything. But many things in our society have changed in the past few decades, including our understanding of how children grow and learn; and the ways we teach children to be capable, responsible, confident people must change as well. Punishment may seem to "work" in the short term. But over time, it creates rebellion, resistance, and children who don't believe in their own worth and capability. There is a better way, and this book is devoted to helping parents and teachers discover it. Because all children (and all parents) are unique individuals, there are usually several nonpunitive solutions to any problem, but parents often don't immediately understand or accept these solutions. Indeed, Positive Discipline requires a paradigm shift—a radically different way of thinking about discipline. Parents who are hooked on punishment are often asking the wrong questions. They usually want to know:

- How do I make my child do what I want her to do?

- How do I make my child understand "no"?

- How do I get my child to listen to me?

- How do I make this problem go away?

Most frazzled parents want answers to these questions at one time or another, but they are based on short-term thinking. Parents will be eager for nonpunitive alternatives when they ask the following questions, and see the results this change in approach creates for them and their children:

- How do I help my child learn respect, cooperation, and problem-solving skills?

- How do I help my child feel capable?

- How do I help my child feel a sense of belonging and significance?

- How do I get into my child's world and understand his developmental process?

- How can I use problems as opportunities for learning—for my child and for me?

These questions address the big picture and are based on long-term thinking. We have discovered that when parents find answers to the long-term questions, the short-term questions take care of themselves. Children do cooperate (most of the time, at least) when they're involved in finding solutions to problems; they will understand "no" when they are developmentally ready; and they listen when parents listen to them and talk in ways that invite listening. Problems are solved more easily when parents use kind and firm guidance until children are old enough to be involved in the process of creating limits and focusing on solutions.

The building blocks of Positive Discipline include:

- **Mutual respect.** Parents model firmness by respecting themselves and the needs of the situation, and kindness by respecting the needs and humanity of the child.

- **Understanding the belief *behind* behavior.** All human behavior happens for a reason, and children start creating the beliefs that form their personality from the day they are born. You will be far more effective at changing your child's behavior when you understand the beliefs behind it. When your child is younger than three, you will also need to understand her developmental abilities and needs.

- **Understanding child development and age-appropriateness.** This is necessary so that parents don't expect behavior of children that is beyond their ability and comprehension.

- **Effective communication.** Parents and children (even little ones) can learn to listen well and use respectful words to ask for what they need.

- **Discipline that teaches.** Effective discipline teaches valuable skills and attitudes, and is neither permissive nor punitive. Millions have found this to be the best method of instilling the social and life skills a child needs to navigate his way through life.

- **Focusing on solutions instead of punishment.** Blame never solves problems. At first, *you* will decide how to approach challenges and problems. As your little one grows and develops, you will work together to find respectful, helpful solutions to the challenges you face, from spilled apple juice to bedtime woes.

- **Encouragement.** Encouragement celebrates effort and improvement, not just success, and builds a long-term sense of self-worth and confidence. Encouragement is such an important Positive Discipline principle that it will be covered in depth in Chapter 11.

- **Children *do* better when they *feel* better.** Where did we get the crazy idea that in order to "make" children behave, we should make them feel shame, humiliation, or even pain? Children are more motivated to cooperate, learn new skills, and offer affection and respect when they feel encouraged, connected, and loved.

DISCIPLINE METHODS TO AVOID

Most parents have done it at one time or another. But if you are screaming, yelling, or lecturing, please stop. If you are spanking or slapping, please stop. If you are trying to gain compliance through threats, warnings, bribes, or lectures, please stop. All of these methods are disrespectful and encourage doubt, shame, and guilt, now and in the future. Ultimately, punishment creates more misbehavior. (There are many studies that demonstrate the long-term negative effects of punishment, but these studies are usually buried in academic journals where parents don't see them.)

"Wait just one minute," you may be thinking. "These methods worked for my parents. You're taking away every tool I have to manage my child's behavior. What am I supposed to do, let my child do anything she wants?" No. We are not advocating permissiveness. Permissiveness is disrespectful and does not teach children to feel connected, capable, and able to contribute to others. **_True discipline guides, teaches, and invites healthy behavior._** As you may have discovered, you can never really control anyone's behavior but your own, and attempts to _control_ your child usually create more problems and power struggles. Later in this book, we offer several methods that invite cooperation (when applied with a firm, connected attitude) while encouraging your toddler to develop a healthy sense of autonomy and initiative.

Life with an active, challenging toddler becomes much easier when you accept that positive learning does not take place in a threatening atmosphere. As research in respected university child development labs has consistently demonstrated, children don't learn healthy attitudes and life skills when they are feeling scared, hurt, or angry. When children feel threatened, they may go into "fight or flight" mode—and because your brain has mirror neurons ("monkey see, monkey do" neurons; more on these in Chapter 3), you may join them there!

Sadly, a child often "misbehaves" because she has lost her sense of belonging or connection. Misbehavior "works" for a very good reason; that is, it regains a parent's attention and involvement, even if that attention is negative. Believe it or not, children don't "act out" to get attention. While all children need attention, what they really seek is safe, secure *connection*. When your child knows that she is securely connected to you, her misbehavior will diminish.

SHE WANTS WHAT SHE WANTS

Q: My sixteen-month-old girl does whatever she wants even though my husband and I have tried various methods of punishment. We've tried saying no, putting her in time-out, slapping her hands, and yelling, but nothing seems to work on her. She throws some pretty bad temper tantrums, too. I feel like we have tried everything. I am opposed to spanking and have given in to hand-slapping as a compromise, but it doesn't work either. My husband thinks we should spank so she knows she has done something wrong and will not repeat it. What do you suggest?

A: You are experiencing the frustration of so many parents who do not understand their child's development. Punishment—no matter what sort you use—is likely to produce what we call the Four R's of Punishment:

1. Resentment
2. Rebellion
3. Revenge
4. Retreat, through:
   a. Sneakiness ("I just won't get caught next time") or
   b. Low self-worth ("I really am a bad person")

Has any young child you know responded in these ways? Brain research suggests that punishment hampers optimal brain development, so it should come as no surprise that the punishments you've tried are not working. Take heart: You have not yet "tried everything." The rest of this book will help you understand why punishment is not effective, and teach you what to do instead.

WHAT CHILDREN REALLY NEED

There is a difference between wants and needs, and your little one's needs are simpler than you might think. All genuine needs should be met. When you give in to all wants, however, you can create problems for your child and for yourself.

For example, your child needs food, shelter, and attachment. He needs warmth and security. He needs to learn he is capable and can contribute. He does not need a tablet computer, a television in his bedroom, a miniature monster truck to drive, or even the color-coordinated baby stroller with built-in DVD player and vibrat-ing seat. He may love staring at a television screen when he is only three months old, yet experts tell us that any kind of screen time at this age can hamper optimal brain development. He may want to sleep in your bed, but if you give him time to self-soothe in his own bed, he will develop a sense of self-reliance and capability. It is true that a child may love and want french fries and sweets, but if he is offered apple slices instead, you will be meeting his nutritional needs, instead of less healthful "wants." You must decide what works in your family: If you give in to unhealthy wants, you could be setting the stage for childhood (and adult) obesity and many future power struggles with a child who feels entitled. You get the idea.

From his earliest moments in your family, your young child has four basic needs:

1. A sense of belonging (connection)
2. A sense of personal power and autonomy (capability)
3. Social and life skills (contribution)
4. Kind and firm discipline that *teaches* (with dignity and respect)

If you can provide your child with these needs, he will be well on his way to life as a competent, resourceful, happy human being.

THE IMPORTANCE OF CONNECTION

"Well, of course," you may be thinking, "everyone knows a baby needs to belong." Most parents interpret this quite simply: He needs love. But love alone does not always create a sense of belonging or capability. In fact, love sometimes leads parents to pamper their child, to punish their child, or to make decisions that are not in their child's long-term best interest.

Children who don't believe they belong become discouraged, and discouraged children often misbehave. Notice the word "believe." You may "know" your child belongs, but if *he* doesn't believe it for some reason (the birth of another baby, being sent to his room without dinner, not spending enough time with a parent, etc.), he may try to get that feeling back in mistaken ways. In fact, most young children's misbehavior (that is, behavior not related to developmental stages) is a sort of "code" designed to let you know that they don't feel a sense of belonging and need your attention, connection, time, and teaching.

It is this deep sense of unconditional belonging and connection that researchers refer to as "attachment," and that is so critical to a child's healthy development. When you can create a sense of belonging and significance for every member of your family, your home becomes a place of peace, respect, and safety.

PERSONAL POWER AND AUTONOMY

Developing autonomy and initiative are among the earliest developmental tasks your child will face. (More about this in Chapter 8.) And while parents may not exactly like it, even the youngest child has personal power—and quickly learns how to use it. If you doubt this, think about the last time you saw a two-year-old jut out his jaw, fold his chubby arms, and say boldly, "No! You're not the boss of me!"

Over and over we hear parents complain about power struggles with "strong-willed" children (we always wonder, "Would they rather have weak-willed children?"): children who won't obey, won't listen, or have temper tantrums. Some of this behavior is typical of a young child's development, as children explore and experiment to discover who they are and what they can do. However, many of these power struggles are just that—power struggles—because parents take power away from children instead of guiding them to develop their inborn power in useful ways.

Part of your job as a parent will be to help your toddler learn to channel his power in positive directions—kind and firm distraction and redirection until he is old enough to help solve problems, to learn life skills, and to respect and cooperate with others. Punishment will not teach these vital lessons: effective and loving *discipline* will.

SOCIAL AND LIFE SKILLS

Teaching your toddler skills—how to get along with other children and adults, how to fall asleep by herself, how to feed and dress herself—will occupy most of your parenting hours in these early years. But the need for social and practical life skills never goes away. In fact, a true sense of self-worth does not come from being loved, praised, or showered with goodies. It comes from having *skills* that provide a sense of capability and resilience to handle the ups and downs and disappointments of life. When your child feels competent and capable, he will also be better able to contribute to the lives of others in his family and community.

When children are young, they love to imitate parents, grandparents, and other caregivers. Your toddler will want to push the vacuum cleaner, squirt the bottle of bathroom cleaner, and cook breakfast (with lots of supervision). As your little one grows more capable, you can use these everyday moments of life together to teach her how to become a competent, confident person. Working together to learn skills can occasionally be messy, but it's also an enjoyable and valuable part of raising your child.

QUESTIONS TO PONDER

1. What does "kind" mean to you? Make a list of behaviors you would describe as kind, or remember an action you witnessed that demonstrated kind behavior.
2. What does "firm" mean to you? Make a list of behaviors you would describe as firm, or remember an action you witnessed that demonstrated firm behavior.
3. Now combine these concepts. What would blend the kind behaviors on your list with firmness? What would help the firm behaviors on your list also demonstrate kindness?
4. What could you imagine doing in a situation with your child (or one in your care) that is both kind and firm? How might being kind and firm at the same time change your relationship with that child?

3

THE MIRACULOUS BRAIN

Helping Your Child Learn

Martin and Rosalie wanted only the best for their baby, Rachel. They spent at least half an hour every day speaking to Rachel while she was still in the womb; they held headphones against Rosalie's bulging abdomen so the baby could learn to appreciate music. When Rachel was born, her proud and ambitious parents brought her home to a nursery equipped with every possible device to speed the learning process. She had special mobiles dancing above her crib; music played constantly; and Martin and Rosalie invested a small fortune in "educational" books, DVDs, and toys. They even purchased a baby carrier with a holder for Martin's iPad and numerous sophisticated educational apps, and were delighted when Rachel seemed to be transfixed by the colorful images. They wanted to give their precious baby every opportunity in life, but is this the best way to achieve their goal?

Jeff and Carol also were eager to teach their son, but they chose a different approach. They spent hours talking, singing, and playing with ten-month-old Gregory. They gazed into his eyes, spoke to him frequently, responded to his cries and gestures, and encouraged him to explore his world. As Gregory crawled among his colorful toys, Jeff or Carol were often on the floor nearby, laughing when Gregory handed them toys and enjoying each new discovery. Evening often found Gregory perched happily on a parent's lap, pointing a chubby finger at the images in a book as Mom or Dad read the story, with lots of different voices and a great deal of laughter. Gregory's parents focused on building a strong and loving connection with their young son—and in so doing, hoped to set the stage for a lifetime of healthy learning and development. Were they?

There are many parents like Martin, Rosalie, Jeff, and Carol, loving people doing their best to get their children off to a good start and help them succeed in school, relationships, and life itself. Until quite recently, however, we had no way of knowing exactly what really worked. How do children learn? Are there ways to help them be more successful and to maximize their potential? Is it wrong to encourage early learning? What exactly is "success"? Do young children need academics, or social skills? Or are both equally important?

THE LIVING, GROWING BRAIN

Experts used to believe that babies were born with brains that were more or less "finished"; all that remained was to fill the waiting brain with the necessary information. Increasing awareness of brain function continues to change the way we understand the human brain (and the "mind" that is part of it)—and how babies and children learn about the world around them. Brain scans have allowed researchers to peer inside the living brain, observe its structure, and discover how it uses energy, blood flow, and special substances called neurotransmitters to think, to perceive, and to learn. What those researchers have discovered is extraordinary and makes it more important than ever for parents and caregivers to understand these critical early years of a child's life.

The human brain begins life as a small cluster of cells in the fetus. By the fourth week of pregnancy, these cells have begun to sort themselves out according to the function they will one day perform and, to the wonder of researchers, have begun to "migrate" to the part of the brain they are destined to occupy. Nature provides the fetus with more cells than it will need; some do not survive the migration, while others join together in a network of connections called synapses.

The experiences and human relationships a child enjoys stimulate and shape the brain, and power the process of creating all the neurological networks that the child will need in life. By the time a child is two years old, his brain has the same number of synapses as an adult's; by the age of three, he has more than one thousand trillion connections—twice as many as his parents and caregivers! By about the age of ten, a child's brain begins to prune away excess synapses (those that haven't been used enough). Then, during adolescence, a "second wave" of pruning and growth begins. The human brain is "under construction" throughout childhood and adolescence; in fact, the prefrontal cortex, which is responsible for good judgment, emotional regulation, impulse control, and other admirable "adult" qualities, is not fully mature until after the age of twenty!

As Daniel Siegel and Tina Payne Bryson write in *The Whole-Brain Child,*

> Everything that happens to us affects the way the brain develops. This wire-and-rewire process is what integration is all about: giving our children experiences to create connections between different parts of the brain. When these parts collaborate, they create and reinforce the integrative fibers that link different parts of the brain. As a result, they are connected in

more powerful ways and can work together even more harmoniously.

Contrary to what we once believed, the human brain never stops growing and never loses the ability to form new synapses and connections. Change may be more difficult as we age, but change—in attitudes, behavior, and relationships—is always possible.

The first three years, however, are especially important; what a child learns and decides about himself ("Am I loved or unloved, capable or not capable?") and the world around him ("Is it safe or threatening, encouraging or discouraging?") becomes part of the "wiring" of his brain. The outside world, which is experienced through a child's senses (hearing, seeing, smelling, and touching), enables the brain to create or change connections. We also know that babies are not the "blank slate" we once believed them to be: "Babies and young children think, observe, and reason. They consider evidence, draw conclusions, do experiments, solve problems, and search for the truth."*

While the brain is amazingly flexible and is able to adapt to change or injury, there are windows early in a child's life during which important learning (like vision and language development) takes place. If those windows are missed, it may become more difficult for a child to acquire those abilities. For some functions, brain development is a "use it or lose it" proposition; for others, such as social skills development, learning continues well into early adulthood. Parents and caregivers shape a child's world, and in so doing, they also shape his growing brain.

NATURE OR NURTURE?

Books, magazines, and research journals are filled with new studies on human genes and their importance in how we live and who we become. Researchers now believe that genes may have an even stronger influence

---

* Alison Gopnik, Andrew Meltzoff, and Patricia Kuhl, *The Scientist in the Crib: What Early Learning Tells Us About the Mind* (New York: Harper, 1999), p. 13.

on temperament and personality than we previously thought. There is evidence that genes influence such qualities as optimism, depression, aggression, and even whether or not a person is a thrill seeker—which may be old news to parents who are forever plucking their daring toddlers from the tops of walls, jungle gyms, and trees!

Parents may find themselves wondering just how much influence they have on their growing child. If genes are so powerful, does it really matter how you parent your children?

The answer is that it matters a great deal. While a child inherits certain traits and tendencies through her genes, the story of how those traits develop is written as your child interacts with the world around her. (Brain researchers call these early reactions and decisions "adaptations.") Your child may have arrived on the planet with her own unique temperament, but how you and her other caregivers interact with her will shape the person she becomes. (More on temperament in Chapter 10.) As educational psychologist Jane M. Healy puts it, "Brains shape behavior, and behavior shapes brains."

It is no longer a question of nature versus nurture: A child's inborn traits and abilities and her environment engage in an intimate, complicated dance, and both are part of who she will become. Even more important are the *decisions* your child will make about who she is and what she can expect from the world around her. Parents, fragile and imperfect, bear the responsibility for shaping a child's environment. Especially in the first years of life, connection with caring and responsive parents and other caregivers is critical for your child. You influence the very structure and wiring of your baby's brain; you influence the person she becomes and the future she will have.

"BETTER" BABIES

You may be wondering whether it is helpful to begin academic teaching early in life, as Martin and Rosalie did with little Rachel. After all, if brains are still growing for the first few years, shouldn't you put in as much information as you can? Perhaps it will surprise you to learn that many brain researchers believe that the best way to provide a good foundation for learning is the old-fashioned way: allowing a child to explore his world through hands-on play.

No one can say for certain how much teaching and stimulation is "enough" for young children—but timing matters. Some researchers believe that it may even be harmful to force children to learn academics too quickly or to absorb concepts that their brains are not yet mature enough to handle. If the brain isn't ready to learn abstract concepts (math, for instance), it may patch together a pathway of connections that is less effective than the one that would have been used later on—and the less effective pathway becomes "wired" in place. Early screen use, such as Martin and Rosalie encouraged with their daughter's iPad exposure, raises concerns because we do not fully understand how it affects developing brain circuitry, not to mention whether the content is developmentally appropriate. There is also growing concern by researchers about the potentially addictive effects of screen time.

Premature emphasis on academics also has an emotional component. Children continually make decisions about themselves and the world around them. When children have difficulty mastering a concept introduced by loving parents or caregivers, they may form the belief "I'm not smart enough." This belief can override optimal development.

There are few absolutes in brain development, however. Each human brain is unique and special, and it is impossible to generalize about what is right or wrong for an individual child. Still, many scholars like Jane Healy believe that our fast-paced modern culture (and some of our "educational" games and technology) may be affecting children's ability to pay attention, to listen, and to learn later on in life.

Experts such as Stanley I. Greenspan underscore the importance of following your child's cues and signals, and responding first and foremost to emotional information. The ability to link feelings with communication (for example, interactions like those of Jeff and Carol with baby Gregory) emerges during a baby's first year of life. Encouraging the growth of real relationships is among the most important tasks of early brain development. (You will learn more about emotional development in Chapter 6.)

"HARDWIRED TO CONNECT": WHAT YOUR CHILD REALLY NEEDS

Babies and young children learn best in the context of relationships. The human brain changes both its structure and its function in response to the nature and quality of the *relationships* each person experiences (rather than the facts, figures, or academic information she acquires). ***What your little one most needs to learn in the first three years of life isn't found on flash cards or electronic screens. Brain development is all about connection with other people, and your child's brain is wired to seek connection from the moment of birth. How you and your child's other caregivers relate to her—how you talk and play and nurture—is by far the most important factor in a baby or toddler's development.*** Magda Gerber refers to infant caregivers as "educarers" and goes so far as to say that the daily tasks of feeding, toileting, and caring for babies are, in fact, the true heart of childcare in these early months and years. Such repetitive activities create the vital bonds and connections growing brains need.

According to Ross A. Thompson,* young children learn best when

---

* A professor of psychology at the University of California at Davis, and a founding member of the National Scientific Council on the Developing Child (www.developingchild.net).

Miraculous Mirror Neurons

Have you ever wondered how your baby learns to clap his hands, wave bye-bye, or "gimme five"? Researchers describe the presence in the human brain of "mirror neurons," which perceive physical action, facial expression, and emotion and prepare the brain to duplicate what it "sees." When you play peekaboo with your baby, his mirror neurons help him figure out how to imitate you. In the same way, when you are angry, excited, or anxious, his mirror neurons will "catch" your emotion and create that same feeling within him. Mirror neurons help explain why we weep, laugh, or get angry with each other so easily. It also explains why what you *do* (the behavior you model) as a parent is so much more powerful than your words in teaching your child. By the way, mirror neurons work in both directions. If you are calm when dealing with your little one, he is more likely to be calm as well, a helpful idea to remember when the inevitable tantrums occur!

they are unstressed and when they live in a reasonably stimulating environment—and, yes, pots and pans are very stimulating. Thompson believes that special stimulation, such as videos and other academic learning tools, is unnecessary (sorry, Martin and Rosalie); in fact, what children really need to grow and develop is *unhurried time* with caring adults, people who will focus on the child and follow his cues without distraction or expectations (keep it up, Jeff and Carol). Remember, both parents and other caregivers can provide this sort of child-centered interaction. It is important to note that this does not mean allowing children to rule the home.

THE IMPORTANCE OF ATTACHMENT

When you connect well with your child—when you recognize and respond to his signals, offer love and belonging, and allow your little one to develop a sense of trust and security—you help your child develop what is called a "secure attachment." This may well be what Rudolf Dreikurs identified as a strong sense of "belonging." Securely attached children connect well with themselves and with others and have the best opportunity to develop healthy, balanced relationships. They are also far more likely to acquire the social, emotional, and intellectual skills parents hope their children will have. It is interesting to note that researchers such as Mary Main have discovered that the best predictor of a child's sense of attachment is her *parent's* level of attachment to his or her own family growing up.* How you understand and make sense of your own history and experiences has a direct effect on your growing child.†

For the moment, however, be aware that there is nothing more important you can give your little one than a strong relationship with you, one built on love, trust, and unconditional acceptance—even when her behavior presents you with challenges. This book will equip you with many practical tools to guide your child's behavior, but there is no substitute for genuine connection.

Long-Term Benefits of Healthy Attachment

Studies that have followed children from infancy to adulthood tell us that healthy attachment is the strongest predictor of many important qualities. Children who have healthy attachments will:

- Be more motivated to learn
- Do better in school
- Have more confidence and sense of self-worth
- Develop good problem-solving skills
- Form healthier relationships
- Become more self-reliant
- Cope with stress and manage frustration well

(From *Early Moments Matter: Small Steps, Long-Lasting Effects*, www.pbs.org/thisemotionallife)

---

* Erik Erikson found that an infant's development of a sense of trust in the first year of life is directly related to a mother's sense of trust in herself.

† The details of attachment are beyond the scope of this book, but it is wise to understand that you cannot give your child what you do not have yourself. Understanding and resolving your own struggles, challenges, and emotional issues can change your interactions and may be one of the greatest gifts you give your child. To learn more about attachment, brain development, and parenting, see *Parenting from the Inside Out: How a Deeper Self-Understanding Can Help You Raise Children Who Thrive,* by Daniel J. Siegel, M.D., and Mary Hartzell, M.Ed. (New York: Tarcher Putnam, 2003).

The Impact of Trauma

There are times when a young child's life is not the peaceful ideal parents dream of. Infants and toddlers can experience stress; sometimes they are exposed to injury, fear, or violence in their homes or communities. Sometimes they must deal with medical treatment or hospitalizations that are frightening or painful. These physically or emotionally stressful experiences are known as *trauma*, and they can have deep impacts on a child's emotional development.

Children exposed to trauma may have difficulty falling asleep, or they may have nightmares. They may seem anxious or withdrawn and may cling to parents and caregivers. They may have violent tantrums triggered by something that seems meaningless to you, such as not getting the particular cup they wanted. They may talk frequently about what they have witnessed, and act it out repetitively with toys or other people. Or they might shut down and refuse to show emotion. Their ability to relax, to learn, and to focus on skills and ideas may be impacted.

Remember: the brain is resilient, and given a safe environment, most children and adults can recover from trauma. The best "medicine" is the presence of patient, loving caregivers who can provide the trust, security, and connection the child needs—for as long as he needs it. It is also important to remove the cause of the stress or violence as soon as possible. Always ask for help, for you and for your child, when you need it.

HOW TO NURTURE A GROWING BRAIN— AND THE CHILD WHO OWNS IT

A young child's flexible brain has the ability to adapt to many different environments and situations. What he learns in his first years determines which synapses the brain will keep and which will be lost. Abuse or neglect in the early years of a child's life may damage her ability to trust and connect with others. On the other hand, children whose early experiences are happy and healthy will build into their growing brains qualities and perceptions that will help them thrive.

Many of the recommendations experts now make are steps wise parents have taken instinctively from the beginning of time. When you understand the true importance of these ways of nurturing a baby, however, you can do them consciously, with confidence that you are providing exactly what your little one most needs from you.

What should parents know? What can you do to give your child a healthy brain—and a healthy life?

RESPOND TO YOUR BABY'S CUES

Responding when a baby cries—providing food, a clean diaper, or a snuggle—is important in helping that baby learn trust, perhaps the most vital early lesson. Parents can respond to an infant's kicking legs and waving fists, smiling back or playing finger games when he is eager for stimulation; and they can learn to recognize when a baby needs quiet time to nap or just to be still. This sort of connection is called "contingent communication" by brain researchers and is one of the most important ingredients in early brain development. (It is also one of the few parenting skills that crosses all cultures.) Learning to hear, interpret, and respond appropriately to your baby's cues is one of your first and most important parenting tasks. Parents who can attune themselves to their little one's signals and needs are well on their way to building a strong relationship.

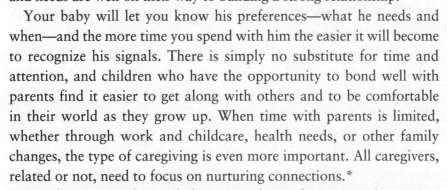

Your baby will let you know his preferences—what he needs and when—and the more time you spend with him the easier it will become to recognize his signals. There is simply no substitute for time and attention, and children who have the opportunity to bond well with parents find it easier to get along with others and to be comfortable in their world as they grow up. When time with parents is limited, whether through work and childcare, health needs, or other family changes, the type of caregiving is even more important. All caregivers, related or not, need to focus on nurturing connections.*

Spending time with your baby, responding to his cues, and nurturing a healthy connection are not the same thing as pampering. Pampering, sometimes called "spoiling," makes your child dependent on you. As you will learn, it is important to meet all of your child's *needs* for love and basic care, but it can be harmful to give in to all her *wants*. As you

---

* Magda Gerber's book *Dear Parent: Caring for Infants with Respect* (Los Angeles: Resources for Infant Educarers, 1998) is a valuable resource for you and your child's caregivers. See the Resources section for details.

gain information and knowledge, remember to access your heart and inner wisdom to find the balance of interaction that is respectful and healthy for you and your child.

TOUCH, SPEAK, AND SING

Studies have shown that babies who are touched, massaged, and held often are less irritable and gain weight more quickly. Holding, rocking, and cuddling a child communicates love and acceptance perhaps better than anything else. Babies, toddlers, even parents need hugs, and a loving hug may be all the "help" your little one needs for many of life's small crises.

Many adults are not comfortable with physical touch. Many weren't hugged or touched themselves, or perhaps the touching happened in the wrong way. Fathers, especially, may feel uncomfortable touching or hugging their children and sometimes substitute roughhousing and wrestling (which can be lots of fun) for snuggling and affection.

While touch helps your little one attach to you, and provides both comfort and stimulation, it should always happen in the right way and at the right time. Asking an older child, "Would you like a hug?" or "May I give you a hug?" will help give them a sense of control over their bodies.

Speaking, too, is important. What grown-up can resist cooing gentle words to a newborn? Talking and reading to infants and young children who obviously can't yet understand your words may not seem important, but these "conversations" stimulate the parts of a child's brain responsible for speech and language development.

Remember that while repetition may be boring to you, it isn't to your child. Babies and toddlers learn through repetition, which is why routines are such an effective and important teaching tool for this age group. You may think you cannot endure reading *Pat the Bunny* one more time—but your little one will remain delighted with the sounds and touchable textures of this old favorite for months. Knowing that you are shaping a healthy brain may give you the patience it takes to tell favorite stories over and over again. Incidentally, television does not have the same effect on babies and toddlers as real speech. Television and screen animation are not conversation, and their frantic, flashy structure may negatively affect a child's attention span and ability to listen. There is no substitute for talking to a child, and no better way for her to learn.

Music also appears to have a powerful influence on growing brains. While little Megan may not care whether it's Mozart or "Silly Songs" she hears, the melody and rhythm will affect her. Music seems to stimulate creativity; our hearts and brain waves tend to speed up and slow down to match the pace of the music we're listening to. In fact, gently bouncing your baby on your lap while you sing or listen to music actually helps wire his brain to "hear" rhythm. There can be few things as delightful as watching a dancing toddler, bouncing to the strains of a classic Hokey Pokey or wiggling to a more contemporary favorite. Don't rely only on recorded music, either. Sing to your young child. (Yes, you can sing—your toddler isn't a critic!) At first, you will sing alone, but before long your toddler will be yodeling along. It isn't noise: It's the sound of healthy brains growing!

Remember, music also soothes. Soft, gentle sounds are as relaxing to children as they are to adults. At rest time or before bedtime, try playing soothing music and watch how your busy baby will begin to slow down and become calm. (Gentle music is a great way to ease into rest periods at childcare programs, too.)

PROVIDE OPPORTUNITIES TO PLAY—AND PLAY ALONG

In these days of busy parents and overburdened caregivers, confinement in infant seats and playpens and time spent in front of a screen often substitute for play. But babies and toddlers are just discovering their bodies—and just forming the vital connections that link brain with action. They are developing their motor control and learning about textures and gravity. They need the opportunity to play actively.

Play truly is a child's work. It is how she experiences her world, learns about relationships, and tries on new roles and personalities. Parents are usually good at taking children places where *kids* can play—we're endlessly on the road to gymnastics, "water babies," or playgroup—but they are often less good at playing themselves, or may believe they don't have the time.

Grandparents often comment that one of the joys they have discovered is that of simply playing with their grandchildren, whether it is being a willing "horsie," gathering flowers and leaves for a fairy hut, or sharing teatime underneath a blanket-covered "fort." Freed from the daily stresses of juggling work, family, and the care of their own young children, grandparents find they can relax and simply play with their delightful grandbabies.

Play is an important tool in building a loving and connected relationship with any child. The toys don't actually have to "do" any-

thing; worthwhile play may mean handing the same brightly colored rattle back and forth and listening to the noise it makes (many, many times). Allow a child to "lead" the play. There is no better way to understand a toddler's world than to play with him.

Your child will need lots of opportunities to exercise his imagination and creativity as he grows. (Sometimes that includes time to play alone.) Children can play with—and learn from—the box the toy comes in, or the pots and pans under the sink. Who needs a battery-operated fire engine that makes siren noises when a child can—and should—do that for himself? The old-fashioned, interactive favorites still serve a valuable purpose; provide building blocks, dress-up clothes, a sandbox, and lumps of clay, then watch as your little one discovers the joy of building, touching, and shaping his world. Better yet, play with him. Get down on the floor and build a fort out of sofa cushions, or play a favorite board game (older toddlers love Chutes and Ladders or Candy Land

and can play well with only a little help from you); have a water fight or play in the mud. Remember, children learn from all of their senses, and having the opportunity to get messy is a valuable part of play—and learning. (You can always clean up together afterward—and that will be fun, too.) You'll be creating special memories and a bond with your child that both of you will treasure, as well as growing vital connections in his brain.

ENCOURAGE CURIOSITY AND SAFE EXPLORATION

Infant seats, baby swings, and playpens may be helpful when you need some free time, but your active toddler needs time and space to work on her sense of autonomy and initiative, and there's no better way than being allowed to roam and explore the house, the yard, or the neighborhood park—with your supervision, of course. (See Chapter 8 for more on autonomy—and childproofing.)

A child's brain grows and is stimulated best by things that she is actively interested in. If your little one shows curiosity about colors and paints, animals, or big trucks, you'll be helping her brain develop by finding ways to explore what she most wants to learn about. Take time to discover what makes your little one sparkle, then create opportunities to explore.

ALLOW PRIVATE TIME FOR YOUR BABY

Please don't get the impression that your baby needs constant stimulation. Babies need private time to explore by themselves. When you see an infant staring at his fingers or playing with his toes, he is exploring. Many babies are content to sit in their infant seats and follow you with their eyes as you occupy yourself with other tasks.

As usual, the key word is "balance." It is good to provide stimulation—talking, cooing, and singing—but not all the time. Overstimulation can actually make a baby crabby, and too much stimulation can be counterproductive for optimal brain development. If your baby turns his

When It's More Than Just the "Baby Blues"

Most mothers experience some emotional dips and swings in the months after giving birth, but a surprising number of mothers experience depression severe enough to interfere with their ability to function and enjoy life. Postpartum depression is no one's fault—but it can have a serious impact on a mother's health and on her child's development.

Postpartum depression can interfere with a mother's ability to enjoy her infant and to respond to cues and signals. Depressed mothers often feel unusually tired and sad, and may be easily irritated or angered by their child's needs. Depression interferes with sleep and appetite; depressed moms may be distracted, and may avoid other people or going out. Depression has serious implications for babies, too: Infants of depressed mothers may become irritable and hard to soothe, be delayed in their speech and development, and eventually develop behavior problems.

If you recognize any symptoms of depression in yourself, please ask for help. There are many ways to treat depression, and life can become much easier with support for you and your little one.

face away from you while you're playing or talking, he may be letting you know that he needs some "quiet time" to rest and regroup. Remember, however, that all babies are not alike. Some are more content with quiet play and calm time than others.

USE DISCIPLINE TO TEACH— NEVER SHAKE OR HIT

Growing brains are extremely fragile. Every day an infant dies or is permanently disabled by being shaken or hit by an angry, frustrated adult. "I would never hurt my baby," you may be saying, but it may come as a surprise to you to learn that harsh criticism, punishment, or shaming may also damage a child's brain and ability to trust you. Remember, those connections that are used most will become permanent; those not used will be lost. All parents make mistakes, and all parents will experience the intense frustration and exhaustion that happen sometimes when you share your life with very young children. When you are aware of the long-term effects of the way you treat your child, you can make choices that will not only teach and provide the structure she needs but allow her to learn that she does belong and have significance—lessons that will last a lifetime.

TAKE CARE OF YOURSELF

How, you may be wondering, do my health and state of mind affect my child's brain? Parents and caregivers are the most important people in a young child's life. The quality of what you have to offer is often affected by your own all-too-human moods and emotions. Stress, exhaustion, or worry affect the way you interact with your baby or toddler—and, consequently, the way she perceives you and herself.

SELECT CHILDCARE CAREFULLY

A child's growing brain does not shut off when he is dropped off at a childcare center. Most parents work outside the home these days, and many babies and toddlers spend the bulk of their waking hours in another's care. Not surprisingly, the same skills that are essential for parents in nurturing developing brains are just as critical for childcare providers. Leaving your child in another's care may be difficult, but it helps to recognize that high-quality care can support a child's development. It is important to be sure that the care your child receives when he is away from you is truly *quality* care. This will be explored in more depth in Chapter 19.

LOVE AND ENJOY YOUR CHILD

Remember, what your child (and all of us) needs to know is that she belongs, that she has a special place in life, and that she has value to those around her. **No matter how busy your life, and how seriously you take your responsibilities as a parent, take time to simply love and enjoy your child.** The quiet moments of wonder, the laughter and giggling, the delight we take in the special qualities, first words, and adorable actions of these new

Encourage Your Baby's Brain Development

- Respond to your baby's cues.
- Touch, speak, and sing.
- Provide opportunities to play—and play along.
- Encourage curiosity and safe exploration.
- Allow private time for your baby.
- Use discipline to teach—never shake or hit.
- Take care of yourself.
- Select childcare carefully.
- Love and enjoy your child.

little people are not wasted time but precious investments in the future of your family. The housecleaning, yard work, and laundry will wait; slow down occasionally and just enjoy the time you have with your child. It speeds by all too quickly.

THE FIRST THREE YEARS LAST FOREVER

The Positive Discipline approach to raising young children fits well with our knowledge of how the human brain develops, and doing your best will almost certainly be "good enough." Awareness is always the first step to action, and knowledge will help you make choices and decisions that are in the best interest of your baby or toddler.* Raising a young child is indeed a serious responsibility. In many ways, a child's first three years last for the rest of his life.

Conscientious, loving parents frequently worry that they won't be able to meet their child's needs, that they will leave some task undone or fail to provide the care and environment that their child's growing brain requires. It may help a bit to remember that none of us is perfect—and you don't need to be. Your baby or toddler doesn't require perfection; he only needs you to be warm, loving, and aware of his needs.

QUESTIONS TO PONDER

1. Think (and perhaps journal) about the family you grew up in. What did you appreciate about your parents? Your other rela-

---

* For more information on brain development and your child's first three years, visit www.parentsaction.org or www.zerotothree.org.)

tives? Your caregivers? What did you wish could have been different? What decisions do you think you made about yourself and others because of the way you were raised? How might you use what you've learned from your own experiences growing up to strenthen your connection with your child?

2. Consider choosing one of the ways described in this chapter to encourage your baby's brain development and focusing on it for one week. For instance, you might decide to focus on touching, speaking, and singing to your baby. The following week, choose another way. How do you think your relationship with your child will be different when you have spent a week focusing on each suggestion?

3. Which do you believe is more important—using technology to stimulate intellectual learning, or focusing on your relationship with your child? Why? Is it possible to balance the two?

4

GETTING TO KNOW YOUR YOUNG CHILD

Martha had a story to tell. She collapsed into a chair and waited impatiently for the other members of her parenting group to stop their chatter and settle down.

The group's leader noticed Martha's exasperation and smiled. "Martha, it looks like you came prepared with something to share. Why don't you start us out?"

Martha sighed and shook her head. "I just don't know what to do," she moaned, the frustration in her voice obvious. "My two-year-old, Daniel, is driving me crazy. He insists on touching things in stores even though I must have told him a dozen times not to touch. He gets angry when I won't read to him or play with him right away—he just can't seem to wait patiently for even five minutes. He's always yanking his hand out of mine when we walk together, and I worry that he'll get away from me or run into the street."

The rest of the group smiled sympathetically and a few heads nodded as Martha told her tale of woe. Other parents had shared such experiences and understood her feelings. "This morning was the last straw, though." Martha paused. "This morning Daniel deliberately lied to me. I've told him I won't tolerate lying, but he fibbed right to my face."

The leader met Martha's eyes and nodded. "I can see you're really upset. What did Daniel say?"

"Well," Martha said, "he told me he saw a lion in the back-yard. Isn't that ridiculous? He knows there isn't a lion in our backyard! If Daniel starts lying now, what will happen as he grows up?"

Another woman spoke up. "I worry, too. What will my child be like as an adult when he does these things now?" Others nodded in concern.

The concerns and confusion these parents are feeling are easy to understand; most parents have similar moments of frustration and disappointment. But young Daniel isn't intentionally driving his mother to distraction. It's very likely, as Martha's parenting group facilitator will undoubtedly explain, that Daniel is simply being his age-appropriate self: an active, curious two-year-old who is learning about his world in the only way he knows.

GETTING INTO YOUR CHILD'S WORLD

Your little one inhabits a vastly different world from yours. One of the first and most important challenges in parenting your baby or toddler is understanding what his world looks and feels like—from *his* perspective—and how his brain and skills are developing. Expecting your child to think, act, or feel the way you do will create all sorts of difficulties and misunderstandings.

One of the best ways of becoming an effective parent—or, for that matter, an effective human being—is to understand the perceptions of other people, to be able to "get into their world." This is especially true for parents of very young children; after all, their world is so different from yours! (Interestingly, your child will not develop this ability, something researchers call "mindsight," until he is approaching adolescence. No matter how intelligent he is, he cannot see the world exactly the way that you do.) Babies are not miniature adults, but they can certainly begin learning about feelings.

A newborn infant arrives in this world from a place where she's been cradled in warmth and safety beside her mother's heart, her every need immediately met. Suddenly, after a convulsive and tiring journey out of her mother's body, she finds herself in a world of heat and cold, loud noises, moving objects, and bright lights. Faces come and go, voices come from all directions, and this new world runs on a schedule she doesn't yet understand. The instant nourishment and comfort are gone; now she must wail loudly for someone to satisfy her hunger or give her comfort. Sleeping, eating, simply functioning—all must be adapted to her new life. It wouldn't be surprising if we somehow found scientific evidence that infants long to return to the womb!

From the moment of birth onward, a child's early months and years are a voyage of discovery. And one of the first things a child must discover is himself. An infant's control of himself moves from the center outward. In other words, he develops the large muscles at the center of his body (working lungs, beating heart) before the small muscles in his extremities. At first he is helpless, doing for himself only the most basic bodily functions, unable even to lift his head or to turn over without help. A baby's very survival depends on his ability to attract an adult's attention to get the care he needs.

As time passes, his control increases. He learns to really see ("*Is that Mom?*") and to track objects with his gaze. One day, he realizes that he can manipulate the hands that flap in front of his face; he can make them move, grab them, and even—oh, bliss!—stuff them into his mouth. Later, he learns that he can grab other things with his fingers and stuff those into his mouth as well.

Many other developmental milestones follow in due time. A baby learns to turn over, scoot, crawl, pull herself up on the furniture, and eventually walk. She becomes a little scientist, exploring everything

she can. Parents sometimes see these explorations as "mischief" and may not appreciate their value to healthy brain development. The last things to be mastered are the delicate skills, like balance and fine motor control, which explains why a five-year-old or even a six-year-old may have such a difficult time mastering the art of tying shoes. Part of becoming an effective and loving parent or teacher means understanding the world of the little ones you're working with and making every effort to get inside it.

UNDERSTANDING YOUR CHILD'S PERSONALITY

What shapes the personality of a human being? Why is one two-year-old peaceful and compliant, eager to please and easy to get along with, while the two-year-old next door seems bent on challenging every rule, pushing every limit, and breaking everything in sight? Children are a product of their parents' genes (nature), and they are undoubtedly influenced by the environment and ideas around them (nurture). Research appears to indicate that genes and inborn temperament traits play a stronger role than experts previously thought, while other research demonstrates that beliefs may actually change DNA.* Perhaps it is more important to realize that while children are shaped by both the raw material they inherit and the forces around them, they also bring to the world something unique to them: their own spirit and identity. These factors, combined with the individual decisions (many of them subconscious) they make along the way about what they must do to survive or thrive, will form their personalities. Such decisions are so important that we will come back to them often as we help you get into the world of your little one.

Have you ever noticed that, despite having the same parents and the same home, children in the same family can be incredibly different?

---

* See Bruce H. Lipton, *The Biology of Belief* (Carlsbad, CA: Hay House, 2009).

That is because each child makes unique decisions based on his or her perceptions of the world. One child may decide, "I like the safety of boundaries." Another child may decide, "I feel thwarted by boundaries." Many of these decisions are made preverbally as "a sense of," rather than through rational understanding. Parents need to take time to get to know—and to accept—their children for exactly who they are.

Remember Martha and two-year-old Daniel? Let's take a look at some points that might explain the behavior this mom finds so frustrating. (We will examine these ideas in more detail in later chapters.)

A CHILD LEARNS ABOUT THE WORLD BY DOING

A child who is "playing" is actually hard at work, trying on new roles and ideas, tasting, touching, smelling, and experimenting with life. Learning is a hands-on experience filled with the enthusiastic joy of discovery. It takes a while (and some parental patience) before children learn where the boundaries lie. Some will accept those boundaries while others will continuously push against them. This doesn't make the "pusher" bad. He simply has a different temperament and will keep his parents busy using kind and firm Positive Discipline.

A CHILD'S BIRTH ORDER AFFECTS HOW SHE SEES THE WORLD

Each child born experiences a different family configuration from that experienced by the children who came before or those who may follow. There are more people in the family, more siblings, and the adult or adults in the family have probably grown or changed in some way. They may be less knowledgeable with a first child, or might have gained a certain amount of perspective (and experience) by the time a new child joins the family.

Maria tells of the drama her daughter Fatima's tantrums would spark, and the way she and Fatima's aunts would try to reason with her, pick her up and beg her to calm down, or get exasperated and join in with their own wails of frustration. By the time Fatima's brother, Miguel, arrived two years later and began having his own tantrums, the rest of the family had calmed down. They had learned from Fatima that tantrums were a normal part of raising a toddler. Because they knew this phase would pass (and would pass more quickly if it wasn't given much attention), they found themselves regarding little Miguel's tantrums as endearing. They would smile, shake their heads, and wait them out. Miguel was born into a different, more relaxed household than was Fatima.

Another aspect of birth order is the presence (or absence) of siblings. A hungry "only" or "firstborn" child usually has an adult available to get him a cracker when he wants it. When there are other children present, that cracker may have to wait until a younger brother gets his diaper changed or a baby sister finishes nursing. A firstborn child may also learn how to do things for himself at an earlier age, while his little sister will have older siblings around to hand out those crackers.

These differences are neither good nor bad, but they do affect children's behavior. The older child who suddenly begins whining and misbehaving when her new baby brother is being fussed over is easy to recognize. The little one who starts clinging to Mom when a sibling goes off to preschool may be less obvious. Whatever the behavior, taking into account the effects of a child's birth order can help you make sense of your child's "misbehavior."*

A CHILD'S DEVELOPMENTAL NEED TO EXPLORE AND EXPERIMENT MAY BE LABELED AS MISBEHAVIOR

Children need secure, loving boundaries in order to feel safe, just as everyone needs strong walls and a roof to feel protected from the

---

* For a more detailed understanding of birth order, refer to the Birth Order section of *Positive Discipline for Preschoolers*, and Chapter 3 of *Positive Discipline*.

weather. Still, any self-respecting child will feel obliged to cruise up to the boundaries you've set and test them occasionally, just to make sure they're firmly in place. He's not deliberately trying to drive you insane; he's either exploring at his age-appropriate level or learning about consistency and making sure adults mean what they say (an important part of trust). Often adults fail to realize that they simply can't reason with a toddler and thus they spend more time talking than acting. No matter how well you use them, words are often little more than sounds to young children. Actions, like removing a child from a forbidden temptation by picking him up and carrying him to another location, provide an unmistakable message. (Some  actions or words, though, may only make matters worse: slapping his hand, yelling "no-no," or engaging in a stare-down may invite a child to keep this entertaining adult involved with him—or to retaliate in kind!) Is all of this testing annoying? Of course. Frustrating? Absolutely! But children are rarely as intentionally naughty as their parents think—they're just acting their age.

YOUNG CHILDREN RARELY MISBEHAVE PURPOSELY

Adults mistakenly read motives—that is, intent—into children's behavior that reflect adult thinking rather than toddler thinking. Some act as though their child lies awake at night plotting ways to drive them crazy. Martha's repeated warnings to her son not to touch things aren't terribly effective; supervision and kind, firm distraction would be more helpful. Toddlers are highly impulsive little people, and warnings are simply overpowered by the desire to touch, hold, and explore. A toddler straining over the edge of his stroller to touch a shiny cup at the bottom of a highly breakable pyramid of cups does not intend to "disobey." The colors on the cup attract his

attention; he reaches for it and wants to examine it. He is a small scientist using his hands, mouth, and imperfect coordination to determine the properties of the marvelous world around him. Your real tasks as a parent are prevention, vigilance—and very quick reflexes.

A CHILD'S PHYSICAL SIZE AND ABILITIES HAVE A STRONG INFLUENCE ON BEHAVIOR

Take a moment sometime soon and put your face on the same level as your child's. What do you see? The world looks a lot different from down there! Seeing an adult's face requires tilting your head backward—an uncomfortable position if held too long. Most of the time, young children gaze out at a world of knees, shins, and feet, and the only reliable way to catch an adult's attention is to pull on his hands or legs! And just imagine how frightening a yelling, pointing parent would look from down there.

Crib mobiles took on a whole new look when someone had the good sense to look up at what a child was seeing. The cute little animals the adult saw swirling through the air looked like shapeless slivers of moving color when seen from below. Today's versions aim visual images downward, emphasizing the bold black-and-white graphics that babies find attractive.

A child's world shimmers with delightful, distracting images, sounds, and textures. The best way to be sure a tiny person realizes that you are talking to her is to make eye contact. Get down on her level, look into those curious eyes, and speak directly to her.

Are you still down on the floor? If another adult is handy, reach up and take his hand for a moment. Imagine going for a nice long walk through the nearest shopping mall in this position. What parents often perceive as defiant yanking away may simply be a child trying to get some circulation back into her hand and arm! In addition, adults have much longer legs than their little ones; children almost always have to run to keep up. No wonder they lag behind us or run away to find their own pace.

It can be frustrating to be a small person whose hands won't quite do the tasks they're expected to. Often children want very much to help, to dress themselves, and to do other tasks around the house, but the sheer mechanics are beyond them. The result is a frustrated, angry child—and a frustrated, angry parent. This does not create a positive atmosphere where learning can take place. How might you feel if everything you tried was a little beyond your ability to succeed—and you were criticized

for the efforts you made? You might give up and start "misbehaving" out of sheer frustration. Later we will talk more about expectations, encouragement, and celebrating small steps.

A CHILD'S CONCEPTS OF REALITY AND FANTASY ARE DIFFERENT FROM THOSE OF AN ADULT

Did you know that when you walk out of your infant's line of sight, you have ceased to exist? That the toy accidentally dropped on the floor has disappeared forever? The concept that objects are permanent hasn't developed yet. Separation anxiety begins when babies understand that their parents always exist, and they don't like being separated from them. As soon as they understand that the toy still exists, they get frustrated and cry when it is taken away.

In the same way, a young child experiments with his imagination in order to explore and learn. Our young friend Daniel may not have seen a lion in his backyard, but he may have seen the neighbor's cat. Or he may have watched a cartoon about lions in the jungle. Or his picture book may have included lions and their cubs. Daniel's lion wasn't a "lie" but the product of a vivid imagination with a dash of creativity. The line between fantasy and reality remains blurred throughout the first few years of a child's life.

Fantasy may also be a child's way of getting in touch with feelings for which he doesn't yet have words, a way of exploring his own inner being. The lion in the backyard may be another way of expressing a fear of being alone. Careful listening (more about that later) and acceptance from his parents will help him to understand his feelings, learn to sort them out, and find healthy ways of dealing with them.

PATIENCE IS A VIRTUE FAR BEYOND THE REACH OF MOST YOUNG CHILDREN

Think back for a moment to when you were a child. Remember how long it took for your birthday to arrive? Have you noticed how much the entire process seems to speed up, the older you become?

Time moves far more slowly for an eager child than it does for an adult. Adults must learn that units of time simply don't have the same meaning for children. For young Daniel, five minutes may seem like an eternity, and he is sure that Mom takes far too long to do everything. Yes, children need to learn patience, but parents need to be patient long enough to let them learn. It's not realistic to expect toddlers to sit still for long periods of time, in church or even for storytelling time.

Jimmy was an extremely bright eighteen-month-old. One night, his parents took him to a drive-in for ice cream. A week later, the family drove past the drive-in and Jimmy shouted excitedly, "We went there yesterday!" His father scolded Jimmy for lying. But Jimmy wasn't lying; his father didn't understand child development, and so didn't realize that Jimmy simply hadn't mastered the concept of time yet. With more understanding, his father would have been delighted at Jimmy's developing memory instead of concerned about his "untruthfulness."

BOYS AND GIRLS: DOES GENDER MATTER?

One of the first questions you're likely to be asked when you announce you have a new baby in the family is "What is it?" These curious folks aren't asking about the species; they're wondering about gender. Is it a boy or a girl? Did you have a preference?

Why does gender matter so much? Well, gender involves much more than whether you dress your baby in blue or pink. There are some significant differences in male and female children (especially early in life); there also may be differences in the ways parents talk, touch, and relate to boys and girls.

In most ways, girls and boys are more alike than different. Boys and girls both need love, belonging, and encouragement. They need to develop good character and social and life skills. Girls and boys need kind, firm discipline and connection with parents and caring adults. Cultural differences and beliefs play an important role in how boys and girls develop. Still, because a baby's brain is exposed to sex hormones during pregnancy, some gender differences appear to be part of the way children are wired.

Understanding Your Child's World

- A child learns about the world by doing.
- A child's frustration due to a lack of abilities or skills may be labeled as misbehavior.
- A child's developmental need to explore and experiment may be labeled as misbehavior.
- Young children rarely misbehave purposely.
- A child's birth order affects how she sees the world.
- A child's physical size and abilities have a strong influence on behavior.
- A child's concepts of reality and fantasy are different from those of an adult.
- Patience is a virtue far beyond the reach of most young children.

THE TRUTH ABOUT BOYS AND GIRLS

You may be surprised to learn that baby boys actually appear to be more fragile at birth than do baby girls. Male infants appear to be more easily stressed and more susceptible to health problems. They are often "fussier" than girls; they cry more easily and seem to have a harder time learning to calm themselves down (what is sometimes called "self-soothing"). Baby boys may be more sensitive to changes in routine, and to parental anger or depression.

They also may experience more separation anxiety and may seem more "emotional" than girls.

Female infants, on the other hand, tend to make eye contact sooner than boys do. They often acquire language skills before boys, and have more mature social and emotional skills in the first few years of life. Girls also may develop fine motor skills sooner than boys. Research has shown that parents tend to speak to, touch, and cuddle female infants and toddlers more often than boys. As children grow into their toddler years, boys appear to be more impulsive; they learn self-control more slowly, they are more physically active, and yes, they tend to be more aggressive, curious, impulsive, and competitive than little girls.* Needless to say, parents and preschool teachers may prefer the more "obedient" behavior of little girls—which can teach little boys unintended lessons about their place in the world.

It's worth remembering that **most gender differences are based on generalizations, and each child is special and unique.** By the time your child goes off to school, these differences will have largely evened themselves out.

PARENTS AND GENDER

Parents have a strong influence on how young children develop gender identity. Your baby wasn't born knowing that he is a boy or that she is a girl—or what those words mean. If the culture insists that boys be "strong and silent" (and unfortunately, it often does), parents may instinctively try to "toughen up" their sons early in life. If girls are expected to enjoy quiet play and develop early writing skills, a parent may overlook her daughter's athletic ability and miss opportunities to encourage it. Please give your child the benefit of all possibilities. Your little girl can be strong, and your son compassionate.

Many children do not fit neatly into "boy" or "girl" categories; in

---

* Susan Gilbert, *A Field Guide to Boys and Girls* (New York: Harper Perennial, 2001).

fact, it is typical at this age for children to experiment with different roles, toys, and identities. For some children, typical gender identities will never be a comfortable fit and they will need patience, encouragement, and deep acceptance as they learn to live in a world that has many expectations for who they will be.

Each culture (as reflected in its music, movies, toys, and clothing) has a great deal to say about how girls and boys "should" look and behave. We associate names, colors, jobs, and even musical instruments with either boys or girls; most of these lessons are absorbed early in life, long before children are consciously aware of what they are deciding. Research appears to indicate that boys *and* girls are healthier when they develop the ability to be both strong and kind, as well as courageous and compassionate.

At some point during your child's early years, take time to explore what *you* believe about gender. What "should" little boys be like? Little girls? How can you best nurture the strengths and sensitivities of your own special little one? Getting into your child's world and understanding his development will help you teach, encourage, and comfort your own unique child.

DEVELOPMENT? OR MISBEHAVIOR?

As you have learned, one of the challenges in parenting a young child is understanding the difference between normal development and intentional behavior. There is no one "right" answer for many everyday parenting dilemmas, but resist valuing quick (often temporary) results over the development of slower (long-term) life skills. There is more and more research demonstrating that nonpunitive methods are more effective in the long term than punishment, even though punishment may seem to generate immediate results. You and your child will both benefit when you and your other caregivers learn all you can about growth and development, and come to know each unique child. Learn to trust your innate wisdom as a parent. No expert or book (including this one) can give you all the answers—although, as you will learn throughout this book, Positive Discipline tools and principles will help you guide and encourage your child during these first important years.

QUESTIONS TO PONDER

1. Take time to think about the behavior challenges you experience with your baby or toddler. How many of those "misbehaviors" can you attribute to her age and development? How many can she actually control?

2. When you were expecting, did you hope for a girl or a boy? Why? What do you believe is important about your child's gender? If your child does not fit your expectations, how can you learn to offer encouragement and connection for the person your child actually *is*?

SECTION TWO

YOUR DEVELOPING CHILD

5

HOW DO I BEGIN?

Positive Discipline Tools

The stage is now set; you and your little one have begun the process of growing and learning together and you now understand why connection, respect, and kindness with firmness are so important. But how do you actually *do* Positive Discipline? If punishment doesn't work, what does? This chapter will give you the tools you need to build a relationship of cooperation and respect with your child, while guiding her to develop the characteristics and life skills that will serve her throughout her life. We will refer to these tools many times in the chapters ahead, and this chapter can become a handy one-stop reference as you begin to guide and influence your child's behavior.

Remember, no tool, no matter how helpful, works all the time for all children. As your own unique child grows and changes, you'll have to return to the drawing board many times, but these ideas will provide a foundation for years of effective parenting. Also, it is important to remember that these tools are not effective if used as techniques to control instead of principles to inspire. The feeling (and attitude) behind what you do is more important than what you do.

Ten Basics for Implementing Positive Discipline

1. Create a connection before a correction.
2. Get children involved:
   a. Offer acceptable choices.
   b. Provide opportunities to help.
3. Create routines.
4. Teach respect by being respectful.
5. Use your sense of humor.
6. Get into your child's world.
7. Follow through with kind and firm action: if you say it, mean it, and if you mean it, follow through.
8. Be patient.
9. Provide lots of supervision, distraction, and redirection.
10. Accept your child's uniqueness.

CONNECTION BEFORE CORRECTION

Because helping children feel a sense of belonging and significance (connection) is the foundation of Positive Discipline, we cannot talk enough about the importance of the relationship you create with your child. Thousands of parents have told us how Positive Discipline has helped them create a more loving relationship with their children (and with the other parent). However, when parents say these tools don't work, often it is because they have not taken the time to truly connect with their child first.

Connection can take many forms. It can be as simple as saying "I love you and the answer is no" or validating feelings: "I know you don't want to stop playing, and it is time for bed." It is helpful to be self-aware and to notice when you find yourself in a power struggle with your child. When that happens, be willing to back away and start over when you have changed your attitude—which will enable your child to change his.

GET CHILDREN INVOLVED

During the first year of life, your child will depend on you for everything. But you may be surprised at how quickly he finds his voice and unique personality. Instead of telling him what to do, find ways to involve him in decisions (in age-appropriate ways, of course) and to draw out what he thinks and perceives. "Curiosity questions" are one way to do this. Ask, "Where do we put your diaper?" "Which book do you want to read?" "What do you think will happen if you push your tricycle over the curb?" or "How should we get ready for childcare?" For a child who is not yet able to talk, say, "Next, we _____," while kindly and firmly showing her instead of telling her.

Offer Acceptable Choices

Having choices gives children a sense of power: they have the power to choose one possibility or another. Choices also invite a child to use his thinking skills as he contemplates what to do. And, of course, toddlers often love it when choices include an opportunity to help. "What is the first thing we should put away when we get home—the ice cream or the orange juice? You decide." "Would you like to carry the blanket or the cracker box as we walk to the car? You decide." Adding "You decide" increases your child's sense of power. Be sure the choices are developmentally appropriate and that all of the choices you give are options you are comfortable with. When your child wants to do something else, you can say, "That isn't one of the choices. You can decide between _____ (repeat the choices available)."

Provide Opportunities to Help

Toddlers often resist a command to "go to the car" but respond cheerfully to a request like "I need your help. Will you carry the keys to the car for me?" Activities that might easily have become power struggles and battles can become opportunities for laughter and closeness if you use your instincts and creativity.

CREATE ROUTINES

Young children learn best by repetition and consistency. You can ease the moments of transition in family life by creating reliable routines for your little one. Routines can be created for every event that happens over and over: getting up, bedtime, dinner, shopping, and so on. Then you can say to your child, "Now it's time for _____." As soon as your child is old enough, get him involved in helping you create routine charts. These are a kind of "map" (not a sticker or reward chart) that can be illustrated with pictures of your child doing the necessary tasks. Once he's older, he will love telling you what's next on his routine chart. If he forgets, avoid telling. Instead ask, "What is next on your routine chart?" Reward charts take away from your child's inner sense of capability, because the focus is on the reward. Routine charts simply list sequences of events, and act as guidelines for common tasks.

TEACH RESPECT BY BEING RESPECTFUL

Parents usually believe children should show respect to adults, but what about adults showing respect to children? *Children learn respect by seeing what it looks like in action.* Be respectful when you make requests. Don't expect a child to do something "right now" when you are interrupting something she is thoroughly engaged in. Give her some warning. "We need to leave the park in two minutes. Do you want to swing one more time or ride the teeter-totter?" Carry a small timer with you or invite her to help you pick out a ringtone on your phone. Then set the timer together for an agreed-upon time. When it goes off, it is time to go.

Remember, too, that shame and humiliation are disrespectful, and a child who is treated with disrespect is likely to return the favor. Kindness and firmness show respect for your child's dignity, your own dignity, and the needs of the situation.

USE YOUR SENSE OF HUMOR

No one ever said parenting had to be boring or unpleasant. Often, laughter is the best way to approach a situation. Learn to laugh together and create games to get unpleasant jobs done quickly. Humor is one of the best—and most enjoyable—parenting tools.

It is amazing how a child who resists a direct order will respond with enthusiasm when that order becomes an invitation to play. Try telling your toddler, "I bet you can't pick up all your little cars before I count to ten," or "I wonder if you can brush your teeth and get into your pajamas before Dad does."

GET INTO YOUR CHILD'S WORLD

Understanding your baby's or toddler's developmental needs and limitations is critical to parenting in the first three years of life. Do your best to be empathetic when your child cries (or has a temper tantrum). He may just be frustrated with his lack of abilities. Empathy involves understanding and connection, not rescuing. If you want to leave the park and your child isn't ready to go, give her a hug and validate her feelings: "You're really upset right now. I know you want to stay, and it's time to leave." Then hold your child and let her experience her feelings before you move on to the next activity. If you were to pamper your child by letting her stay at the park longer, she would not have the opportunity to learn from experience that she can survive disappointment—and she might be learning that you can be manipulated.

Getting into your child's world also means seeing the world from her perspective and recognizing her abilities—and her limitations. Ask yourself occasionally how you might be feeling (and acting) if you were your child. It can be illuminating to view the world through a smaller person's eyes.

FOLLOW THROUGH WITH KIND AND FIRM ACTION: IF YOU SAY IT, MEAN IT, AND IF YOU MEAN IT, FOLLOW THROUGH

Children usually sense when you mean what you say and when you don't. It's usually best not to say anything unless you mean it, are willing to do it, can say it respectfully—and can follow through with dignity and respect. Sometimes the fewer words you say, the better! This may mean redirecting your child or showing her what she *can* do instead of punishing her for what she *can't* do. It also might mean wordlessly removing a child from the slide when she refuses to leave, rather than getting into an argument or a battle of wills. When this is done kindly, firmly, and without anger or words, it will be both respectful and effective.

BE PATIENT

Understand that you may need to teach your child many things over and over before she is developmentally ready to understand. For example, you can encourage a young child to share, but don't expect her to understand the concept and do it on her own right away. Sharing requires time, practice, and better-developed impulse control. When she refuses to share, rest assured that this doesn't mean she will be forever selfish. It will help to understand that she is acting age-appropriately. Don't take your child's behavior personally and think your child is mad at you, bad, or defiant. Act like the adult (sometimes easier said than done) and do what is necessary without guilt and shame.

PROVIDE LOTS OF SUPERVISION, DISTRACTION, AND REDIRECTION

Minimize your words and maximize your actions. As Rudolf Dreikurs once said, "Shut your mouth and act." Young children need constant supervision. If a child heads toward an open door, quietly take her by the hand and lead her to where she needs to go. Show her what she *can* do instead of what she can't do. Instead of saying, "Don't hit the dog," show her how to touch the dog nicely. When you understand that children don't really understand "no" the way you think they should, it makes more sense to use distraction, redirection, or any of the respectful Positive Discipline methods.

ACCEPT YOUR CHILD'S UNIQUENESS

Remember that children develop differently and have different strengths. Expecting from a child what he cannot give will only frustrate both of you. Your sister's children may be able to sit quietly in a restaurant for hours, while yours get twitchy after just a few minutes, no matter how diligently you prepare. (Refer to Chapters 9 and 10 on

My Child Won't Listen!

Q: My two-year-old is so stubborn. No matter how I talk to him, he just refuses to listen to me; he only wants to do what he wants. If I tell him it's time for bed, he ignores me and keeps right on watching TV. I don't seem to be able to get him to do anything unless I get angry—and I always feel terrible after I lose my temper. How can I get him to listen to me?

A: This is one of the most frequent complaints we hear from parents: "My child won't listen!" (When most parents say "My child won't listen," what they really mean is "My child won't obey.") It's unlikely that there is anything wrong with your son's hearing; he simply doesn't want to do what you are telling him to do. There are many ways to engage your child's attention and cooperation—this chapter is filled with them. You can also try some of the tools already mentioned: asking (rather than telling) him to do something; getting down on his level before speaking; creating a bedtime routine chart; setting a timer and then following through with kind and firm action; and, if necessary, carrying him to his room. Believe it or not, his refusal to "listen" is working for him: it's keeping you busy with him for long periods of time. Most parents lose their tempers from time to time. When this happens, apologize and ask for a hug, then think about how to get a different result next time.

temperament and developmentally appropriate behavior for more on this subject.) That being the case, you may decide to save that fancy meal out for a time when you can enjoy it in adult company—or for when your children have matured enough for all of you to enjoy it together.

It may help to think of yourself as a coach, helping your child succeed and learn how to do things. You're also an observer, learning who your child is as a unique human being. Never underestimate the ability of a young child. Watch carefully as you introduce new opportunities and activities; discover what your child is interested in, what he can do by himself, and what he needs your help with in order to learn.

RETHINK "TIME-OUT"

Many parents use something called time-out, but few really understand what it is or how best to use it with young children. If you've ever heard a parent say to a defiant toddler, "I've had it! Go to time-out and think about what you did," or "That's one . . . that's two . . . ," you may wonder where time-out fits with the Positive Discipline approach.

Positive time-out (very different from *punitive* time-out) can be an extremely effective way of helping a child (and a parent!) calm down enough to solve problems together. In fact, when you are upset or angry, you lose access to the part of the brain that allows you to think clearly, so time-out is an especially appropriate parenting tool—when it is positive and not punitive, and is used to teach, encourage, and soothe. But there are several points that need to be made regarding time-out for young children.*

---

* For expanded information about time-out, see *Positive Time-Out and Over 50 Ways to Avoid Power Struggles in the Home and the Classroom,* by Jane Nelsen (New York: Three Rivers Press, 1999).

- **Time-outs should not be used with children under the age of three and a half to four years of age.** (If they aren't old enough to help design a time-out spot, they aren't old enough to use it.) Until children can link cause and effect and begin to think logically, which begins at around age two and a half (and is an ongoing process that even some adults have not fully mastered), supervision and distraction are the most effective parenting tools. Even when children reach the beginning stages of rational thought, they do not have the maturity and judgment to make logical decisions.

Most parents have at one time or another found themselves in a heated debate with someone who only comes up to their kneecap—and most will admit that reason, lecturing, and argument just don't work. Your child may be able to read the energy of your feelings and understand that you want something; he may even be able to guess what that something is. But he does not understand the logic of your arguments in the way you think he does.

It is heartbreaking to see young children sent to punitive time-outs when they are not developmentally able to understand what it is all about. A punitive time-out increases the probability that young children will develop a sense of doubt and shame instead of a healthy sense of autonomy. (See Chapter 8 for important information on the development of autonomy versus doubt and shame.)

- **Children do better when they feel better.** Even younger children can benefit from an opportunity to "cool off," especially if you go with them. We know of one mother who used "positive time-out" successfully with her eighteen-month-old child. That it "worked" was undoubtedly due to her attitude. She would say to her child, "Would you like to lie on your comfy pillow for a while?" Sometimes he would just toddle off to his pillow and lie down until he felt better. If he hesitated, she would ask, "Do you want me to go with you?" This mother understood the purpose of positive time-out—to help children feel better so that they can do better, not to make them feel bad in the hope that feeling bad will inspire them to do better (it doesn't), or to "think about what they did" (they can't).

• **Your attitude is the key.** Your child is more likely to be focused on what *you* did (and the emotion behind it) than what she did. At this point in their young lives, children need lots of guidance without the expectation that they will be able to absorb and use what they are learning right away. In most cases, time-out should not be used at all with a child younger than three—unless it is being modeled by adults. Sometimes just asking for a hug is a quick "time-out" that will help you both feel better.

• **Create a calming space *with* your child.** If you do decide to try positive time-out with your child, let him help you set up a safe, comfortable area where you can go together. This could be as simple as a favorite chair where your child can sit on your lap while you sing a calming song or read a book. No, this is not rewarding misbehavior. It is understanding that learning to manage feelings takes time and practice. Pillows, stuffed animals, or favorite soothing toys may help. Before the age of three and a half, you might find it helpful to say, "Let's go to your cool-off spot to read a book or listen to music until we feel better." Your child may not understand the purpose of time-out, but she will sense the "energy" behind your words and will respond accordingly.*

---

* You may find it helpful to read *Jared's Cool-Out Space,* by Jane Nelsen, Ashlee Wilkinson, and Bill Schorr, with your child. Watching Jared create and use his "cool-out space" may inspire your child—and you! Available at www.positivediscipline.com.

• **Model positive time-out by creating your own "cool-out space."** When you feel overwhelmed, you might say, "I need to go to my special place for a few minutes until I feel better. Do you want to come with me?" It will take a while for the meaning of what you are doing to sink in, but your child will eventually discover that "cooling out" is helpful for everyone.

• **Be sure to have more than just time-out in your toolbox.** No parenting tool works all of the time. There is never one tool—or three, or even ten—that is effective for every situation and for every child. Filling your parenting toolbox with healthy, nonpunitive alternatives will help you avoid the temptation to punish when your child challenges you—and he undoubtedly will. The more you know, the more confident you will feel as you cope with the ups and downs of life with a young child.

> *Georgia sighed in exasperation—this was Amanda's third tantrum this afternoon. Two-year-old Amanda was having a rough day; Luke, her older brother, had invited a houseful of friends over to play for the afternoon and Amanda hadn't been able to take her usual nap. Now, cranky and miserable, she had ripped half the pages from Georgia's new magazine, then swept it off the table. She gazed up at her mom with stubborn defiance—and a trembling chin.*
>
> *Georgia was tired herself. She stifled the desire to lecture her small daughter and drew a deep breath. "Would you like to curl up in your special corner with your blankie?" she asked Amanda.*
>
> *Amanda only shook her head and sat down in a heap amid the torn pages of the magazine.*
>
> *"Well, how about playing with your dollhouse?"*

Georgia asked helpfully, reaching out to take Amanda's hand and lead her to her favorite toy.

Amanda yanked her hand away and let her little body go limp on the floor, shaking her head vehemently.

Georgia sighed again and sat down near her daughter. Let's see, she thought. What else did they suggest in that parenting class—something about asking for help?

Georgia rose and gave Amanda a weary smile. "You know what, honey?" she said as kindly as she could. "I need to start dinner—and I sure could use some help. You can lie here and rest or you can join me in the kitchen and help me wash the lettuce—it's up to you." And with that, Georgia walked into the kitchen.

For a few moments, the sniffling and kicking from the family room floor continued. Soon, however, a small, tear-streaked face peered around the kitchen corner. Amanda looked uncertainly at her mom, but Georgia just smiled and gestured toward the sink.

Encouraged, Amanda went to get her little stool, dragged it over to the sink, and began dunking lettuce leaves in the water. By the time Amanda's dad arrived home, harmony had been restored: Georgia had helped Amanda clear away the ripped magazine, and Georgia, Luke, and Amanda were working companionably together to set the table. Georgia was glad that positive time-out wasn't the only tool in her parenting toolbox.

It is often true that what works with young children one day will not work the next. But if you've taken the time to know your child and to learn all the different ways there are to teach and encourage, chances are good that you will find *something* that works—just for today.

• **Always remember your child's developmental stage and capabilities.** Understanding what is (and is not) age-appropriate behavior will help you not to expect things that are beyond the ability of your child.

> *Chuck and Susie took their eighteen-month-old twin boys to a band concert featuring their seven-year-old daughter as a flute soloist. The twins were fascinated with the concert—for about ten minutes. Then they found other ways to entertain themselves. One twin started crawling under the seats, and the other soon joined the fun. Chuck took the twins outside and spanked them for not sitting still. The twins cried loudly and could not be taken back inside for the rest of the concert. Chuck was very disappointed that he missed his daughter's solo, his daughter was disappointed that her father didn't hear her, and Susie and the twins were upset about the spanking. Everyone was miserable.*

It is a sad thing when children are punished for doing things that are developmentally appropriate, even though they are not *situationally* appropriate. It is unreasonable to expect young children to sit quietly for long periods of time. However, it is not okay to allow children to disturb others. Since Chuck and Susie didn't choose to leave their twins with a caregiver, it would have been more effective for them to take turns taking their children outside so they could take turns hearing parts of the concert. It was not appropriate to punish the children, but it would have been helpful to provide a distraction, such as bringing coloring supplies to play with or picture books to look at. This kind of advance planning makes it more likely that your child will be able to behave appropriately.

LET THE MESSAGE OF LOVE GET THROUGH

We often ask parents in workshops why they want their children to "be good." After a few moments of head-scratching and blank stares, they tell us that they love their children and think that they will be happier people if they are "good"—or that they will be miserable if they become "spoiled brats." So they punish (or reward) in the name of love. But do their children feel loved? Positive Discipline means learning to be kind and firm at the same time, which nurtures your connection with your child while teaching skills and appropriate behavior.

Even the most effective nonpunitive parenting tools must be used in an atmosphere of love, of unconditional acceptance and belonging. Be sure you take time for hugs and cuddles, for smiles and loving touch. Your child will do better when he feels better, and he will feel better when he lives—and can learn life's lessons—in a world where he knows he belongs and is taught with kindness *and* firmness.

QUESTIONS TO PONDER

1. Think about a relationship where you feel a sense of acceptance and belonging. What allows you to feel that way? What hinders your sense of belonging? Now think about your child's sense of belonging. What creates it? How might her behavior change if she truly felt a sense of connection to you?

2. Consider a time when your child misbehaved or "didn't listen." After reading this chapter, can you think of any Positive Discipline tools which might have made a difference in that situation? Decide what you will do the next time this behavior occurs. Journal about the differences for you and for your child.

6

THE DEVELOPMENT OF EMOTIONAL SKILLS AND LANGUAGE

Have you ever watched a parent cradle an infant, gaze down into his face, and coo words of love? What does it all mean to the baby? He can't understand the words; how does he learn to recognize the feelings? How do feelings and vague impressions grow into words, thoughts, and real communication? How does your baby learn to give and receive love?

EMOTIONS AND CONNECTION

Babies and very young children read nonverbal cues, facial expressions, and emotional energy to learn about the world of relationships. An infant does not understand all the complex meanings and concepts contained in the word "love," but she does learn to interpret the world around her. In some families there is little connection, security, or trust. In most, however, a baby experiences trust and connection, with adults who hear and respond to her cries and signals for attention. She senses that the hands that touch her are gentle and caressing, and the voice that speaks to her is

warm and soft. Mom or Dad looks into her eyes and holds her attention (until she looks away as part of her innate ability to "self-soothe" from all the excitement). She feels the gentle rain of kisses that tickle her feathery hair. She recognizes familiar smells that communicate the approach of special people, and she senses the environment of caring that supports her in her new life. These events convey a feeling of "love" to a young child, and she responds with similar feelings and behavior.

A young child's brain is growing connections throughout the first years of life, and the interactions this infant has with the world around her are shaping the way she will grow and develop. Isn't it wonderful that the things we instinctively long to do with babies—touch, tickle, smile, love—are the very things that nurture health and happiness?

CHILDREN ABSORB THE ENERGY OF FEELINGS

The nonverbal signals you send your child are far more powerful than your words. Young children are acutely sensitive to nonverbal communication. Infants "tune in" to human faces and actively seek connection with the adults around them. When Mom sits down to nurse feeling annoyed, tired, or cranky, her baby squirms, fusses, and won't settle into nursing. A baby as young as a few weeks of age can sense the tension in her mother's body, feel the rigid muscles in her arms, and hear the thumping of her heart as she lies close to her mom's chest.

Alicia enjoyed quiet mornings and afternoons with her three-week-old baby, Julian. Her husband was at work and their older children were in school. Julian slept much of the time. During his waking moments, after being fed and diapered, he seemed content to watch his mother move about the kitchen. Alicia was certain those brief smiles were not gas.

Every day, however, around four o'clock in the afternoon, Julian would start to fuss. Holding and cuddling did not seem to comfort him. Could it be that the baby sensed the stress his mother was feeling about getting dinner on the table and taking care of the older children when they came home from school? This seemed to be a reasonable explanation, because the baby would calm down as soon as the busy evening had passed and Alicia was able to relax.

CREATE A CALM ATMOSPHERE

It is both wonderful and a bit unsettling to have an infant or very young child around the house. Because little ones are so directly attuned to the emotional states of their parents, it is helpful (if not always possible) when you are able to relax, stay calm, and find ways to build a loving, trusting connection with your child. Your family won't suffer if you have simple dinners while adjusting to a new baby (and helping him adjust to you). A calm atmosphere is much more pleasant—and much healthier—for everyone. You can be more sensitive to your baby's moods and needs when you slow down and take time to read the energy of all the members of your family.

After a tiring day at work, Manka made her daily trek to the childcare center to pick up her infant son, Tahir. She hurriedly gathered up the baby and his various belongings, rushed through traffic, and, once home, settled Tahir into his high chair with a snack. Since she usually arrived home before her husband, she immediately set about fixing dinner. This was the worst hour of the day for mother and son. Tahir fussed, squirmed, and pushed his crackers onto the floor. Manka cut herself as she tried to slice the vegetables, spilled too much spice into the pan, and was thoroughly exhausted and frustrated by the time her husband walked through the door.

Manka's husband, Sundar, felt pretty miserable himself, coming home to a squalling baby, undercooked or overcooked meals, and a wife who spent the evening complaining. Watching her husband crush the crackers into the floor when he went over to hug Tahir didn't help Manka's mood.

One evening, Sundar pushed aside his plate of soggy vegetables. He gazed across the table at his weary wife and began to discuss their miserable evening routine. An understanding smile on his face, he assured Manka that he would be glad to make sandwiches for both of them if he could come home to a more relaxed wife and child.

Manka felt relieved. She admitted that she felt overwhelmed preparing the elaborate meals they had both enjoyed before Tahir's birth. The next evening, when Manka entered the house with Tahir in tow, she put down all of the bags, papers, and toys she had carried in with her. She gave Tahir a big hug and snuggled with him in the rocking chair, where they spent the next half hour playing tickling games, cooing and smiling at each other. When Sundar walked through the door, he found Tahir giggling as Manka nibbled his toes. Tahir shrieked with laughter as his dad joined in the fun. A short while later, a relaxed family enjoyed toasted cheese sandwiches washed down with hot cups of canned soup. Food hadn't tasted this good in far too long.

Tahir and Manka needed time to reconnect each day far more than anyone in the family needed gourmet cooking. By slowing down and allowing time to make the transition from the hectic daily routine to their family time at home, Manka was able to tune in to Tahir's needs—and her husband was able to share the evening's tasks. The entire family thrived as the energy in their home improved.

TANTRUMS: EMOTIONAL MELTDOWNS

Everyone has feelings. In fact, researchers tell us that emotion (not logic or reason) is the energy that runs the human brain. Still, emotions are not mysterious forces that take over and cause difficult or embarrassing behavior. Emotions are simply information, and are intended to help each of us make decisions about what we need to do to stay healthy and safe. There's no denying, however, that strong emotions can be challenging. Like it or not, all young children have tantrums from time to time. Understanding why tantrums happen—and how to deal with them—can help you remain calm and composed in the midst of even the most severe emotional storm.

Nicholas's family walked through the shopping mall together. Two-year-old Nicholas was holding the last bite of his cookie in one hand and a new box of crayons in the other when he spied a display of stuffed Easter bunnies in a store window. He darted off, pointing to the display and dropping the crayons in his haste. Mom and Dad followed him to the store window, retrieving the spilled crayons. They admired the bunnies together. Not surprisingly, Nicholas wanted one. "Nicky's bunny!" he said, pointing to a particularly jolly blue specimen. His parents agreed that the bunnies looked lovely and suggested that perhaps another day he might get one.

Nicholas wasn't satisfied with this answer. He fell to the floor, a writhing mass of pumping legs and pounding fists, wailing with a noisy sincerity that would impress any passing Hollywood producers. Mom glanced around in embarrassment while her husband stood over young Nick, telling him to get up right now! Nick landed a random kick on Dad's knee. Dad's voice got louder than Nick's. Mom, meanwhile, wished she had a bag to put over her head. Surely, everyone was watching and thinking what horrible parents they were.

In fact, Nick's parents aren't horrible at all—and neither is Nick. They were sailing along pretty smoothly until the bunnies intervened. Nick's parents tried to respond to him in ways that did not invite a power struggle; they had given him one special treat already and they responded to his demands calmly. So why did Nick throw a tantrum? Is he a spoiled brat? Does he "just need a good spanking"? No. The most likely answer is that Nick threw a tantrum "just because"—he wants what he wants and he wants it now. He has no understanding of concepts like *reasonable, practical,* or *delayed gratification.*

Tantrums are loud, highly visible, and embarrassing (at least to adults). They are also quite normal. Young children have all the feelings adults do. They feel sad, excited, and frustrated, but they lack both the words for those feelings and the skills (and impulse control) to cope with them. In fact, the part of the brain that is responsible for emotional regulation and self-calming (the prefrontal cortex) is not completely mature until a person is twenty to twenty-five years old. **If you think about how hard it can be to control your own feelings, you shouldn't be surprised that your toddler will rarely be successful at it.**

Once adults understand why children's overloaded senses sometimes flash into tantrums, they can quit feeling responsible for them. Sometimes, no matter what you say or do, your child will get overwhelmed and throw a tantrum. Adults can learn not to add to the chaos. Remember those mirror neurons? It is unfortunate (but all too human) that Nick's dad got into the act by throwing a tantrum of his own. Nick's tantrum will pass quickly but it may take his parents—now carrying their howling son to the car—longer to recover their equilibrium.

GIVING IN IS NOT THE ANSWER

You may be wondering, "Okay, then what am I supposed to do when confronted with a temper tantrum—especially in public?" Giving in may stop the tantrum for the moment, but it has some negative long-term effects.

What do you think your child is learning and deciding when he has a tantrum and you give in? Our guess is that he has just learned a negative life skill: do whatever it takes to get your way. He may be deciding, "I'm loved when I get what I want—and I know how to get people to give me what I want." Children repeat what "works."

Instead, follow the advice of Rudolf Dreikurs, one of the earliest parenting teachers. Dreikurs advised parents to "shut your mouth and act," remembering that what you do isn't as important as the attitude *behind* what you do. You might pick up your screaming child and carry him to the car. Do this with a calm, kind, and firm manner—which may require several deep breaths to calm yourself down first. Allow him to have his feelings; in fact, you can even empathize with him, and label those feelings so he begins to understand them. "You're really disappointed that we didn't buy the blue bunny."

There are three reasons to avoid lectures:

1. He can't "think" when his brain is flooded with emotions.
2. Words are often like throwing fuel on the flames.
3. Silence prevents a second meltdown—yours!

When he does calm down enough to be able to hear your words, avoid scolding. Breathe with him. Give him time to reboot his brain. Validate his feelings. In time, he can learn to soothe his own difficult emotions.

THE IMPORTANCE OF SELF-CALMING

Brain researchers tell us that when we "lose it" (and all parents do from time to time), the prefrontal cortex effectively "disconnects,"

> ### The Brain in the Palm of the Hand
>
> Dr. Daniel Siegel has a simple and creative way of explaining what happens in your brain when you get upset, and why calming down is the first important step to solving a problem with your little one. You can see a video online of Dr. Siegel explaining "the brain in the palm of the hand" (www.youtube.com/watch?v=DD -lfP1FBFk). It is well worth the two minutes it takes to watch.

leaving us with input from only the parts of the brain responsible for emotion and physical sensation. And because all humans have mirror neurons, anger and tantrums are contagious. None of us does his or her best work when angry.

The first step in dealing with a tantrum (either your own or your child's) is to calm down. Breathe deeply and count to ten. Researchers tell us that focused, calm breathing helps the brain "integrate"—that is, the brain reconnects and the ability to think clearly and look for real solutions is restored. Once you have taken time to cool off, help your child do the same. And he *does* need your help: Emotional regulation is a skill that will take him years to master.

HELPING YOUR CHILD CALM DOWN

Young children lack the ability to recognize and manage their emotions, and punishing them for this inability isn't fair or helpful. If your child is three years old or a little older, you may be able to use *positive* time-out (which you learned about in Chapter 5) as one way to teach her to calm down when she is angry or unhappy.

Focus on soothing a child younger than three before dealing with problems. Gentle touch, rhythmic breathing, or soft music may help her regain control. It is also okay to simply allow her to have her feelings until they dissipate, without trying to change them or fix them. If you are calm enough, sit nearby and send out loving energy without interfering. Remember, the goal is to help her calm down, not to punish her or make her "think about what she did."

Baby-Sized Overload

Marjorie and Karen's attempts to soothe their youngest daughter with walking, singing, and stroking only made her cry harder. When they finally put her down, she seemed relieved. She would cry a minute or two, then relax and fall asleep. Their well-meaning stimulation actually prolonged her distress; what she really needed was time alone.

Remember, crying is communication for infants, *not* misbehavior. Each parent must learn to interpret the message her child is sending. Crying does not always mean the same thing; it is not reinforcing negative behavior to respond to a baby's cries. Sometimes the appropriate response is to let a child release tension by crying. Eventually, parents will learn what the crying means—and that may depend on the overall atmosphere and sense of belonging a child experiences.

Be sure your child is safe and healthy, then decide what (if any) action is called for. Little ones will learn to manage their emotions more quickly when they are given time to practice in a safe, responsive environment.

WHAT ABOUT HEAD BANGING?

Q: I have three girls, ages five, three, and two. I am wondering how I can stop my two-year-old from having temper tantrums or hurting herself. I've already tried ignoring the tantrums. If she doesn't get what she wants, she falls to the floor and begins to bang her head, sometimes very hard. I don't know what to do. Please help.

A: Tantrums, head banging, holding one's breath—all are very common in young children who aren't getting their way. All are very upsetting to concerned parents. Sometimes these behaviors are the means by which a child vents her frustration. Your two-year-old may also have discovered that these behaviors "work"—in other words, they get her something she believes she needs: the object of her demands, or your attention and involvement. Two-year-olds are developing autonomy and want the right to make their own choices—even when they lack the skills to do so appropriately.

If you're worried that your daughter may bruise herself by banging her head on something hard, pick her up and, without saying anything, move her to a softer spot (the carpet, her bed, a pillow). You might try saying, "I'd like to work on this with you, but we can't

Weathering the Storm: What to Do During a Tantrum

What can parents and caregivers do to help a child through a tantrum? Here are some suggestions:

- **Calm yourself down first.** Example is the best teacher, and you will respond to your child's intense emotions more effectively when you are calm. Take a moment to breathe deeply. Once your child is safe, walk away for a few seconds to gather your own resources. Do whatever it takes for you to remain kind and firm.
- **Provide safety and damage control.** While tantrums may be part of living with young children, damage and injury need not be. It may be wise to move a child to a safer location or, if you are in a public place, to a more private corner. Without yelling or lecturing, calmly move out of your child's reach any objects that may be thrown or damaged.
- **Resist trying to "fix" a tantrum or coax a child with rewards.** Offering to give a child a disputed item teaches him that tantrums are a good tool for getting his way. Remember that tantrums are normal but giving in to demands will only earn you more tantrums. Remain kind, calm, and firm, and let the storm blow over.
- **Avoid getting hooked by your child's behavior.** Tantrums are rarely as personal as they seem. Remember that your child is not being malicious or "bad," and lacks the ability to fully control his emotions.

---

talk when you're so upset." (Even if she doesn't understand all the words, your calm tone of voice will communicate with her.) Then let her know you are available when she's calmed down. Make sure she's in a safe place, and take some deep breaths to calm yourself. It will take time, but if you're kind and firm, she'll get the message that you can't be manipulated by tantrums, tears, and threats.

ACTIVE LISTENING: GIVING NAMES TO FEELINGS

Children constantly send nonverbal messages. Their facial expressions, gestures, and behavior provide clues to perceptive adults about what

Surviving the Storm: What to Do After a Tantrum

After a tantrum, try the following:

- **Allow emotions to settle.** Give your child a quiet moment to cool down and catch his breath. Talk quietly about what happened and reassure your child that while his behavior may have been inappropriate, you love him very much.

- **Reconnect.** Children may need a hug after such a powerful emotional storm. Tears and sniffles often follow tantrums as the child clears out the overload of emotions. A wordless, comforting hug may help both of you feel better.

- **Help your child make amends.** When everyone has calmed down, any damage should be addressed. Thrown items can be picked up, torn papers gathered and discarded, or pillows stacked back on the bed or sofa. Adults may offer to help a child with these tasks. It may also be appropriate to help your child repair additional damage, such as a broken toy. Recognize your child's abilities and development and don't expect things she can't do, but allowing her to squeeze some glue, run the Dustbuster, or put tape on a torn book may help her feel a sense of self-control again and give her a very real way to learn about making things right.

- **Forgive and forget—and plan ahead.** Once the tantrum is over and the mess has been cleaned up, let it go. Concentrate on your relationship and, if you can, on recognizing what led up to the tantrum. Prevention is often the best way of dealing with children's emotional outbursts. Tantrums may happen when children have missed naps or meals, are in unfamiliar surroundings, or are coping with stressed-out adults. Understanding your child's temperament and daily rhythms will help you both avoid many (though probably not all) of these outbursts.

they are feeling. An eighteen-month-old child cannot tell you, "I'm feeling tired, confused, and frustrated that I can't reach the cookie jar." He doesn't have the words to express such a complicated sequence of thoughts and feelings. What you might hear are wails and shrieks accompanied by a toy thrown to the ground, a crumpled-up face, and a small body collapsing on the floor.

A parent may feel understandable frustration of her own, and may express that frustration with harsh words. Or she can choose to help her child understand his feelings, give them a label that will help him to identify them in the future, and open the door to a way of dealing with the situation at hand.

Mom might respond like this: "I can see that you feel frustrated because you can't reach the cookie jar. I feel frustrated when I can't do something, too. Let's figure this out together." Once a child's feelings are named, validated, and understood, he usually feels better and is more willing to work on solutions. In this instance, Mom and her son figured out that the cookie jar could be placed on a lower shelf within easy reach. They also decided to fill the cookie jar with healthy snacks, such as fruit slices or raisins, so he could help himself anytime. Your child may not always hear or respond to your words, but saying them can help you change your attitude.

Remember, your child was not born with a vocabulary for his emotions. He cannot identify feelings with words and may not understand exactly what his feelings are. *Active listening—the art of noticing a child's feelings and identifying them calmly and clearly with words—is an important step in teaching your child to manage both his emotions and, eventually, his behavior.* Even when your child is too young to understand the words themselves, you will be offering clues to the often confusing world of feelings. The day will come when he begins to connect his own emotions with the words you offer and no longer needs to "act out"—at least not as often.

GENDER AND EMOTIONAL LITERACY

For reasons we don't understand clearly, girls often acquire social, language, and emotional skills sooner than boys do; boys are often more easily upset (and harder to soothe) than girls. In addition, in many cultures, boys hear messages about emotional expression that may make it more difficult for them to identify and manage their own feelings.

Numerous researchers—such as William Pollock, Dan Kindlon, and

Michael Thompson—have noted that while little girls are expected to cry, giggle, and express their feelings, adults and peers (intentionally or unintentionally) may give little boys the message that openly expressing emotions such as sadness, fear, or loneliness is "weak." When they take a tumble and hurt themselves, they are often told something like "You're okay," when they don't *feel* okay at all. On the other hand, girls are likely to be offered cuddles and gently soothed.

Research has also shown that parents talk more often to daughters than to sons about feelings. (In fact, many parents talk more to girls overall, using more words per day than they speak to boys—and the number of words spoken per day is an important ingredient in school readiness.) With less guidance and encouragement, little boys often develop the belief that having feelings is "wrong."

Interestingly, while there are indeed gender-based differences in the human brain, emotional sensitivity is not among them. Boys have exactly the same feelings that girls do, and the same need to learn emotional awareness and regulation skills. Kindlon and Thompson call this "emotional literacy," and believe that an inability to identify and express emotions may be one reason why boys are at greater risk during adolescence for depression, drug and alcohol abuse, dropping out of school, and suicide; it may also explain the high frequency of anger in both adolescent boys and adult men. Cuddling, touching, and talking about feelings will not make your son "weak"—these actions *will* help your son become a healthy young man. Practice active listening; use lots of "feeling words" in conversation. As your little boy grows up, you will find ways to teach him to understand what he feels—and to choose behavior that is respectful and appropriate.*

---

* For more information, see *Raising Cain: Protecting the Emotional Life of Boys* by Dan Kindlon and Michael Thompson (New York: Ballantine, 1999), and *The Everything Parent's Guide to Raising Boys* by Cheryl L. Erwin (Avon, Mass.: Adams Media, 2006).

DEALING WITH ANGER AND DEFIANCE

There is, perhaps, no emotion that causes more parental concern than a child's anger. Young children express anger in ways their parents find alarming: having temper tantrums, throwing objects, yelling, hitting, kicking, even biting. (Biting is a common way for children who aren't yet verbally skilled to express anger or frustration.)  All human beings have feelings—lots of them—and all of us, adults and children, need ways to express and understand our feelings.

Does this mean parents should tolerate hitting, yelling, or kicking as acceptable expressions of anger? Of course not. Actions that harm others (or oneself) are not appropriate ways of expressing feelings. Parents and teachers can make an effort to get into the young child's world and understand it. They can practice active listening to validate and clarify feelings, and they can then teach children to express their anger (which may be justified) in acceptable ways.

Children learn by watching adults. Parents model how to deal with strong feelings when they stand quietly and take some deep breaths instead of reacting immediately to upsets; when they respond to a child who tries to hit without hitting back; or when they walk over to a child, get down on his eye level, and request that he stop a behavior rather than hollering from across the room.

Children learn about anger by:

- Watching how adults behave when angry

- Experiencing how others treat them when angry

- Learning to identify feelings of anger within themselves

It is tempting to respond to anger with anger—to join in the yelling, send kids off to a punitive time-out, or otherwise try to "fix" the angry child. These responses usually escalate the conflict and destroy any opportunity there might have been to teach, to understand, or to find a workable solution to the problem. Ironically, parents may model the opposite of what they want to teach. It is difficult to teach a child to control his behavior if you can't control your own. Remember, your little one does not have the same understanding of anger that you do. He needs your help both to identify his feelings and to learn to manage and express them in appropriate ways. How can parents and caregivers help an angry child?

> ### How Should You React When Your Child Is Angry?
>
> - Use words to label your child's feelings.
> - Validate the feelings.
> - Provide appropriate ways for your child to express his feelings.

USE WORDS TO LABEL YOUR CHILD'S FEELINGS

Use a calm voice and "reflect" to your child what he is feeling. You might say, "Boy, you look angry! I see that your chin is sticking out, your eyebrows are all scrunched up, and your fists are clenched." Giving these clues helps a child make the connection between how he feels and what he is doing. Obviously, real understanding takes time, but it's never too soon to start.

VALIDATE THE FEELINGS

Emotions are generated deep within your child's brain. He does not "choose" his emotions, and there really is no such thing as a "wrong" feeling—something many adults have yet to learn. Your child has reasons for his feelings, even when he does not consciously know what those reasons are. Begin teaching your child that his feelings are always okay, but some actions are not. Try saying, "It's okay to be mad—I'd feel pretty mad, too, if I were you. It's not okay to hit me or hurt yourself. What would help you feel better?" Remember, we usually *do* better when we *feel* better. Lessons learned now about recognizing and managing feelings will benefit your child his entire life.

PROVIDE APPROPRIATE WAYS FOR YOUR CHILD TO EXPRESS HIS FEELINGS

What might an angry toddler do to manage his anger? Well, it might help to roar like a dinosaur, scribble on paper with markers, run around the backyard, or knead a ball of playdough. These provide physical outlets

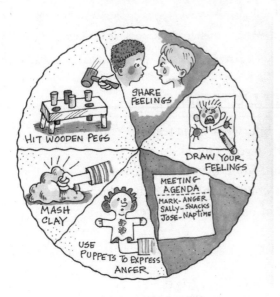

for emotional energy. Parents usually discover that anger expressed in healthy ways dissipates much more quickly; in fact, they often find themselves giggling with the same toddler who was so furious only moments before. (Hitting or punching pillows or other objects sometimes escalates anger rather than reducing it. Pay attention to what your child is learning if you choose this approach.)

Our senses can provide calming pathways, too. Taking deep breaths, smelling flowers, listening to soft music, stroking a soft teddy bear, or splashing in a basin of water can all be restorative.

A WORD ABOUT "BLANKIES" AND OTHER SECURITY OBJECTS

Closely tied to a child's feelings of trust and security is one accessory of young childhood that has passed into folklore: the security blanket. Linus, in the cartoon strip *Peanuts,* carries his everywhere, even using it to zap his obnoxious older sister. Children the world over rely on scraps of blanket, favorite stuffed animals, or imaginary friends to help them feel secure—and parents the world over often wonder if it's healthy to allow them to do so.

With a little thought, it's easy to understand how intimidating a place this world of ours can be to a very young child. A child's attachment to his blankie can be very strong; it often has its own feel and taste, and a child can usually tell if an attempt is made to replace or switch the favorite object. Many parents have had the alarming experience of leaving a teddy or blankie at the grocery store or in a motel, then having to make an emergency return trip with a hysterical child.

Feelings of insecurity and fear, while they can be upsetting for parents, are like all other emotions. They are just feelings and can be handled with active listening, warmth, and understanding. If sleeping with a special blanket or a stuffed animal helps a child relax and feel cozy, is there truly any harm in it?

Some children never adopt a blankie or stuffed animal, preferring instead to suck on their thumbs or on a pacifier. Monica believed that her children would not suck their thumbs if they had plenty of opportunity to suck at the breast. However, the one child she had nursed on demand sucked her thumb until she was six. Monica had to admit, "So much for that theory!"

Pacifiers can be a helpful way to allow an infant to satisfy her need to suck, and they can provide security (and peace) during times of upset or stress. In fact, a child who appears to have given up her thumb or pacifier often resumes the habit if the family moves, if she changes childcare settings or caregivers, or if there is some other upheaval in her life. Most parents eventually wonder if thumb sucking or using a pacifier is wise, especially as a child grows older. The American Association of Pediatrics recommends the use of a pacifier at nap and bedtime during the first year of life. Research has shown that its use can decrease the incidence of SIDS (Sudden Infant Death Syndrome). They specify that the pacifier should not be introduced until breastfeeding is securely established, and that a child not be forced to use a pacifier if she resists.

When the use of a pacifier is discontinued by age five, dental effects are typically reversible. If you have concerns about sucking needs, especially where teeth and orthodontia are concerned, you may be able to put your fears at rest by talking to a pediatric dentist. As a general rule, the less fuss adults make, the sooner the issue tends to be resolved. As they grow older, children are often willing to restrict use of their security objects to bedtime or naptime, especially if they have experienced understanding and acceptance from their parents. Most children, left to themselves, give up their blankies or pacifiers of their own free will, usually by the age of six.

WEANING FROM THE PACIFIER

Q: I would like to know if you have any suggestions about how to get my two-and-a-half- and four-and-a-half-year-old children to stop using a pacifier. I have never worried about it before and let them use it whenever they wanted, because I know it comforts them and I did not see any harm. But I took Luke, my older boy, to the orthodontist today because he has a large overbite that is affecting his speech and teeth. The orthodontist did say that the pacifier was definitely adding to the problem.

So, I guess it is time for weaning. I want to make sure that I do this in the kindest, most respectful way possible. I think I need to do the same with his little brother, Jake, because it would be hard for Luke to see his brother still using a passy. Suggestions, please!

A: Some parents have found it effective to "lose" the passies and have faith in their children to survive—which they do. When you allow your children to experience minor "suffering" (very different from "*making* them suffer"), they can develop their "disappointment muscles" and learn from experience that they can be resilient. In the long run, this will help them feel more capable. You might try talking with Luke about why his passy isn't good for him, and make a plan together for giving it up.*

Several weeks later, this mom told the following story: "Well, I sat down and talked to Luke about it and asked him how he wanted to let go of his passy. He immediately said he wanted to gather them all up, wash them, and put them in a ziplock bag to give to my sister for when she eventually has a baby. He was so sweet! So we did it, with his little brother following along as usual. They whined a little in the afternoon and just a little at night, but I reassured them and that was it. It was pretty painless. This morning Luke ran in and said, " 'I knew I could do it!' "

"My little girl's blankie sort of fell apart," said another mom. "It literally disintegrated until she was down to a few shredded pieces. It became a bother for her to find these fragments and so the blankie passed quietly into history. Actually, I gathered up a couple of these pieces and tucked them into my jewelry box. I couldn't part with them. I plan on adding them to a quilt for my grandchild someday." It is amazing how many parents who lamented their child's attachment to a blanket keep a small scrap as a memento long after their child has abandoned it.

LANGUAGE SKILLS AND COMMUNICATION

Most parents eagerly await their children's first words, sharing them with friends and family and recording them for posterity in baby books and journals. Parents smile over innocent mispronunciations and other manglings of the language, and rejoice when a child can make herself understood consistently.

---

* "The Push," a short film based on a story by David McNally, may help you understand this concept. You can find it at www.eaglesneedapush.com.

Babies generally do not begin to understand the meanings of words until they are six or seven months of age, and most don't say their first words until ten to eighteen months. Long before that time, however, a baby will turn toward a familiar voice, smile into a parent's face, or reach with delight for favorite people. It can be frustrating to try to communicate with and understand a young child who can't yet express his feelings and ideas—and it is frustrating for the child as well!

Like most other developmental skills, the acquisition of language takes place at different rates for different children. If your child seems

alert and responds well to you, chances are that all is well, even if she doesn't have much to say—yet. (If you are concerned about your child's speech development, talk to your pediatrician. Some children do experience delays in speech and language; therapy with a trained speech therapist can be helpful.)

It is worth knowing that children learn language best by being spoken to often and given lots of opportunities to respond. The cooing to newborns that is instinctive to parents the world over actually introduces a baby to the sounds of her native tongue and will help her to synchronize those sounds with lip movements.

Holding a running conversation as you stroll down the grocery aisle about the bright red apples, whether or not you are out of peanut butter, or if salmon would be nice for dinner tonight does not mean you expect your four-month-old to take over shopping anytime soon. This kind of conversation accustoms his ear to language, in the same way that those age-old nursery rhymes teach children to recognize the rhythms and sounds of spoken words—and to duplicate them when the time is right. No matter how exhausting it can be, a toddler's endless stream of "why" and "how come" questions should be answered calmly. As one three-year-old reminded his exasperated mom, "That's how little boys learn!"

THE IMPORTANCE OF TALK

Language—the words you speak and the way you speak them—shapes your very thoughts. Most researchers believe that acquiring language skills is critical to the development of thinking, problem solving, and memory retrieval. Unfortunately, educators and researchers worry that the ability to use language well (and to think critically) is declining. Why?

The biggest culprit may be our hectic, harried lifestyles and how parents choose to use the time they do have with their children. Time in which to sit and read or to talk with one another is all too limited. Children are propped in front of mobile devices and televisions while parents fix dinner, do chores, or work at home. Children may learn a cartoon character's theme song or recognize letters and numbers, but contrary to most parents' belief, they do not learn language by watching a screen. ***Language skills require connection, attention, and the interaction of real conversation.***

All too often, adults' words to children are strictly functional. "Get into your pajamas," "Eat your dinner," or "Don't hit your sister" may be all the conversation some toddlers hear. Other children spend many waking hours in childcare centers where overburdened caregivers may value silence and compliance, not budding language skills.

TEACHING LANGUAGE

Many parents believe that there will be time "later on" to teach words and language skills, but most language learning takes place in the first three years of life. What can parents and caregivers do to give little ones the best chance of learning language now—and succeeding in school later on?

How Can You Encourage Language Development?

- Talk to children.
- Encourage children to "talk back."
- Read lots of books out loud.
- Turn off the technology—at least most of the time.

TALK TO CHILDREN

Most parents instinctively know the sort of verbal play that infants and young children need. Word games, nursery rhymes, and simple songs are wonderful ways to acquaint babies with the mysteries of language. Let children hear your voice; speak to them often. Sing the old-fashioned nursery rhymes. What you say is probably less important than giving them the opportunity to experiment with sounds and words. As your children get older, telling stories is a great way to help children follow a story line, learn word meanings, and stretch their ability to visualize and imagine—all crucial parts of later learning and school readiness.

ENCOURAGE CHILDREN TO "TALK BACK"

No, we don't mean that sort of back-talk. But it is important to give children the opportunity to talk to you, to other adults, and to other children. At first, children's "speech" may consist of sounds, single words, and gestures, but as you encourage them ("what" and "how" questions are one helpful way), their ability to speak to you and to communicate ideas and feelings will grow. Adults (and older siblings) are sometimes impatient with young children, and rush to finish their sentences for them or anticipate their needs. Do your best to be tolerant and give your little one space and time to communicate.

READ LOTS OF BOOKS OUT LOUD

Reading aloud to young children may be the most helpful activity parents can do. Even babies can be propped in your lap to gaze at the pages of a colorful board book, and toddlers usually love to cuddle up and read stories. As you read, become the characters, changing your voice and providing sound effects, and encourage your child to do the same. Include books that have more text and encourage your child to form his own pictures for the words you read; or use picture-only books that allow you to invent your own stories together. Storytelling, too, can be a wonderful way to instill language and creativity. Telling stories from your own history or sharing stories from your culture can nurture budding language skills and build connection with your little one.

Reading can become a favorite part of a toddler's day, and young children are usually eager to soak up the fascinating worlds books can open. Three-year-old Kevin's mother was astonished when he "read" a favorite Berenstain Bears book to her one day. He had memorized the words, the voices—and the right places to turn the pages. Barbara was thirteen months old when her favorite aunt sat down to read a book about flowers with her. Barbara gazed intently at the picture, pulled the book into her hands, and put her nose against the page for a long sniff. Her aunt was amazed at how well Barbara understood the connection between the picture of a flower on the printed page and the fragrance of a real flower.

As your child grows older, share with her the books you loved when you were her age, or check with friends for titles their children have enjoyed.* Make reading together part of your bedtime routine. Many parents find that this cozy ritual lasts far beyond toddlerhood and provides a time of warmth and closeness for years to come.

TURN OFF THE TECHNOLOGY— AT LEAST MOST OF THE TIME

Television, apps, and games may actually change the way a child's brain functions, and the constant background noise of the TV can delay

---

* Boys may not always find books fascinating, especially when female caregivers are doing the choosing. Check out www.guysread.com for recommendations of books the males in your life will enjoy.

Is My Child Okay?

Pediatricians know that parents are often the best judge of a child's development. Because early intervention is essential in the treatment of many developmental delays and disorders, your instincts—and concerns—about your child are always worth paying attention to, *especially* in the first three years of life. (More on special needs in Chapter 20.) For instance, the incidence of autism and autism-related disorders has risen dramatically in recent years.* Communication, language, and emotional development may provide important clues about a child's development. While only a trained specialist can diagnose problems,† the following questions may help you decide if your child needs help:

- Does your child recognize and respond to familiar faces?
- Does he use his finger to point at or show you something?
- Does your child turn his head toward you when you say his name?
- Does he imitate your actions, gestures, and facial expressions?
- Does he make eye contact with you?
- Is your child interested in other children, people, or objects?
- Does he respond to your smiles, cuddles, and gestures?
- Does your child rock, bounce, or spend long periods of time staring into space?
- Does your child try to attract your attention to his own activities?
- Is your child unusually insistent on routines, predictability, or specific objects?

Children demonstrate these responses at different ages, but if you answered yes to a good number of the above questions, you probably have nothing to worry about. If you answered no to many of them and your child does not seem to make progress, you might consider talking to your doctor. Although "symptoms" do not necessarily indicate a problem, early intervention is critical. If you suspect that your child is not developing on schedule or connecting easily with his caregivers, do not hesitate to talk to your pediatrician.

---

* According to a 2014 study by the Centers for Disease Control and Prevention, autism now occurs in approximately one out of every sixty-eight births.

† For free downloadable month-by-month or annual milestone checklists, go to www.cdc.gov/ncbddd/actearly/milestones.

a child's speech development. The American Association of Pediatrics discourages screen media exposure for children under the age of two.

It may help to remember that most language and emotional development takes place naturally, *when parents and caregivers make time to play and talk with children.* Take a deep breath, relax, and remind yourself to enjoy these years. It's never too late—or too soon—to begin.

QUESTIONS TO PONDER

1. Think about the last time your child had a tantrum in a public place. (Most do eventually!) What was uppermost in your mind: helping your child calm down and learn emotional management skills, or wondering what observers might be thinking of you? Do some journaling about how your child's meltdowns affect you, and what you can do next time to remain calm and helpful.

2. Because young children are more visual than verbal, charts and pictures can be helpful tools. Make an "anger wheel of choice" with your child (if she is old enough) to help her learn to self-soothe. (See the example on page 99.) Make a simple pie chart with six or eight sections; in each section, draw a picture of something that helps your child calm down and feel better when she's angry or unhappy. Some suggestions might be water play, cuddling with a security object, listening to an audiobook, or something similar. Invite her to help you color the wheel or decorate it with glitter; then post it in a spot where she can see it easily. When she is angry or upset, invite her to look at the chart and select one way to feel better.

3. No one likes to be told what to do—including your child. Practice reframing your directions and commands ("Brush your teeth," "Put on your jacket," "Pick up your toys") as questions: "What do you need to do so your teeth won't feel slimy?" "What should you put on so you won't be cold outside?" "What do you need to do before dinner?" The message is the same, but questions invite children to think for themselves and are often received much better than commands. Try it and see!

4. Do some journaling about feelings. Do you believe that some feelings are okay to have, while others are not? Are there feelings you think your son or your daughter should not have? What did you learn from your own parents and teachers about boys, girls, and feelings? Is there anything you want to do differently with your own child?

7

TRUST VERSUS MISTRUST

"Can I Count on You?"

In his pioneering work on emotional development (work that has been validated by numerous studies), Erik Erikson identified critical tasks that all humans must master. The first critical task, a sense of trust versus mistrust, is developed during the first year. To develop a sense of trust, an important part of a secure attachment, a baby must learn that his basic needs will be met consistently and lovingly. These needs include proper nutrition, a comfortable temperature, dry diapers, adequate sleep, and lots and lots of touching, holding, and cuddling.

It's important to note that the development of trust, like all developmental tasks, will not be resolved once and for all in the first year of life. Instead, it will be built upon and expanded many times in the years ahead as you and your child face new challenges together. However, a sense of mistrust can create a foundation that will be difficult (though not impossible) to overcome in future years. For that reason, knowing how to help your child develop a sense of trust is very important.

Many parents feel confused about the difference between meeting

their babies' needs and spoiling—and they're sure to hear many points of view. Opinions range from "Put your baby on a strict schedule (after all, he or she has come to live in your house and there is no reason to change your life too much)" to "Forget about your life; hover around your baby and try to anticipate every need and whimper." Neither extreme is likely to work well. Understanding the importance of your child developing trust instead of mistrust is a key factor in finding the right balance for you and your baby.

A neglected baby (one whose basic needs for food, comfort, and loving touch are not met) will develop a sense of mistrust in life, what we now call an "insecure attachment." Perhaps surprisingly, an extremely pampered baby may also develop a sense of mistrust, because he has never had to practice much patience or self-reliance. As with so many aspects of parenting, the best solution is creating a healthy balance.

DEVELOPMENTAL APPROPRIATENESS IN THE FIRST YEAR OF LIFE

Part of dealing with young children's behavior in a way that achieves positive outcomes involves knowing what is "developmentally appropriate," a term we use to describe the characteristics and behaviors that are typical of children at certain ages. The more you know about the psychological, intellectual, and physical development of your child, the more you will know about what is developmentally appropriate and the better your ability to get into your child's world and influence his early decisions and behavior.

CAN YOU SPOIL A BABY?

At some point during a baby's first weeks and months, his parents will hear the admonition, "Don't pick the baby up every time he cries—you'll spoil him!" But most parents feel uncomfortable allowing a baby to cry, especially for long periods of time. How will you know when to hold your baby and when to allow him to sort life out for himself?

Developing trust—and having a secure attachment—means a child believes "I am loved and wanted here, no matter what." This task outweighs everything else in those first hectic weeks, and it is *always* important to respond to a baby's cries and signals, and to decide whether your little one needs food, a clean diaper, or comfort. She is deciding what "works" (from the viewpoint of a very young, immature, and unskilled person) by observing how you react to her actions. Early in a baby's life, she needs you to respond consistently and to offer her love, comfort, and care.

Sometime during the first year, infants begin to form beliefs about themselves and other people, and about how to get what they believe they need. (Some believe this process may even begin in the womb.) At this point, babies may learn to cry in order to get attention. There is nothing wrong with wanting and getting attention. However, there's an old rule of thumb about this: If you feel like you're being manipulated by your child—you may be!

If parents do not respond consistently to a baby's cues, that baby may decide he doesn't belong and cannot trust the adults in his life. This can damage the attachment that is so critical for social, emotional, and intellectual development. But if parents pamper a baby, picking her up at every whimper and never allowing her to experience her feelings or learn to soothe herself, that baby may decide life is best lived by getting others to do things for her. Time will help you discover how to respond to your own baby, but remember: she will need time and space to practice skills. Crying isn't fatal, no matter how frustrating or irritating it may be, and letting your baby fuss a bit isn't bad parenting—especially after the first few months. Truly getting to know your own child is your first crucial task. If in doubt, err on the side of attachment and engage in the challenging process of "weaning" when your child develops language skills.

Alisa adored her four-month-old baby, Matthew, and loved to hold him, but she didn't want to be manipulated by her charming little guy. So she took her mother-in-law's advice and let the baby "cry it out"; she stopped going in to pick him up when he awoke crying. This seemed to work well, and eventually Matthew and his mom slept more soundly. But one night little Matthew cried for over an hour, refusing to settle down and sleep. Finally, desperate for some rest herself, Alisa went in to check on him and discovered he was running a 104-degree fever. She realized that while she didn't want to pamper her baby, she did need to respond to be sure his basic needs were being met. She also decided to wait until he was older to work on teaching him resilience.

Learning the difference between what an infant truly *needs* and what he simply *wants* causes considerable anxiety for parents, but as your understanding increases so will your confidence. As we have said before, it is important to meet all of your child's needs, but not all of her wants. When a child lives in an environment where she experiences large doses of connection, she will not be traumatized by small doses of disappointment. **You will need to use your head and your heart to be an effective parent.** The more information you have, the more you can trust your head. The more you know how important it is to enjoy your child, the more you can trust your heart. When in doubt, always trust your heart.

UNIQUENESS, SELF-TRUST, AND PARENT CONFIDENCE

To say that people are different and unique isn't new or profound, but it is easy to forget. With time, you will discover parenting tools that feel comfortable and effective for you. What does all this have to do with the development of trust or mistrust? Erikson found that a primary factor in the development of a child's trust is her sense that her primary caretaker—usually her mother—has confidence in herself.

Trust Versus Mistrust

During the first year of life, a child begins to learn the fundamental concept of trust, the first important stage of emotional development. If she cries, does someone come? If she's hungry, cold, or wet, will someone help? Do the routines and rituals of daily life happen predictably? It is through these simple experiences that she will learn to trust and rely on her parents.

Without this basic sense of trust, life becomes far more difficult. Children who have been shuttled in and out of foster homes during their early years, or who have been denied affection and consistent care, often refuse to make eye contact or respond to even the most loving attempts later on. It can take a great deal of patience and determination to instill the sense of trust that was stunted during these children's early years.

Most of us know people who have a hard time trusting themselves or others, and who seem to have little faith in their ability to influence what happens to them. Will your child go through life with a sense of trust or mistrust, faith or doubt? Much depends on how he is treated in the first year of life (and the subconscious decisions he makes about his experiences). The development of a sense of trust begins in this critical first year and will continue as your child grows.

Because self-confidence is so important, we want to repeat that most mothers find they can trust themselves more when they have a basic understanding of child development and parenting skills—and faith in their own instincts. This is one reason that parent education can be so important. When you have learned all you can about child development, age-appropriate behavior, and nonpunitive methods to help your child thrive, you will feel more confident about your ability to understand and care for your child.

Children develop a sense of trust when someone consistently responds to their cries, but do not misinterpret this to mean that your child will be traumatized if you don't respond to every whimper.

Parents soon learn to recognize the differences in a baby's cries—whether she is hungry, hurt, or angry. Sometimes a baby will cry to release excess energy; allowing her to cry until she settles may actually help her learn to self-soothe. When parents think they have to help their children get to sleep by rocking them, nursing them, or giving them a bottle, or even lying down with them, their children may learn manipulation skills instead of trust (in themselves and in their parents). This does not mean that falling asleep in Grandma's arms while being rocked is going to damage your child. Always remember that balance is better than any extreme.

It takes knowledge and confidence (and faith in your child) to know when it is okay to allow her to experience a little discomfort in order to develop a sense of trust and confidence in herself. Remember that no parent is born knowing where this balance lies—and mistakes allow us to fine-tune our knowledge. Pay attention not only to your baby but also to your own feelings and wisdom, and chances are good that you'll soon know what works best for your child.

ROUTINES AND RITUALS

These early months and years represent a time of constant change. Any mom with a newborn can testify that her daily routines change drastically from day to day, because everything is new, for both infants and their parents. For a child to develop trust, life must become predictable, and that is the role of routines. Establishing routines is an important part of a parent and child's first months and years together. By the age of three months, most babies have settled into a predictable schedule. If a mother is nursing, the three-month point seems to be the time when growth spurts that cause fussiness cease. Milk supply now meets the child's needs. But routines will be tested along the way as a child grows and develops—for example, when she is ready to give up naps but you aren't ready to give up that quiet time for yourself.

Daily activities, when done in ways that can be counted upon, form the backdrop of predictability and connection that becomes a child's life experience. When we see things in this context, it makes sense that whenever there is disruption in our lives—from a move, to a divorce, to the chaos caused

by natural or man-made disasters—our sense of safety is reestablished by following familiar routines, allowing us to resume our trust in the world around us. The early activities of caregiving may not seem critical, but these simple everyday acts shape our lifelong ability to trust.

Rituals, though not very elaborate in these early years, do contribute important elements to the strengthening and development of trust. Mom gently bouncing her baby and cooing after nursing, Dad making smacking sounds with his lips to coax a smile before offering the baby his bottle, or an older sister singing "Twinkle, Twinkle, Little Star" at bedtime—all are rituals that add texture to a young child's life and begin to define it. They confirm his experience of the world as a predictable and trustworthy place, and tell him that he is secure and safe. As he grows, the rituals of family celebrations and traditions will continue to add joy and a sense of connection to his life.

ENJOY YOUR CHILDREN AND YOURSELF

Life throws plenty of curveballs to all new parents, from ear infections to worries about unpaid bills, but if you forget to enjoy special moments, learning new skills and adjusting to life with a developing child can seem like a heavy burden. Do we really need to mention the importance of enjoying your children? We think so. Sharing your life

with a child, especially during his first year of life, can be an overwhelming experience. Everything is new, the baby is demanding, and you may have moments when you worry if you're doing it "right." Your baby will sense your worry and doubt, and his growing sense of trust may be hindered. Use this opportunity to increase your trust in yourself—remembering that it is not helpful to take mistakes too seriously. It is helpful to learn from them with gratitude. When built upon the foundation of enjoyment, awareness, and education, confidence will filter through your heart and you will know what to do. (Yes, you really will!)

MAKING ENJOYMENT A PRIORITY

How can infants develop a sense of trust if they don't feel the energy of enjoyment from their parents or caregivers, and know that they are loved, wanted, and appreciated? Maya Angelou said it all on an *Oprah* show: "Do your eyes light up when your children walk into the room?" When your child is an infant, make sure your eyes light up when you walk into his presence—and continue to do so for the rest of your life.

Ask yourself this question when circumstances get in the way of simply enjoying your child: "What difference will this make ten years from now?" Whether or not the house is clean, the lawn is mowed, or the furniture is waxed won't make any difference; on the other hand, time you spend with your partner and your child will make all the difference in the world!

Help Your Infant Develop a Sense of Trust

- Meet all your baby's needs.
- Learn the difference between needs and wants.
- Avoid pampering (meet all needs, not all wants).
- Learn about developmental needs (social, intellectual, and physical).
- Learn parenting skills (including long-term results of what you do).
- Have confidence and trust in yourself and your child.
- Enjoy your child.

QUESTIONS TO PONDER

1. Take a moment to journal about your own confidence as a parent. What parts of caring for your child allow you to relax and enjoy the process? What tasks make you feel tense or overwhelmed? How might your relationship with your child be different if you were able to relax more often? What would allow you to develop confidence as a parent?

2. Are there times you feel you're being manipulated by your child? Do you believe it's necessary to constantly hold or carry your child? How easily can you tolerate her crying and attempts to self-soothe? In what ways does learning about her need to develop trust help you relax and give her space to learn?

8

AUTONOMY VERSUS DOUBT AND SHAME

"I Can Stand on My Own Two Feet (But Don't Abandon Me!)"

The second of Erik Erikson's critical tasks (a sense of autonomy versus doubt and shame) is developed during the second year of life. Understanding this will help you find more joy than frustration in the many antics of your toddler. What do toddlers want to do? Just about everything: explore, touch, examine, put their fingers in sockets, play with the remote control, empty cupboards of every pot and pan, play in the toilet, unravel the toilet paper, eat lipstick, spill perfume, and investigate everything they can get their hands on.

What happens when parents don't allow a toddler to explore, or slap their child's hand when he touches something he is not supposed to touch? He may develop a sense of doubt and shame that haunts him in later life. Shame, it turns out, is one of the most toxic emotional reactions a person can have, and does not inspire trust, confidence, or closeness.

Well-meaning parents who have not learned about this important developmental phase may not know that too much confinement and punishment, or constantly referring to the "terrible twos" with irritation, can instill doubt and shame instead of a sense of autonomy—even though this sense of doubt and shame does not show up until later in life. Notice that we said a *sense of* autonomy—not autonomy itself.

Erik Erikson used the words "sense of" to describe a tendency in one direction or the other. A "sense of" also describes the confidence or confusion young children may experience when they don't have the language or maturity to explain what is happening. Erikson believed that between the ages of one and three, children have the opportunity, with the help of their parents, to begin their quest for a sense of autonomy that is stronger and healthier than feelings of doubt and shame.

A sense of autonomy is critical in healthy development; it is autonomy that gives a child confidence and the ability to pursue his own ideas and plans. Not surprisingly, a young child's desire for autonomy presents some challenges for parents (as anyone who has shared a home with a toddler can testify), but children cannot thrive without it. Your child's search for a sense of autonomy will continue throughout his childhood, but the foundation is established in his second and third year. A strong sense of trust initiated in the first year, and a strong sense of autonomy developed in the second and third years, also build the foundation for healthy self-worth.

WHAT IS AUTONOMY?

Since a strong sense of autonomy is so important, you need to know what it is and how to help your toddler develop it. The dictionary defines "autonomy" as independence or freedom, having the will of one's actions. "What?" you might ask. "Give my toddler independence and freedom? My toddler is still a baby who needs to be dependent on me!" The truth is that your toddler needs both autonomy *and* healthy dependence on you. He needs a balance between the security provided by parents and home, and the freedom to discover his own capabilities.

This is illustrated beautifully by Harry F. Harlow's classic research using monkeys and their young. In Harlow's study, the mother monkeys took their babies into a room full of toys. The baby monkeys clung to their mothers while they surveyed the interesting toys. Eventually, their need to explore took over and they left their mothers to play with the toys. Periodically, they would return and jump into their mothers' arms for another dose of security before going back to their play. Children, too, need this gentle blending of safety and freedom. Too much freedom could be dangerous and threatening for a toddler. Too little freedom hampers healthy brain development and may stunt a developing sense of autonomy.

ENCOURAGING AUTONOMY WITHOUT BEING PERMISSIVE

It is easy to misunderstand what autonomy means for a toddler. Possessing autonomy does not mean that a child no longer needs guidance and safe boundaries. She does. It does not mean that she should rule the house and do whatever she wants. She shouldn't. The development of autonomy requires freedom *within* safe boundaries, and kind and firm guidance, so your child can begin her important journey toward independence.

Autonomy does not mean that a child is prepared to make decisions about life situations. Asking a child whether he wants to hold the keys or your purse gives him a healthy opportunity to experience his own power. Asking him whether he would prefer this preschool or that one, whether the family should visit Grandma's at Thanksgiving, or whether he would mind if Mommy and Daddy go to a movie tonight may lead him to believe he is (or should be) in charge. Such decisions are adult responsibilities. Burdening children with too many choices—or the wrong sorts of choices—creates demanding, anxious tyrants. This is ineffective—and possibly harmful—parenting.

HOW TO SAFELY PROMOTE AUTONOMY

Because autonomy is such an important step in healthy development, you may wonder just what your role should be in promoting your little one's self-confidence without exposing her to undue risk. One of the more persistent debates about parenting in early childhood concerns childproofing a home: removing poisons, plugging electrical sockets, latching kitchen cabinets, putting valuable or fragile items out of reach of young hands, and otherwise making the home environment safe for a child to explore. The importance of developing a child's autonomy is an excellent argument in favor of childproofing your home. Some adults fret that childproofing fails to teach children about restraint. Remember that this is the age for supervision: self-restraint will come later. Young children are developmentally programmed to explore, and lack impulse control. If you ignore developmental needs and limitations, stress is the most likely result. The accompanying conflict and power struggles will not teach your child anything helpful.

There are many things a child should not be allowed to do—like running with Grandma's crystal vase or taking Dad's hammer to the goldfish tank. Many adults believe the best way to teach toddlers not to touch things or do what they shouldn't is to slap their hands. Not so. One childcare director who was leading a parenting class was asked how he kept children away from things they should not touch. Without any hesitation he said, "If they shouldn't touch it, it is not within their reach." Pretty simple, really. Grandma's vase belongs on the mantel and Dad's hammer should be stored in a toolbox. (The fish will thank you.)

Homes are not always easy to rearrange, but there is still much you can do to provide a safe and exploration-friendly environment. Try covering those tempting remote controls or computer keyboards with a small cloth or towel. Limit access to what your toddler can reach and offer something appropriate to explore instead, such as lower drawers filled with pots and pans or plastic containers. Block access to wires and other forbidden objects by placing a basket of tempting toys in front of them.

Think for a moment. Toddlers would not be normal if they didn't want to explore and touch. They're doing their developmental job, and it is an important ingredient in their sense of autonomy. Does it make sense to punish them for doing something that is normal and important for healthy development? Slapping and spanking is far more likely to create a sense of doubt and shame than healthy autonomy. Effective parenting can help children learn limits without creating doubt and shame.

One mother insisted that she had to spank her child when it was a matter of safety, such as running into the street. She was asked if she thought a spanking would teach him well enough that she could allow him to play near a busy street unsupervised. She had to admit it wouldn't. When she was asked, "How about a hundred spankings? Would that teach him so you could let him play near a busy street unsupervised?" She had to admit that she wouldn't let her toddler play near a busy street no matter how often he had been spanked. She knew instinctively that he lacked the maturity and judgment to handle such danger on his own, and that spanking was not effective teaching.

TEACH WITHOUT EXPECTING YOUR CHILD TO UNDERSTAND—UNTIL HE IS READY

What this mother *can* do is teach her child about the dangers of a busy street—without expecting him to understand until he is older and can grasp the meaning of what he has been learning. She can hold his hand while walking near a busy intersection, ask him to look up and down the street to see if any cars are coming, and have him tell her when he thinks it is safe to cross the street. Even when he understands that it is safe to cross the street only when no cars are coming, he will still need supervision until he is much older—at least six to ten years old, depending on your community.

This method of teaching follows the same principles of how children learn to talk. No one expects an infant to understand all the loving things parents say to her. Parents don't expect their toddler to understand the first books they read to her. However, they recognize that their children will never learn to talk or understand stories unless they hear a lot of talking and reading—for as long as it takes.

AUTONOMY AS A LIFE SKILL

Imagine awaking from a deep sleep and discovering that you are in an unfamiliar new world and must learn not only how your own, brand-new body and emotions work but how the people around you live—and what they expect from you. Learning to survive and thrive would require a great deal of courage.

Just being a toddler takes courage, something that is innate in young children unless parents instill a sense of fear. Little ones are born with the

courage and energy to set about exploring how their world works. It's a task fraught with perils—from a parent's point of view. Actually, parents and toddlers make a good team. A toddler is happy to climb on the couch, and parents can be ready to catch him when he gets too close to the edge.

Healthy autonomy is a balance between protecting children and allowing them to explore and test the world they will inhabit. How much is too much? How will you know when you (and your child) have the balance right?

THE NEED TO EXPLORE IN A SAFE ENVIRONMENT

An important part of the development of autonomy during the second year of life lies in the maturation of the muscle system. Providing a safe environment for exploration is one of the best ways to help toddlers develop autonomy as well as healthy muscles. As they explore, they exercise their muscles and enhance muscle maturation by experimenting with such activities as climbing, holding on, and letting go. (Yes, dropping that spoon over and over is helping them develop both their sense of autonomy and their muscle control.) Children who are confined too much will not have the opportunity to develop a strong sense of autonomy. Their brains may not develop the important pathways that come from exploring, and testing what they can and cannot do.

> *Jenny did not know about the importance of helping her toddler develop a strong sense of autonomy. She was an artist who loved to paint during the day when the light was good. Her daughter, Dani, seemed content to sit in a high chair eating crackers for long periods of time. When Dani would tire of the high chair, Jenny would move her to a playpen or windup swing. Dani was rarely allowed to roam around the house.*

Jenny was not a "bad" parent. She felt thrilled and lucky that Dani seemed so content with her confinement, and that she could get so much painting done. Jenny didn't understand that she was hindering Dani's development of autonomy, brain development, and muscle control by not giving her more opportunities to explore.

Positive Discipline methods help children develop a sense of autonomy and brain development, as well as the characteristics and the life skills they will need when they no longer depend on adults. Children, from birth through the preschool years, *always* need adults around. They also need opportunities to begin learning the attitudes and skills required to eventually make decisions and solve problems on their own.

PUNISHMENT EQUALS DOUBT AND SHAME

Punishment is something that a more powerful person does to a less powerful person with the hope of creating a change in behavior. Unfortunately, punishment does not foster a healthy sense of autonomy, and it does not teach life skills. Still, *not* punishing seems to require a real shift in attitude for many parents. Punishment (spanking and shaming children for doing things that are developmentally appropriate) fosters doubt and shame. Children will experience enough self-imposed doubt and shame as they encounter the real limits of their abilities.

Real discipline is *teaching*. Punishment does not teach helpful skills or attitudes. Do not slap hands, spank, or use shaming words, such as "bad girl." A young child often does not understand the connection between what she did (reach for an electrical cord) and the response (a quick slap). Many parents have had the unsettling experience of reaching for a child with love and having that child cringe away in fear, as if a slap is on the way. This is certainly not the sort of relationship that fosters trust and closeness, and certainly not what most parents would choose.

Children may experience frustration at not being allowed to play with your smartphone or to turn the dials on the stove. This is what Erikson called the real "crisis" of this stage of development. But adding punishment to the natural crisis is like pouring salt on a wound. The frustration is greatly eased when parents remember to be kind when they are being firm. Children feel the difference.

TEACHING TODDLERS?

Not only *can* you teach a toddler, you *must*. Encourage autonomy by asking questions, and encourage your toddler to ask questions too. Skip the lectures. They invite avoidance or resistance, while questions invite thinking and participation. Toddlers can understand more than they can verbalize. Asking questions such as "What might happen if we cross the street without

To Spank or Not to Spank

Q: When my son was three years old, he was very good. The few times he was bad, I used to take him to his room and put him on the time-out chair and it worked. Now my daughter is three. She is always bad. I've done everything I can think of. The time-out chair didn't work, so I tried telling her no, taking away toys, talking about why she was bad, and even hugging her a lot, saying what she did was bad and she should try not to do it again. The only thing left to do is spank. I never spanked my son, and my mother never spanked me. I don't know if I should. If I do spank, which way is best? Should I use my hand or a belt? Should she be standing or over my knee? I want to do what is best for my daughter.

A: Parents need to understand that their children are never "bad," even though they may get into mischief. When parents understand developmental appropriateness, Erikson's social and emotional stages of development, and temperament, even the definition of "mischief" will shrink. Your daughter is not "bad" any more than your son is perfect—they have different temperaments. (And even though your son's temperament is easier to deal with, we worry that he might become dependent on the approval of others or fail to develop healthy self-worth. Children are not developing appropriate autonomy and initiative if they do not go through lots of exploring, experimenting, and testing of the rules.)

Your daughter sounds normal for her temperament, not "bad." The problem is that when punitive methods are used with "normal" children (who can have any of a wide range of different temperament types), it is the *punishment* that creates defiance, rebellion, and power struggles. All of the methods you have been using are punitive. (You are even turning hugs into punishment by telling her she is bad while hugging her.) We're glad you have avoided spanking. Many research studies have shown that over time, spanking creates even worse behavior.

So what should you do? Here are just a few of the many Positive Discipline tools you could try:

1. Create a connection before correction: "I love you, and it is not okay to do what you are doing."
2. Ask for her help: "Sweetie, I need your help. What ideas do you have to solve this problem?" This question often invites cooperation instead of resistance.
3. Turn it around and ask her how you can help her: "What do you need right now?"
4. Tell her you need a hug. This is often enough to stop the spiral of discouraging behavior.
5. Kindly take her hand and lead her to what she should do. If she resists, smile warmly and keep moving in the direction of what needs to be done.

looking first?" helps with language development, thinking skills, and a child's sense of autonomy.

SHOW WHAT *TO* DO INSTEAD OF WHAT NOT TO DO

Many toddlers go through a hitting stage. Believe it or not, when they do this they are not really misbehaving. It could be that they are frustrated and don't have the skills to accomplish their goals. Many are just exploring possibilities by hitting (such as what happens when they hit the water in the tub). Have you ever watched parents hit children while telling them not to hit? Parents may also scold and say, "We don't hit!" Watch the twinkle in a child's eye and you can just imagine her saying, "Yes, we do. We just did."

Instead of hitting back or scolding, it is more effective to show a child what to do rather than what not to do. Increase your supervision during the hitting pattern of behavior. Quickly catch a hand that is poised to hit and say "Touch nicely" while showing her what this looks like.

> *Eighteen-month-old Cecelia was going through a hitting phase. She would hit her mother in the face "for no reason at all." Mom was just holding her. She would also hit the dog. Mom became more vigilant at supervision and started catching her in the act. She would gently guide Cecelia's hand to stroke her face while saying, "Touch gently." Mom would catch Cecelia's hand as she started to hit the dog, and would guide her hand to stroke the dog while saying, "Touch nicely."*
>
> *After this scene was repeated four or five times, Cecelia would raise her hand to hit and then look at her mom with an impish grin. Mom would say, "Touch nicely"—and Cecelia would.*

DEVELOPMENTALLY APPROPRIATE BEHAVIOR

> *Patsy had her arms full. The diaper bag was slung over one shoulder, two overdue library books were gripped in one hand,*

and the car keys dangled from one finger. Patsy's other arm cradled her two-month-old baby son. "Come on, Marissa," she called to her two-and-a-half-year-old. "It's time to go to the library. Let's get in the car."

But Marissa wasn't having anything to do with the idea. She stood miserably at the top of the porch steps with her arms stretched out toward her mother. "Up!" she insisted.

Patsy sighed with exasperation. "You can walk," she said encouragingly. "Come on, sweetie—Mommy's arms are full."

Marissa's small face crumpled. "Can't walk," she wailed, collapsing in a pitiful little heap. "Uuuuppp!"

Patsy sighed and her overloaded shoulders sagged. Was it wrong to ask Marissa to use her own two legs? Would she feel unloved if Patsy didn't pick her up?

Marissa wants to be carried but she does not *need* to be carried, unless she is exhausted or ill. It is developmentally appropriate to carry an infant but less appropriate to carry a toddler. Understanding Marissa's need for healthy autonomy will help her mother decide when to carry her and when to allow her to struggle on her own.

Suppose you have a toddler who wants to be carried to the car. Instead of carrying her, you may stoop down, give her a hug (you may need to put a few things down first), and tell her you are sure she can walk to the car by herself. If she still whines to be carried, you might say, "I'll hold your hand and walk slowly, but I know you can do it." Even better, enlist her aid. "I really need your help. Will you carry my book?" Voilà! The tears dry up and everyone proceeds to the car, with mom carrying one less item.

Yes, it seems easier to just pick her up and carry her to the car. Helping children develop the confidence and life skills they need is not always easy or convenient. But who said parenting would be easy? It need not be so difficult, either. Successful parenting is often a matter of knowing what is effective and what is not.

DISTRACTION AND CHOICES

Since it is normal and developmentally appropriate for toddlers to explore and want to touch, it is wise to provide them with areas where they can do so safely. In the kitchen, you might have a cupboard full of plastic containers, wooden spoons, and other items that can't hurt or be hurt by your child. In the living room, you can provide a box of special toys.

When your child wants to touch something that shouldn't be touched or cannot be placed out of reach, such as a potted orchid, kindly and firmly pick him up and remove him from that item and place him by the toy box. Don't slap or say "No!" Instead, tell him what he can do. "You can play with your toys. Look at the big truck. I'll bet you can make it move."

It is also important to realize that words alone will not be effective in managing your child's behavior—or keeping her safe. Rather than saying "No!" or "Don't touch that!" from across the room, get up and go to your child. Make eye contact, then use kind, firm *action* to move her away from forbidden or dangerous objects. Relying on words alone often teaches children that they can safely ignore you. After all, there's not much you can do from across the room.

Toddlers are interested in exploring so many things that it is not difficult to use distraction at this age. When a toddler wants to touch something that isn't appropriate, offer a substitute—or a choice of substitutes. "You can't jump on the couch. Would you like to play with your truck or help me wash the dishes?" "It is time for bed. Which story do you want me to read when you've put on your pajamas?" "I need to talk on the phone now. You can play in your drawer (prepared in advance with age-appropriate items) or the pan cupboard while I'm on the phone." One mom kept several activity baskets on top of her refrigerator, which came down only during phone calls. When she

The Triple A's of Autonomy

Attitude

1. Change your perception. Recognize your child's developmental abilities, then calm yourself before responding.
2. Recognize your child's limited understanding. "No" is an abstract concept and one that toddlers do not fully understand.
3. Accept that developmental timetables differ. Each child will develop in his own unique way.
4. Value the *process*, not only the *product*. Make time to enjoy getting there or doing something, instead of focusing only on the destination or outcome.

Atmosphere

1. Provide opportunities for practice. Accept that skill-practice can be messy. Support mastery by making tasks child-friendly with scaled-down implements and small, easy steps. Remember, your child is growing brain connections.
2. Encourage thinking. Involve your child in planning by asking "what" and "how" questions.
3. Allow appropriate power. Provide reasonable chances to say no.
4. Avoid power struggles. Give a hug instead of engaging in yes/no shouting matches.

Action

1. Be kind *and* firm. Follow through by doing what you say you will do.
2. Teach by doing. Talk less, avoid lectures, and *act* instead.
3. Show children what to do instead of what not to do. Again, avoid lectures and teach by modeling appropriate behavior.
4. Offer limited choices (all of which are acceptable): "Do you want to wear the red pajamas or the blue ones?"
5. Avoid open-ended choices, such as "Do you want to go to bed?" with its potential, unacceptable "no."
6. Use redirection and distraction—as many times as it takes.

Tools for Developing Healthy Autonomy

• Provide security *and* opportunities to explore.
• Remove dangerous objects and create safe boundaries, then let go and allow your child to investigate his world.
• Use distraction, redirection, and kind, firm action to guide your toddler's behavior rather than slapping, spanking, or words alone.
• Allow your toddler to run, climb, and develop healthy muscles in a safe space.
• Recognize the difference between your child's *wants* and *needs*; you should always respond to his needs, but using good judgment about when to provide what he wants will help him learn character and life skills.
• Teach skills *and* provide careful supervision.
• Focus on connection, love, and relationship.

wanted to talk on the phone, she brought out a basket. Her daughter eagerly looked forward to a chance to play with these special toys. With simple additions—such as a new ball, a different-sized block, or a puzzle—the baskets remained intriguing. Offering choices and using distraction are simple and respectful responses to a toddler's need for guidance.

UNCONSCIOUS LIFE DECISIONS

One thing children do not consciously understand and cannot verbalize is the unconscious decisions they are constantly making about themselves, about the world, about others, and about how they need to behave in the world to survive and thrive. They are making decisions based on their interpretation of their life experiences, and these early nonverbal, emotional responses or "adaptations" become part of the wiring of a child's brain.

When you distract your child by removing her from what she can't touch and guiding her to what she can, what will she decide? She will probably realize that it is okay to explore, to try new things, and to learn about the world around her—and that some things are off-limits.

I BLEW IT!

Sometimes parents feel guilty when they discover new information, especially when it seems to point out mistakes they may have made. You may be saying, "Oh my goodness! That's what I did! Have I ruined my child forever?" Absolutely not. As we say over and over, mistakes are wonderful opportunities to learn—for adults and for children.

Sometimes you will need to tell your child about your mistakes and start over. "Honey, I thought the best way to show you how much I love you was to do everything for you. Now I know that is not the best thing for you. It may be hard for both of us, but I need to help you learn how capable you are. I have faith in both of us. We can do it!" And it's true. Don't waste any time on guilt. You will continue to make mistakes; so will your child. Isn't that exciting? If your child isn't talking yet, you can convey the same message through the energy of your attitude and confidence.

Understanding the importance of this developmental stage can help parents learn the skills and provide the atmosphere (at least most of the time) that encourage children to develop competence and capability that will serve them all their lives. Parents can also interact with their children (most of the time) in ways that invite them to make healthy decisions about themselves, others, and the world. Notice we said "invite." We can never be sure how individuals will interpret their own life experiences and what they will decide about them. Notice, too, that we say "most of the time." None of us—parents or children—gets it right all the time. Teaching, loving, and acting respectfully most of the time really is enough.

A child may still feel frustrated and upset about not being allowed to touch whatever she wants. She may even have a temper tantrum. However, when supervised with firmness and kindness, she will have a much different feeling (and make different decisions about herself and about you) than when she is forced or punished.

Children who are encouraged to develop a sense of autonomy usually make healthier decisions later in life. Children who are not allowed to develop a sense of autonomy will more often make decisions based on doubt and shame, which does not lead to the skills and attitudes you want your child to have.

LOVE AND ENJOYMENT

Understanding how important it is for a child to develop autonomy can help parents recognize that neither overprotection nor overindulgence is the best way to show the love children need. Instead, parents can have fun showing love by watching freedom and independence develop in their children and by enjoying the promise of confidence and courage in years to come.

QUESTIONS TO PONDER

1. Look around one room or area of your living space and identify the things your child should not touch. Decide how to move these items out of reach, or how to make them less accessible. Repeat with each room or area of your home.

2. Take time to journal about your own reactions to your child's desire for autonomy. How do you feel when she wants to do things on her own? How do you react? Is there anything you might want to do differently to encourage her sense of competence and confidence while still keeping her safe?

9

UNDERSTANDING AGE-APPROPRIATE BEHAVIOR— AND HOW TO MANAGE IT

Me do it!" This is the cry of the eager two-year-old who is trying to tell us, "I'm ready for big-time autonomy." Although a sense of autonomy is an important step on the developmental path toward confidence and capability, it certainly creates challenges for parents. After all, wouldn't life be much simpler if your child would just do what you tell him to?

There is a difference between "misbehavior" and behavior that grows from a child's inborn, developmentally appropriate need to learn and explore. Just because a behavior is age-appropriate, though, doesn't mean it isn't messy, frustrating, or challenging. You must still respond to it. Understanding age-appropriateness will keep you from taking your child's behavior personally, and from reacting in ways that stifle his growing sense of himself.

Jeremy is almost three years old, and while his parents often laugh that he is a "handful," they delight in their son's curiosity and willingness to experiment with and experience the world around him. Jeremy's mother discovered him one bright morning making a cake in the kitchen; he had stirred milk, raisins, two eggs (with shells), cereal, and lots of flour in the largest bowl he could find. Jeremy's dad found him a few days later using pliers to investigate the inner workings of the vacuum cleaner. Jeremy, his parents have decided, needs invitations to help in the kitchen, a set of his own small tools (and nonelectrical objects to experiment with)—and lots of supervision. Despite the occasional mess, they're happy to know that their son finds his world a fascinating and welcoming place.

Marcus is also nearly three years of age, but Marcus's world is a different sort of place from Jeremy's. Marcus is most comfortable in front of the television. New people and places frighten him, although his parents often encourage him not to be "so shy." Marcus loves the computer and tried to help his dad with his work, but something happened to Dad's files and Dad got mad. Marcus would like to work in the garden with his mom, too, but after he dug a whole row of small holes, taking out mom's newly emerging sweet peas in the process, she sighed the big sigh that Marcus hates and told him to go play in the house. It feels safer to Marcus not to have too many ideas, and to simply watch TV instead. When people raise their voices, he hunches into a small ball. It will take some time and a lot of encouragement for Marcus to show his curiosity again.

AUTONOMY AND "DEVELOPMENTAL APPROPRIATENESS"

Two- and three-year-olds like Jeremy and Marcus see the world as an exciting and fascinating place, especially as they develop more autonomy and a greater physical and intellectual capacity to explore. At the same time, however, they are often frustrated when they find they do not have the skills or abilities to accomplish what they want. Children may respond to these frustrations by withdrawing and adopting a sense of doubt about their ability to "conquer the world." Adults can help develop toddlers' confidence (and guide their behavior) by providing a range of opportunities, time for training, and encouragement for the many things children *can* do as they gain a sense of healthy autonomy.

IS THIS REALLY MISBEHAVIOR?

Parenting a toddler will be much less frustrating when parents respond to the intention *behind* the behavior. This is often more easily said than done, especially when you're face-to-face with a two-year-old in a temper. Still, the following concepts may help you work effectively with your child's development:

- "Defiance" looks (and feels) much different when you understand that a child is struggling to develop a sense of autonomy. Her perception of a situation is almost certainly different from yours. Does this mean that it's okay for your two-year-old to shout "No!" in your face? No, but it may mean that you should calm yourself down and think, instead of shouting "No!" back. (Such encounters usually go more smoothly when only one of you is having a tantrum.)

- It makes sense that a child doesn't listen to you when you understand that his developmental urges have a "louder voice." He doesn't intend to disobey or to forget what you've asked; your requests and instructions are simply overwhelmed by his own needs and developmental process. Kind actions, rather than words or punishment, are what is needed.

- It makes sense to use kindness and firmness, as well as problem-solving skills, to find appropriate solutions (as Jeremy's parents did) instead of punishment or useless lectures ("How many times do I have to tell you?") when you understand developmental appropriateness. Kindness shows love and respect for your child's needs and limitations. Firmness provides structure, teaching, and safety. Focusing on solutions addresses underlying skill development, is consistent with the current understanding of brain development, and is based on maintaining dignity and respect for all.

Adults may also need a slight attitude adjustment. Parents are often disappointed or angry when their young children don't live up to their expectations. Two- or three-year-olds are too little to do things  perfectly (as Marcus's parents discovered). It is certainly simpler and faster for you to do things *for* your child (or without him) instead of taking the time and having the patience to help him do things himself (or, at least, with you). But which is more important: ease, speed, and perfection, or helping children develop confidence, perceptions of capability, and strong life skills? That's what healthy autonomy is all about.

Parenting is rarely quick, tidy, or efficient. Too many parents want confident, courageous, cooperative, respectful, resourceful, responsible children, but they don't understand what children need in order to develop these characteristics. With training, two-year-olds can dress themselves, pour their own cereal and milk (from child-sized containers), and help set the table. They can learn to help out at the grocery store, hand out prayer books at church, or pick up litter at the park. Learning these skills is an important part of developing a sense of autonomy and experiencing positive contribution.

SKILLS ARE LEARNED, NOT INBORN

No one is born with the ability to eat with a spoon. There are no genetic codes that enable a child to ease her arms into narrow coat sleeves. Even child prodigies cannot carry a full cup of juice without losing a drop or two. Skills are learned, not inborn. When you understand that *all* skills require training, you can begin to see your child as a competent learner with unlimited potential, instead of a clumsy little burden.

One of the most exciting insights of brain research tells us that brain connections strengthen with repetition. This applies directly to skill development. Your child won't perfect the art of fitting her feet into her shoes on the first try. It requires regular repetition of this act to achieve proficiency. Her brain is linking up new connections while she gains mastery over her wiggly fingers and squirmy toes. Research has taught us that knowledge and experience are inseparably entwined; each increases the other. When you teach your child to master tasks step-by-step and provide lots of opportunities to practice, you will be raising a competent, confident child.

SKILLS VERSUS SPILLS

The long process of learning skills provides lots of opportunities to spill, drip, and dump. Think of a typical activity, such as pouring morning cereal and milk. Teaching a skill is easiest when you modify the task to help your little one experience success.

The cereal box is big and unwieldy; so is the milk carton. But you can adjust both so that your child can practice autonomy and learn new skills. Serve milk in a little pitcher or measuring cup, repackage cereal in small containers, and place everything at a convenient height. Demonstrate pouring the cereal, then add the milk. At first, let your child hold her hands on yours (to get a feel for the task), then rest yours lightly on top of hers as she repeats

Understanding Developmental Appropriateness

These parenting fantasies thrive when parents lack understanding about developmental appropriateness. Do you recognize any of them?

1. Believing that your child should listen to you and do what you say.
2. Believing that your toddler should be obedient and understand when you say "no."
3. Hoping your child will be "good" because you are tired and don't want to be bothered.

The truth is . . .

1. Toddlers are often too busy following their own developmental blueprint to stop and do what you say.
2. "No" is an abstract concept that cannot be understood by toddlers at the advanced level parents think they can understand.
3. Children are always "good," but they are not always obedient—especially during the development of autonomy.

Five Ways to Provide Skill Training for Your Child

1. Plan ahead—or expect resistance ahead.
2. Involve children in the planning process.
3. Offer limited choices.
4. Ask curiosity questions to encourage thinking.
5. Follow through with dignity and respect.

the movements. Finally, stay nearby and encourage her efforts. Celebrate as your child gradually masters these new skills.

GOING PUBLIC

With time for training, children can learn to behave in those famous child development laboratories: public places. Taking time for training can involve many strategies. Consider the following tools to help your child learn to behave in public places.

Plan Ahead—or Expect Resistance Ahead

Young children live in the present moment. And, like many adults, they often find transitions and changes difficult to deal with. A shift from playing with blocks in the living room to rolling along in a grocery basket takes considerable adjustment, and some children find it easier than others do.

When moving from one activity or location to another, planning ahead is critical. Your young explorer may want to climb under the clothing racks, sneak a peek at the world from the top of the beauty salon chair, or mount an expedition to discover what lies around the corner—any corner. Do your best to think through any potential problems and plan for them *before* taking your toddler out in public. Be sure to carry along small toys and snacks to provide entertainment and nourishment, too.

Involve Children in the Planning Process

You might set the stage something like this: "We are going to eat with Aunt Annie and Cousin Jamie at the restaurant. Before we get there,

what will you do in the car?" (If a child is prever-
bal, use simple language to describe the event. If
she is verbal, allow her to supply the answers as the
planning proceeds.) Mention the car seat, buckling
in, and playing with toys en route. You can explore
the coming occasion with your child using simple
questions and descriptions.

Invite your child to picture the setting or
describe it for her: sitting in the chair, drawing
with special crayons, and eating her lunch. What
will she be allowed to order? Must she eat things she doesn't like? Bit
by bit, the picture grows. Use simple, clear language to explain your
expectations—and keep them realistic.

It is more effective to ask a child questions (inviting her to think for
herself) than it is to tell her what to do (and invite resistance or power
struggles). You might ask, with genuine curiosity, "When we go out
to eat, is it okay to throw your food? What about running around the
restaurant? Can you grab the sugar container?" If she thinks these
behaviors are acceptable, you can take the opportunity to teach her
about behavior in public places. Focus more on *do's* and/or *choices*
than on *don'ts*. "Food is for eating." "Do you want to sit quietly at
the table with everyone and eat your lunch, or go sit in the car with
me for a while?" Inconvenient? Yes. Good training? Yes. Kindness
and firmness at the same time help children understand that you mean
what you say and will follow through with action. (Remember, "Let's
Pretend" is often a painless, enjoyable way to establish limits and
expectations.)

Be sure your plans account for your child's individual temperament
as well as the social situation. How long can she sit still during a meal?
What activities are available? Will there be time to play with her cousins? Perhaps this outing would be better held at a pizza joint than at an
elegant restaurant. Remember, plan for success and realize that your
little one will need more than one practice session before she masters
these skills.

Offer Limited Choices

Choices can support a child's growing sense of autonomy, but they must be appropriate and clearly defined, and all of the choices must be choices *you* can live with. For example, the following choices might cause problems:

- "Would you like to go to childcare today?" (This is the adult's responsibility and often isn't a choice but a necessity.)

- "What would you like to do today?" (The child needs some hints here. Are we talking coloring, baking cookies, watching television all day, or taking a trip to Disneyland?)

- "You may pick out any toy you want; you get to choose." (Does this include the $200 motorized kiddie-car or a toy machine gun? Be sure you can keep the promises you make. It is usually wise to think carefully before speaking.)

Ask Curiosity Questions to Encourage Thinking

Children do not develop a strong sense of autonomy when parents and teachers spend too much time talking—telling children what happened, what caused it to happen, how they should feel about it, and what they should do about it. "Telling" may keep children from seeing mistakes as opportunities to learn, or may send the discouraging message that children aren't living up to adult expectations. Lecturing often goes over children's heads because they're not ready to understand the concepts adults are trying to establish—and they usually discover they can simply tune adults out (unintentional training in the art of not listening).

Last but not least: **Telling children what, how, and why teaches them what to think, not how to think.** Parents are often disappointed when their children don't develop more self-control, but they may not realize they are not using parenting skills that encourage self-control. If you take responsibility for your child's actions, he will never learn to take responsibility for himself.

A powerful way to help children develop thinking skills, judgment skills, problem-solving skills, and autonomy is to ask them, "What happened? What were you trying to do? Why do you think this happened? How do you feel about it? How could you fix it? What else could you do if you don't want this to happen again?" (Remember, these skills depend on language—and language takes time to learn. You can and should talk with your child about these ideas, but her response will be limited for a while.)

When children are younger, they need more clues as part of the curiosity questions. For example, if a two-year-old gets stuck on her tricycle, she will be encouraged to think for herself if you ask, "What do you think would happen if you got off and backed up?" This is different from *telling* her to get off and back up. Even a question that contains clues invites thought and a decision.

Follow Through with Dignity and Respect

Again, we want to stress that permissiveness is not the way to help children develop autonomy. One of the most important aspects of teaching your child is your willingness to follow through with both kindness and firmness.

What might follow-through look like in the restaurant meal described earlier? Mom might explain in advance that if her daughter has trouble remembering how to behave in the restaurant, they will have to leave. Kind and firm follow-through means that if she misbehaves, Mom will take her out to wait in the car together while the others in the group finish their meal. It is not respectful (or helpful) to scold or spank while removing her. A parent can either say nothing or say firmly (but kindly), "I'm sorry you didn't feel like sitting quietly in the restaurant today. You can try again next time."

"Out of Control"

Q: My two-and-a-half-year-old son is out of control! He won't respond to the words "Wait, please!" If I don't jump at his every command, he throws a fit or goes on like a broken record, repeating over and over again what he wants. Lately he has been so defiant when we go out in public. He will kick, hit me, and scream at the top of his lungs to get what he wants. Last time it was because I told him we had to leave the jungle gym at the park. He didn't want to leave, and made such a scene that everyone was watching. What do I do in this situation? I don't believe in hitting him, yet I don't appreciate being hit and humiliated like this, either.

A: Some people would call your toddler "spirited"; others might label him "strong-willed." Whatever you call him (and it is best to avoid labels), trying to control him will never work. There are three ways you can increase cooperation:

1. Your child does not understand "Wait, please!" in the way you think he does. This is an abstract concept that is in direct opposition to his developmental need to explore his world and his growing sense of autonomy. He should not be allowed to do anything he wants, however. Say "Wait, please" and stop occasionally when you go for a casual walk together. Do this playfully to help him experience this concept. He may still have trouble stopping immediately, but practice will make it easier for him to understand and cooperate with you more often.

2. Instead of telling him what to do, find ways to involve him in the decision so he gets a sense of *appropriate* personal power and autonomy. For example:

a. Give him some warning. "We need to leave in a minute. What is the last crayon color you want to use today?"

b. Use a timer to provide a cue. Carry a small timer around with you. (Young children love inexpensive timers shaped like chickens and apples, and enjoy carrying them.) Let him help you set it to one or two minutes. Ask him what it means when the timer goes off. Agree when he says "time to leave" and do so.

c. Give him a choice that requires his help. "Do you want to carry your book to the car, or do you want to carry my keys? You decide."

d. Help him visualize the next activity. "What is the first thing we should do when we get home?"

3. If these don't work, you may need to take him by the hand and lead him to the car. Every time he resists, stop pulling, stand still, and let him tug your hand until he stops resisting. Then move toward the car again, letting your arm go slack every time he resists. If he tries to wiggle his hand free, hold it gently but firmly, continuing to give slack. This may seem like a seesaw, but when he catches on that you are going to be both kind and firm, he will probably go with you. If not, you may need to pick him up and carry him to the car while ignoring his kicks and screams (and the looks other adults give you). The key is to avoid the "emotional hook" (that feeling parents get that they have to "win," enforce their will, or impress onlookers). Do what is required to complete the task rather than demanding total compliance.

Giving a child the chance to try again is reasonable and encouraging. It is not reasonable to say, "I'm never taking you out to eat again—or anywhere else, for that matter!" Not only is this statement unreasonable, but who really wants to follow through on such threats? This does not demonstrate kindness or firmness, nor does it inspire trust.

Yes, it is inconvenient for you to miss your meal while using kind and firm follow-through; and yes, your child may not like it. But you also have a choice. Which is more important, a restaurant meal or the self-esteem and confidence your child will develop by learning appropriate social skills? Action is far more effective than words with young children. When you follow through with kindness and firmness, your child will learn that you say what you mean and that you will do what you say—important elements of trust and respect.

SUPERVISION

It bears repeating that safety is one of the most important considerations during the first years of life. Your job is to keep your child safe without letting your fears discourage her. For this reason, supervision is an important parenting tool for little ones, along with the usual kindness and firmness, while guiding and teaching your child. Children do not "learn" from nagging and lectures; they learn from teaching and respectful, firm actions. Save your breath and supervise.

DISTRACTION AND REDIRECTION

Redirection and distraction are among the most simple—and useful—parenting tools for living with toddlers.

Thirteen-month-old Ellen was crawling rapidly toward the dog's dish—one of her favorite "toys"—when her dad spotted her. He called out her name firmly. Ellen paused and looked back over her shoulder. Her dad gathered her up and carried her across the room to where her barnyard set was waiting.

"Here, sweetie," he said with a hug. "See what the pigs and cows are up to."

If Ellen chooses to head for the dog's dish again, her dad can intercept her and direct her toward a more acceptable object—again. Acting without lecturing or shaming avoids a power struggle and lets Ellen learn by experience that Dad won't let her play with the dish.

What if Ellen keeps returning to the forbidden dish? How many times must a parent redirect a child's attention? Well, as many times as it takes—and that is often more than parents like. (Of course, Dad can also move the dish to the laundry room where the dog can get to it but Ellen cannot.) Kindly but firmly directing Ellen toward acceptable objects, and continuing to do so until she gets the message, allows you to respond to her behavior in ways that do not punish, shame, or invite a battle of wills.

After her parenting class on developmental appropriateness, Lisa reported to her classmates, "I sure do have a happier home since I stopped yelling at Justin. The things he does that used to make me angry are now fascinating to me. I think he'll get an A in autonomy. I will also get an A in kind and firm distraction because I'm getting lots of practice!"

WHEN NOTHING SEEMS TO WORK

We have heard parents cry out in frustration, "I have tried all of these suggestions and nothing works!" Sometimes our advice can sound patronizing, especially when we say "Avoid the emotional hook." Each of us can tell you that she was hooked by a child more than once.

It may not sound helpful, but sometimes you need to feel your frustration and allow yourself to have a tantrum. You can have your feelings without feeling guilty, just as we suggest you let your child experience his feelings. Hopefully, you can also find a friend with a shoulder to cry on.

Do your best to remember that who your child is today is not who he will be forever. In Chapter 21, we share suggestions on the importance of self-care; sometimes taking care of yourself is the best thing you can do while you wait out the frustration. Meanwhile, we will keep encouraging you to have faith in your child and in yourself.

QUESTIONS TO PONDER

1. List two things you and your child struggle over repeatedly. How could you change the environment to reduce or eliminate these hassles?
2. What could you do to distract your child from forbidden items while acting in a kind and firm way, instead of continuing to repeat these struggles?
3. What emerging skills are implied in these power struggles? Are they within your child's developmental capabilities? Are they skills that will benefit your child as she grows? Is there a way you could allow your child to practice these skills in a positive, productive way?
4. Keep a list of things you can do to help you survive those times of complete frustration.

10

TEMPERAMENT

What Makes Your Child Unique?

Most parents cherish a fantasy about having "the perfect baby" or "the perfect child." The conventional description of this ideal baby is one who doesn't cry or fuss often; who sleeps peacefully through the night, takes long naps, eats her food without spitting it out (or up); and who can happily entertain herself, gurgling and cooing angelically at her crib mobile. "Oh," we say when confronted with one of these enviable specimens, "what a good baby." Does this mean that babies who don't fit this description are "bad"?

THE MYTH OF THE PERFECT CHILD

Of course, there is no such thing as a "bad" baby or child, even though most don't fit the fantasy description. Babies are born with different, unique personalities, as any parent with more than one child knows. In fact, we worry about the "fantasy child." As she grows up, this child may not feel secure enough to test the status quo and find out who she is when apart from her parents and teachers; she may be afraid to

make mistakes or risk disapproval. Still, some babies do fit the fantasy description, feel secure, and aren't afraid to make mistakes. They are called "easy" children.

Each child is born with a unique style of processing sensory information and responding to the world around her. Stella Chess and Alexander Thomas investigated the miracle of personality in their longitudinal study of the nine aspects of temperament they identified in children.

These temperaments—the qualities and characteristics that contribute to individual personalities—describe a child's "personal style." Researchers believe that many temperament traits are inborn, part of each child's "wiring." However, the way parents interact with their babies and toddlers appears to have a strong effect on how these inborn tendencies actually develop. It's a complex process, one that we don't yet fully understand.*

While attitudes, behavior, and decisions may change with time and experience, temperament appears to be part of us for life. No temperaments are good or bad, right or wrong—they are just different. Understanding your child's unique temperament will help you work *with* her to learn, to grow, and to thrive.

THE STUDY OF TEMPERAMENT

Scientific investigation of temperament theory began in the late 1960s, and continued into the '70s, with a longitudinal study of two basic temperaments, active and passive. This study revealed that these temperaments were lifelong characteristics; in other words, passive infants tended to become passive adults, while active infants tended to become active adults.

Chess and Thomas expanded the temperament theory significantly, even though their nine temperaments all fit under the general headings

---

* For more information, we recommend *Know Your Child* (New York: Basic Books, 1987) and other related works by Chess and Thomas.

of active and passive. In the years since Chess and Thomas began their work, additional researchers, such as Jerome Kagan and Mary Rothbart, have devoted time and study to temperament, developing additional techniques to measure inborn traits in infants and toddlers. There are now numerous ways to describe and measure temperament; we have chosen to include the original nine temperaments of Chess and Thomas because they are easily understood by parents and care-givers, and easily observed in children.

When parents truly understand temperament, they can respond to children in ways that encourage development and growth. **With understanding and acceptance, parents are equipped to help children reach their full potential, rather than try-ing to mold them into fantasy children.** Knowing your child's unique temperament (and, perhaps, your own) will enable you to teach and connect with her more effectively. Keep in mind, however, that your child's temperament will have many variations, and that your expecta-tions may turn into self-fulfilling prophecies. Use the following infor-mation to increase your own understanding and to build a stronger connection with your child—not to predict behavior.

THE NINE TEMPERAMENTS OF CHESS AND THOMAS

The nine temperaments are activity level, rhythmicity, initial response (approach or withdrawal), adaptability, sensory threshold, quality of mood, intensity of reactions, distractibility, and persistence and atten-tion span. (Some of these temperaments overlap a bit, so don't worry about trying to measure them precisely.) All children possess varying degrees of each characteristic. The following sections will describe what each temperament looks like in real life. (You may want to think about children you know as we examine these aspects of temperament.)

1. Activity Level
"Activity level" refers to the level of motor activity and the propor-tion of active and inactive periods. For instance, an infant with high

activity might kick and splash so much in his bath that the floor needs a good mopping afterward, while a low-activity infant may smile happily while enjoying the sensations of his bathwater. Activity level will influence a parent's interactions with a child. For instance, parents of active children will often have to be more active and alert themselves.

Barry's mom lay next to her six-month-old on a beach blanket, pleading for his cooperation. "Could you just stay still for a few minutes?" she asked, as more sand from a vigorously kicking foot sprayed her face.

Two years later, Barry's brother, Jackson, arrived and Mom found herself tiptoeing into the nursery at regular intervals. She would place her finger next to baby Jackson's nose to reassure herself that he was still breathing. After raising Barry, she could not quite believe that a baby would sleep for such long stretches of time. Barry and Jackson were her introduction to the differences in temperament.

If your little one has a high activity level, you will want to provide lots of opportunities for safe exploration and play. (Be sure to childproof your home first!) He may need some active play before settling down to focus on a task. A less active infant or toddler may need to be invited to go exploring; you can use bright toys, interesting noises, and smiles to gently encourage him to interact with his world. When making plans, taking activity level into account will help you prevent problems and provide appropriate movement for your child's needs.

2. Rhythmicity

"Rhythmicity" refers to the predictability (or unpredictability) of biological functions, such as hunger, sleeping, and bowel movements. One infant might have one bowel movement daily, immediately after breakfast, while another infant's schedule seems different each day.

One child might eat her biggest meal at lunch, while another child prefers dinner—or a different meal each day!

> *Carla was so proud: she thought her little Jackie was toilet trained by the time he was two years old. She put him on his toilet chair several times a day, and he obligingly produced a bowel movement each morning and urinated on each succeeding visit. But Jackie wasn't toilet trained—his mom was trained. Jackie was so regular that when his mom remembered to put him on his chair, he performed. When she got busy and forgot, she was rewarded with a poopy mess to clean up.*

If your little one expects meals or naps at predictable times each day, you will be tempting fate if you disregard his schedule. Taking your child's rhythmicity into account will ensure you have the food (or the potty chair) available when needed.

3. Initial Response (Approach or Withdrawal)

This temperament describes the way a child reacts to a new situation or stimulus, such as a new food, toy, person, or place. Approach responses are often displayed by mood expression (gurgling, smiling) or motor activity (swallowing a new food, reaching for a new toy). Withdrawal responses look more negative and are expressed by mood (crying, fussing) or motor activity (spitting food out, pushing a new toy away). Learning to parent your unique child means recognizing these cues and responding in encouraging, nurturing ways.

Some babies are open to just about any new experience—new foods, new people—while others are more reluctant.

> *Ted traveled several weeks each month as part of his job. When he returned home and attempted to pick up Isabelle, his new daughter, she would stiffen, resist, and begin crying. Ted felt devastated. He adored his baby girl. When he learned*

about temperament, he recognized that his daughter reacted to changes of any kind with initial alarm. He began to take a gentler, more gradual approach after his prolonged absences. While his partner held Isabelle, Ted tickled the baby's feet, stroked her arms, and talked softly to her. Though Isabelle was still slow to warm up, this method allowed her more time to adjust. In the meantime, Ted no longer felt rejected and could be sympathetic to his daughter's needs.

If your child welcomes new experiences, celebrate: It will undoubtedly make life together easier. If your little one takes longer to adjust, however, you can look for small steps to help him adjust to change and new situations without taking his reactions personally.

4. Adaptability

Adaptability overlaps with approach and withdrawal, and describes how a child reacts to a new situation over time—her ability to adjust and change. Some children initially spit out a new food but accept it after a few trial tastes. Others accept a new food, a new article of clothing, or a new preschool far more slowly, if at all.

When Jenna's baby son arrived, his older sister and brother were already in grade school and involved in a whirl of sports, music lessons, and other activities. Because of their busy schedules, the baby was rarely at home for a regular naptime. But that posed no problem. This baby was a highly adaptable child, perfectly content to curl up and sleep wherever he happened to be at the time, whether at a basketball game or in the grocery cart.

Meanwhile, Jenna's neighbor, Kate, often found herself looking for rides for her eight-year-old son when his activities occurred during her baby's naptime. If they weren't home at the proper time, baby Ana fell apart, crying, whining, and fussing. Ana wouldn't fall asleep anywhere except in her own bed. She would stay awake well past midnight if her family happened to be away from home. Ana had low adaptability, and all the family members suffered when they didn't take her temperament into account.

It is tempting to try to force your child to adapt to your busy schedule—after all, most parents have far more to do than there are hours in the day. But wise parents learn to craft their schedules with their child's adaptability in mind. It may take two days instead of one to get all your errands done, but isn't it more important (and far more pleasant) to have a calm, cheerful child both days?

5. Sensory Threshold

Some children wake up every time a door opens, no matter how softly, while others can sleep through a carnival. The level of sensitivity to sensory input (touch, taste, vision, smell, and hearing) varies from one child to the next and affects how they behave and view the world.

When Mallory was eight months old, her grandmother took her outside to play. The day was warm, the new lawn springy and soft. But the moment Mallory's knees touched the grass, her bottom popped into the air. She balanced herself with her hands and feet clutching the ground, avoiding contact between her bare knees and the tickly grass.

That same afternoon, Mallory's cousin, Nellie, arrived for a visit. Nellie's mother plopped her down on the grass, and Nellie crawled off, not even slowing down when she crossed a gravel pathway. Nellie's high sensory threshold allowed her to be an intrepid explorer, while Mallory's response to new textures and experiences produced more caution.

Time and experience will teach you about your own child's sensitivity to physical sensation and stimulation. Does your child like noise and music or does he become fussy? Is he mesmerized by bright, flashing lights, or does he turn his face away? Does he gulp down new foods

Sensory Processing Disorder

Some children are deeply influenced by sensory input; in fact, in some cases, a child's brain may have difficulty making sense of visual, auditory, or other sensory information. One child may find his socks "painful" or his shirt "too tight," while another child does not respond strongly to any stimulation. Some children may rock, spin, or bang their heads in an effort to generate sensory input, and find these startling actions comforting. Any of these children may have "sensory processing disorder" (sometimes known as "sensory integration dysfunction") and can benefit from a variety of therapies that will help them make sense of sensory information and feel more comfortable.

If you suspect that your child reacts differently to sensory input than other children the same age, it may be wise to ask your pediatrician for an evaluation. (For more information, visit www.spdfoundation.net.)

or only nibble at them (or spit them out entirely)? Does he like to be touched and hugged, or does he wriggle away from too much contact?

If your child is more sensitive to stimulation, you will need to go slowly when introducing new toys, new experiences, and new people. Soft light and quiet will help him calm down, and he may become nervous or irritable in noisy, crowded places (such as birthday parties, amusement parks, or busy malls). A less sensitive child may be more willing to try new experiences. Provide him with lots of opportunities to explore and experiment.

A child with a low sensory threshold may need a few moments alone to cry and release the tensions built up during a busy afternoon before settling down to fall asleep. It is respectful to provide this child with a quiet environment with books, stuffed animals, or soft music. It would not be appropriate to continue cooing to, cuddling, and generally overstimulating this little one. His sister, with her different sensory threshold, may thrive on lullabies, peekaboo games, and noisy family members careening through the halls.

6. Quality of Mood

Have you ever noticed that some children (and adults) react to life with pleasure and acceptance while others can find fault with everything and everybody? One baby might favor her family with smiles and coos, while another feels compelled to cry a bit, just "because."

Baby Brent smiled happily when his mom tickled his toes. When he was a toddler, his grin would melt her heart—and he grinned in response to just about every interaction. Then baby Craig was born. Instead of smiling when she tickled his toes, Craig would cry. He didn't seem to think anything was funny, and appeared to be in a sour mood most of the time. As an adult Craig still smiles rarely, yet he is a loving father and son. Brent, as an adult, is also a loving father and he still loves to laugh.

Parents of less-sunny little ones can take heart. Those tiny scowls are not in response to you or your parenting skills. Be sensitive to his mood, but take time to stroke your sober little fellow, massage his round cheeks, and share your own sunshine with him. As he grows, help him to see the world for the lovely place it is.

If your baby beams a happy face to the world, enjoy the gift her temperament brings to your life. Don't rain on her parade. Take a moment to savor the day through her rosy outlook.

7. Intensity of Reactions (overlaps with Quality of Mood)

Children often respond to events around them in different ways. Some smile quietly or merely take a look, then go back to what they were doing; others react with action and emotion. Some children wear their hearts on their little sleeves; they giggle and shriek with laughter when happy and throw impressive tantrums when angry. Some barely react to outside events, and may need your encouragement to get involved in play or other interaction.

At playgroup, Maya's hair was pulled by an inquisitive classmate. The teacher panicked, sure from the way Maya howled that she required a trip to the emergency room. When the same miscreant pulled Juan's hair, Juan hardly looked up from his blocks, swatting the other child's hand away as though it were no more than a gnat alighting nearby.

Maya's mom has learned to sit quietly, waiting until Maya's initial reaction subsides to evaluate the seriousness of the situation. Juan's mother becomes truly alarmed when he cries loudly, knowing how much it takes to elicit such a response. Both children and parents have learned to interact differently based on the intensity of each child's reactions.

As you get to know your child's unique temperament, you will be able to shape his environment in a way that allows him to feel safe, connected, and curious.

8. Distractibility

"If I sit my toddler down with a box of blocks, he won't notice anything else in the room," says one father. "Well," says a mother, "if someone walks by while my baby is nursing, she not only looks but stops sucking until the person is gone." They may not realize it, but these parents are actually talking about their children's "distractibility," the way in which an outside stimulus interferes with a child's present behavior and his willingness (or unwillingness) to be diverted.

Joe heads for the video game console every time he enters the family room. His sitter picks him up, carries him to his toy box, and sometimes even succeeds in distracting him for a moment or two. But minutes later, he sets his course for the game console with an accuracy any pilot would admire. Joe's ability to remain

single-minded and focused may be a great strength someday; for now, his weary sitter must make yet another trip to remove his fingers from the console's buttons (or figure out a way to make it inaccessible to Joe's persistent advances).

Ben picks up his dad's smartphone, bringing it to his open mouth for a taste. Dad intercepts the phone, tickling Ben and substituting a piece of toast. Ben gurgles, hardly noticing that the object clutched in his hand has changed. Ben's distractibility makes him an easy child to watch, while Joe's sitter is working up the courage to ask for an increase in pay.

Distraction and redirection are great tools to use with a toddler—if that toddler is easily distracted and redirected. Rather than becoming frustrated about your child's distractibility (or lack thereof), look for ways to make her environment safe and easy to explore, focus on solutions to the problems you encounter, and recognize and accept her inherent temperament.

9. Persistence and Attention Span *(overlaps with Distractibility)*
"Persistence" refers to a child's willingness to pursue an activity in the face of obstacles or difficulties; "attention span" describes the length of time he will pursue an activity without interruption. The two characteristics are usually related. A toddler who is content to tear up an old magazine for half an hour at a time has a fairly long attention span, while another who plays with ten different toys in ten minutes or less has a short one. Again, no combination is necessarily better than another; they're simply different and present different challenges in parenting and teaching.

Baby Edith has spent the past half hour sitting in her high chair, lining up rows of Cheerios. Sometimes she finds one big enough to fit onto her finger. Her twin sister, Emma, did not even make it through breakfast before her cereal, bowl, and cup hit the floor. Emma dismantled the pot-and-pan cupboard, explored the heating vent, and had to be retrieved from a foray into the bathroom—all while Edith patiently arranged her Cheerios. Emma might become a brilliant sportscaster, her dexterity enabling her to keep up with rapidly changing game configurations and split-second moves. Edith could have a future as a researcher, where an attention span that extends for long periods would be a valuable asset when monitoring trays of petri dishes. It is important to understand that both girls' temperaments can be strengths in the right situation. Wise parents and caregivers will help Emma and Edith maximize the potential of their inborn temperaments by providing teaching, nurturing—and lots of supervision.

Development? Or Disorder?

Q: My son is three years old. He is incredibly active; he won't take a nap, hates to sit and look at a book, and is always in motion. I try to keep him occupied, but he goes through every toy in his toy box in about five minutes. My sister says he probably has attention deficit disorder because he's "hyper" and has such a short attention span; she says I should put him on medication. What should I do?

A: At this age, your son's behavior is more likely to be due to his inborn temperament and developmental abilities than it is to a disorder like ADD or ADHD. Your son seems to have a high activity level, less persistence, and a short attention span. While this certainly creates challenges for you as his parent, you will help him best by accepting his temperament and finding ways to create structure and routine, to use kind, firm teaching, and to keep him active and engaged. ADHD cannot be diagnosed reliably until a child is at least six years of age. Many of the Positive Discipline tools will help your active child cope with home and classroom responsibilities, whether he has ADHD or not.

If your child is less patient and persistent, there are ways you can help her get along in a sometimes frustrating world. When you must wait quietly at a doctor's office, be sure you bring something to engage her attention. Break challenging tasks into small, achievable steps. When she gets frustrated, let her know that you understand her feelings. And be sure to nudge that persistent, less distractible little one to try new things. When you can, give her time to satisfy her curiosity without rushing her.

"GOODNESS OF FIT"

Chess and Thomas (and other researchers) emphasize the importance of "goodness of fit"—finding the balance between a child's needs and those of the people she lives with or who care for her. It will be less frustrating for both of you (and easier to work toward "goodness of fit") when you understand your child's temperament. Children experience enough stress in life as they struggle for competency and belonging. It does not help to compound that stress by expecting a child to be someone she is not.

Understanding a child's temperament doesn't mean shrugging your shoulders and saying, "Oh well, that's just the way this child is." It is an invitation to help a child develop acceptable behavior and skills through patience, encouragement, and kind, firm teaching, while keeping the unique needs of her temperament in mind. For instance, a child with a short attention span will still need to learn to accept some structure. Offering limited choices is one way to be respectful of the child's needs, and of the "needs of the situation" (behavior appropriate for the present environment).

In the same way, it is important to understand your own "personal style" and to recognize that no matter how much you love your child, your temperament and hers may not mesh easily. Working out a match between your temperament and needs and your child's is critical to goodness of fit. If your child has an irregular sleep pattern and you can hardly keep your eyes open after ten at night, you have a poor fit. An understanding of temperament can help you adjust and create a better fit. The key is to find *balance*. Your baby might not sleep through the night due to her temperament, but she can learn to entertain herself when she wakes up. You may need to learn to stagger over and offer a gentle stroke or pat on the back, whisper a few loving words, then allow her to get back to sleep on her own.

The first step is to determine what will work for all family members, with no one's needs being ignored. (This includes your needs. It is not in a child's best interest to have an exhausted, crabby parent.) Yelling at, threatening, or totally ignoring a wakeful child is also not helpful.

A child with low distractibility will need patient preparation to switch from one activity to another. Planning ahead becomes a vital tool to smooth the way for transitions. A low-regularity parent living with a high-regularity toddler must learn to plan meals at predictable intervals, develop routines for daily activities, and establish a more defined rhythm for her day. Her child must learn to cope with occasional revised plans, survive on a cracker or two when a meal is delayed, and develop personal flexibility.

The good news is that parents and children *can* adapt to each other. Our brains are designed to respond and adapt to the world around us; and patience, sensitivity, and love can help all of us learn to live peacefully together. Finding balance takes time and practice, but learning to accept and work with the individual, special temperament of your child will benefit you both as the years go by.

Positive Discipline skills are appropriate for children of all temperaments, because they are respectful and invite children to learn cooperation, responsibility, and life skills. An understanding of temperament will also help you understand why different methods may be more or less effective, depending on the temperament and needs of your child.

INDIVIDUALITY AND CREATIVITY

Parents and caregivers may not be aware of how they squelch individuality and creativity when they (often subconsciously) buy in to the myth of the perfect child. It is tempting for adults to prefer the "easy" child, or to want children to conform to the norms of society. Egos often get involved. You may worry about what others think, and fear that your competency may be questioned if your children aren't "good" in the eyes of others.

One of the primary motivators for the studies of Chess and Thomas was their desire to stop society's tendency to blame mothers for the characteristics of their children. Chess and Thomas state, "A child's temperament can actively influence the attitudes and behavior of her parents, other family members, playmates, and teachers, and in turn help to shape their effect on her behavioral development." In this way, the relationship between child and parents is a two-way street, each continuously influencing the other.

What if the mother whose twins behaved so differently had been two different mothers? It would have been easy to decide that quiet, focused Edith's mother was very effective, while active, busy Emma's mother "just couldn't control that child!" It may be wise to ask yourself occasionally, "Are you looking for blame, or are you looking for solutions?" It is not reasonable or respectful (nor is it effective) to blame your child for behavior caused by her temperament. The more you know about temperament and effective parenting skills, the better you will be at finding solutions that help your child develop into a capable individual, despite her differences and uniqueness.

WORK FOR IMPROVEMENT, NOT PERFECTION

Even with understanding and the best intentions, most parents struggle occasionally with their child's temperament and behavior. You may lack patience yourself, or get hooked into *reacting* to behavior instead of *acting* thoughtfully. Awareness and understanding do not mean we become perfect; mistakes are inevitable. However, once you have had time to cool off after a mistake, you need to apologize and then resolve it with your child. He's usually more than willing to hug and offer forgiveness, especially when he knows you'll do the same for him. It is important to help your child work for improvement, not perfection. You can give this gift to yourself as well.

KINDNESS AND FIRMNESS

Rudolf Dreikurs continually made a plea for parents and caregivers to use kindness *and* firmness with children. (You may have noticed that we mention it frequently, too!) An understanding of temperament underscores its importance. Kindness shows respect for the child and his uniqueness. Firmness shows respect for the needs of the situation, including a child's developing need to learn social skills. By understanding and respecting your child's temperament, you will be able to help him reach his full potential as a capable, confident, contented person. And there's a bonus: you will probably get a lot more rest, laugh more, and learn a great deal about yourself and your child in the process.

QUESTIONS TO PONDER

1. Following are the nine aspects of temperament. On each line, put a dot in the place that best represents your child's temperament. Then, with a different-color ink, put a dot on each line to represent your own temperament. How well does your temperament match that of your child? How might that affect your interactions? You can also place dots to represent your partner or other children.

1. Activity Level

High activity ———————————————————— Low activity

2. Rhythmicity (predictability of physical functions)

Predictable ———————————————————— Unpredictable

3. Initial Response (reaction to something new)

Approach ———————————————————— Withdrawal

4. Adaptability (ability to adjust to change over time)

Adapts quickly ———————————————————— Adapts slowly

5. Sensory Threshold (sensitivity to sensory stimulation)

Very sensitive ———————————————————— Less sensitive

6. Quality of Mood

Optimistic ———————————————————— Pessimistic

7. Intensity of Reactions (response to events)

Intense reactions ———————————————————— Mild reactions

8. Distractibility (willingness of a child to be distracted)

Highly focused ———————————————————— Easily distracted

9. Persistence and Attention Span (ability to stay focused on an activity for a length of time)

Persistent/long attention span ———————————————————— Gives up/short span

2. What ideas does understanding your child's temperament give you about setting up helpful routines? About helping your child adjust to change? About solving problems in your home?

3. If your temperament is not a good "fit" with that of your child, how can you take care of yourself so you can remain as patient and flexible as possible? (Remember, caring for yourself is an

important part of caring for your child.) What modifications might improve the goodness of fit between different temperaments?

4. Journal about changes you might make in your daily routine that will help you and your child function better, individually and with others. Choose one or two small steps to try this week.

SECTION THREE
YOUR CHILD'S WORLD

11

THE ART OF
ENCOURAGEMENT

Nurturing Self-Worth, Confidence,
and Resilience in Your Child

Rudolf Dreikers once said, "Never do anything for a child that the child can do for himself." Children develop a healthy sense of self-confidence and a belief in their own capability through experience and practice. It is developmentally appropriate to meet the needs of a crying infant by comforting and soothing him, but a frustrated toddler (or older child) will develop strong skills when you help him learn to help himself instead of doing too much for him.

Glenda gives Casey a glass of milk with his lunch. He looks at the glass and scowls. "Don't want this glass," he announces.

Glenda sighs in exasperation; then she recognizes an opportunity to teach her small son. "If you want another glass," she says gently, "what do you need to be able to get it?"

Casey isn't particularly interested in learning at the moment.
"Can't reach it," he whines.

Glenda says, "Hmm. How could we solve this problem?"

This new prospect captures Casey's imagination. He stops whining and thinks about it. "Climb and reach it?" he asks.

"That might be unsafe," Glenda says."What about putting the glasses on this lower shelf?"

"Yes!" says Casey, with a big smile on his face. Within a few minutes they rearrange the low shelf with three glasses that Casey helps to choose. He selects one, carries it to the table, and, with obvious pride, pours his milk from the old glass into the new one (creating several puddles in the process).

Instead of becoming annoyed, Glenda recognizes another opportunity for teaching. After Casey enjoys a few sips of his milk, she says, "I notice a few spills. What do you need to do now to clean up the milk that spilled?"

By now, Casey is feeling very capable. He jumps up from the table, gets a sponge from under the sink, and wipes up the spilled milk. He leaves the sponge on the table.

Now Glenda checks Casey's engagement with the process. It's possible that a lesson about sponges would be better left for another time, but Casey seems happy and interested today. So Glenda asks, "Do you know what happens to a sponge when we leave milk in it?"

Casey looks closely at the sponge but doesn't see anything happening. He is curious. "What?" he asks his mom.

Glenda explains, "The milk turns sour and makes the sponge stinky." Now there's a word Casey likes! Glenda has his full attention."We need to rinse out the sponge in the sink really well before putting it back under the sink. Would you like to practice rinsing the sponge?"

Casey never turns down an opportunity to play with water. Glenda shows him how to squeeze the sponge by twisting it, and Casey happily spends the next fifteen minutes standing on his small stool and rinsing the sponge.

Time-consuming? Yes! Is it worth it? Absolutely. Casey has learned that his needs and desires are valid and that he is capable of taking care of them himself. **It takes more than kind words to build self-worth; it takes "competency experiences," moments when you and your child accept a challenge—and succeed.** Casey's mother took the time to teach him the skills he needed to feel capable rather than arguing with him or giving in. She encouraged his sense of competence and had faith in his ability to master the task—with a few puddles. This is kind and firm, developmentally appropriate discipline in action. It is also a demonstration of genuine connection and encouragement.

LIVING WITH—AND LEARNING FROM—MISTAKES

Parents and children are alike in one important respect: they never stop making mistakes. It doesn't matter how much you learn or how much you know. As human beings, we all sometimes forget what we know and get hooked into emotional responses—also known as "losing it." Once you accept this, you can see mistakes as the important life processes they are: interesting opportunities to learn.

Wouldn't it be wonderful if you could instill this attitude in your child so she wouldn't be burdened with the baggage you may carry about mistakes and "failures"? Many children (and adults) short-circuit the lifelong process of developing a healthy sense of autonomy (and fail to develop the courage it requires to take risks and try new things) because they are afraid to make mistakes. Asking curiosity questions (which usually begin with "what" or "how") to help your child learn from her mistakes will make a tremendous difference as she works her way through the learning process.

"LIKE A PLANT NEEDS WATER . . ."

Rudolf Dreikurs reminds us that children need encouragement like a plant needs water. (And don't we all?) Learning the fine art of encouragement is one of the most important skills of effective parenting. Experts who study human behavior and development tell us that a healthy sense of self-worth is one of the greatest assets a child can have. Parents who know how to encourage, have faith, and teach skills are best able to help their children develop a sense of self-worth.

SELF-WORTH AND RESILIENCE: WHERE DO THEY COME FROM?

Self-worth is, quite simply, the confidence and sense of capability each person has in him- or herself. Self-worth comes from feeling a sense of belonging, believing that you're capable (because you have experienced your capability—not because someone else tells you that you are), and knowing your contributions are valued and worthwhile. **_Parents can't give their child a sense of self-worth; each child must grow it for himself._**

Self-worth gives children the courage to take risks in life and to welcome new experiences—everything from tackling the stairs with unsteady steps, to making friends at the childcare center, to trying out for the basketball team or honors orchestra later in life. Children

with a healthy sense of self-worth have learned that it is okay to make mistakes and learn from them, rather than thinking a mistake means they are inadequate. Children who lack self-worth fear failure and often don't believe in themselves even when they possess wonderful talents and abilities.

An important part of self-worth and confidence is a quality known as resilience. "Resilience" is defined in the Merriam-Webster dictionary as "the ability to become strong, healthy, or successful again after something bad happens." It is unlikely that any of us will make it through life without "something bad" happening, and the ability to bounce back, to try again, and to persevere in the face of challenges is a critical part of emotional and mental health. How can you nurture resilience in your child?

TELL ME A STORY . . .

There is one aspect of resilience that deserves special mention. It is a simple thing that most adults do without any prompting: telling stories. All children love to hear stories—especially their own! Stories like "On the day you were born . . . ," "When you used to sleep at Grandma's house while Mommy worked at night . . . ," or "I remember the time Uncle Peter took you to the zoo . . ." all reinforce connections for a child. Not only do children love these stories and want to hear them over and over again, but these stories encourage the development of coping skills and resilience, even when children experience disruptive or traumatic events. In fact, a child who has heard these family stories is more likely to show resilience in the face of trauma than one who has not. Stories anchor a child in ways that make the stress of outside events more manageable. You cannot protect your child from every eventuality, but it is encouraging to know that you *can* provide a foundation of resilience through a strong sense of self and family—and stories can do that.

MISTAKES PARENTS MAKE IN THE NAME OF "SELF-ESTEEM"

Parents (and teachers) may try to nurture "self-esteem" through praise or by teaching children to parrot slogans such as "I am special." Remember, though, that children, even very young ones, are making decisions about themselves and the world around them. All too often, these efforts backfire, leading children to form beliefs that are not in their long-term best interest. Before we look at effective ways to build self-worth, let's look at some methods that don't work.

Ineffective Methods for Building Self-Worth

- Trying to give children self-worth through excessive praise and pep talks
- Overprotecting or rescuing children
- Telling children they're "smart"
- Wanting children to be "better" (or just different)

TRYING TO GIVE CHILDREN SELF-WORTH THROUGH EXCESSIVE PRAISE

Praise can actually be discouraging instead of encouraging. When parents constantly tell a child, "You're such a good girl! I'm so proud of you!" that child may decide, "I'm okay only if someone tells me I am." She may feel pressure to be perfect in order to avoid disappointing her parents. Or she may give up because she believes she can't live up to the praise and the high expectations that usually go along with it. In the long term, praise doesn't have the positive effect most people think it does. A little praise may not hurt, but it probably won't help as much as parents hope.

OVERPROTECTING OR RESCUING CHILDREN

One of the most common reasons children visit a therapist's office these days is anxiety. There are many valid reasons to worry about a child's safety and health in this dangerous world, but so many parents are *so* worried that children find it impossible to take even acceptable risks (like playing at a friend's house or walking to the mailbox). Remember, your child has mirror neurons; if you believe that the world is a scary place, your child is likely to agree with you and to avoid new experiences, which is not a good recipe for confidence and resilience.

Many parents worry that their children will suffer if they have to deal with discomfort or disappointment, but the opposite is true. Overly protected children may decide, "I can't handle problems. I can't survive disappointment. I need others to take care of me and rescue me." Or they may decide that it's easier to let others take responsibility for them. Either way, overprotected and "overhelped" children rarely develop the competence and self-confidence that might help them handle life's challenges as they grow.

TELLING CHILDREN THEY'RE "SMART"

It's wonderful to celebrate your child's gifts and accomplishments and to celebrate his progress along life's path. But some parents, in an effort to encourage their children, bombard them with a constant stream of "You're so smart!" It turns out that this bit of praise in particular can have unexpected consequences.

Carol Dweck, author of *Mindset: The New Psychology of Success,* has done extensive research on this subject. Rewarding a child for a trait like intelligence can create a "fixed" mindset and cripple a child's ability to tackle challenges. In Dweck's words,

> After seven experiments with hundreds of children, we had some of the clearest findings I've ever seen: Praising children's intelligence harms their motivation and it harms their performance. How can that be? Don't children love to be praised? Yes, children love praise. And they especially love to be praised for their intelligence and talent. It really does give them a boost, a special glow—but only for the moment. The minute they hit a snag, their confidence goes out the window and their motivation hits rock bottom. If success means they're smart, then failure means they're dumb. That's the fixed mindset.

Instead of valuing being "smart," encourage your child to learn from mistakes, to enjoy challenges, and to love the *process* of learning—regardless of the result.

WANTING CHILDREN TO BE "BETTER" (OR JUST DIFFERENT)

Since the primary goal of all children is to feel connected and accepted, it may be devastating when a child believes that her parents don't love her unconditionally. When the mother of Travis, an active, high-energy child, repeatedly says, "I wish you were as calm and well-behaved as Johnny," Travis may decide, "I'm not good enough. It really doesn't matter what I do—my mom doesn't like me." Remember, **a misbehaving child is a discouraged child. There is nothing as encouraging and effective as loving, unconditional acceptance.** This does not mean that parents must applaud their children's misbehavior and weaknesses; it does mean that parents can help their children best when they accept them for who they are, with all their unique strengths and weaknesses.

THE ART OF ENCOURAGEMENT

Praise is like junk food. It is sweet, mass-produced, and often neither personal nor meaningful. Little smiley faces that say "great kid" or "good job" can be stamped on any child's hand. Real encouragement is more selective, noticing and validating the uniqueness of each individual.

> Little Amy waited until her twelfth month to make her walking debut. Her family had traveled across the country to visit grandparents in Florida. One afternoon with her parents, grandparents, and siblings gathered around, Amy decided the time to display her skills had arrived. She grinned at her family, then relinquished her hold on the sofa and with heart-stopping wobbles took her first steps, straight into Grandma's eager arms. Her family was ecstatic. "You can do it!" they called, their faces wreathed in smiles. "That's it. Just take it slow. Just a little further. Go, Amy! You've got it! Hooray!" Amy's grin almost split her face in two as she basked in her family's love. Now, that's encouragement!

The praise version might have sounded more like this: "Good girl! What a clever darling! Aren't you precious?"

Many parents become confused about the difference between praise and encouragement, so let's take a closer look. In the scene described above, encouragement focuses on the task, while praise focuses on the person. Many children, when praised, form the belief that they are "good" only if they accomplish a task. Praise usually requires a successfully completed task, while encouragement speaks to the effort. In other words, praise is often conditional, while encouragement is unconditional.

Oddly enough, too much of a good thing can be discouraging. When children receive cheers for every little thing they do, it is easy for them to develop the belief that they are loved and accepted only when others are cheering, clapping, and offering endless attention.

WHAT IS YOUR CHILD DECIDING?

An important way to understand the difference between praise and encouragement is to get into your child's world. Notice if your child is depending too much on the opinion of others, a dangerous result of praise. On the other hand, little ones love an audience and often enthusiastically invite you to "Watch me! Watch me!" It isn't necessary to obsess about the difference between praise and encouragement. Just be aware of the decisions your child may be making. Do your statements convey conditional or unconditional love and support?

One approach is to ask yourself if your words could only be said to this person at this time. You can say "Great job" to the barber, the dog, and your partner, all in the same breath. You can't use "Thank you for giving me such a flattering haircut," "You found your bone—how yummy," or "That shade of blue looks really nice on you—it's different than the shade you usually wear" interchangeably. If your words are unique to the person, place, or situation, they are more likely to be encouragement.

SHOWING FAITH

Amy's family offered her encouragement most effectively by allowing her to experiment with the process of walking—and by not intervening unnecessarily. Amy's family might have chosen to rescue their fragile baby. Grandma might have called out, "Be careful. Quick, someone, catch the baby." Mom or Dad might have swooped in to hold Amy's hand, block her path, or pick her up. Older brother might have grabbed Amy from behind to steady her.

There was a risk that Amy might fall, but Amy's family gave her the chance to take that risk. **_Risks imply the possibility of failure, but without risk there can never be success._** Amy took a risk and managed her first steps. No praise could replace her feeling of accomplishment in that moment. Self-worth is that experience of "I can do it!" You help your children build self-worth when you balance your need to protect them with their need to take risks, tackle new challenges, and explore their capabilities.

Balance, however, is essential. Imagine a parent believing that his child should never be discouraged from exploring her environment. Perhaps he feels that limiting her activities will frustrate her curiosity. So when little Michelle heads into the street, Dad runs to the intersection and flags the cars to a stop, allowing Michelle to stroll contentedly among the fenders. This is not encouragement. What Michelle needs is supervision and lots of teaching about the dangers of intersections, lest she decide to try crossing the street when Dad isn't there to play traffic cop.

Encouragement does not mean remaking the world to fit your toddler's every whim. Kindly and firmly removing a child from the street does limit her exploring; it also protects her from danger and does not allow her to believe wandering in the street is safe. Wise parents weigh their children's choices and environments to determine which experiences offer opportunities for growth and which are simply too dangerous. Allowing a child to take reasonable risks (like climbing on the monkey bars) and learn new skills (such as stirring the scrambled eggs—with your supervision, of course) is encouragement. Facing challenges and experiencing success builds a strong sense of self-worth.

LOVING THE CHILD YOU HAVE

Most of us have dreams of who our child will be. You may hope for a child who is quiet and thoughtful, or energetic and outgoing, or who possesses some other combination of qualities and talents. You may even want a child exactly like yourself. (Parents and children do not necessarily come in matched sets!)

Janice had dreamed of her child's babyhood. She was delighted to have a little girl, and she had painstakingly furnished the nursery in pastel-colored lace and ruffles. She bought ribbons and bows for her daughter's almost-invisible hair; she filled drawers with adorable little dresses. She cleaned up her own favorite dolls and added several more, preparing herself to share all sorts of blissful times with her daughter.

The little girl in question, however, had other ideas. She was not a cuddly child, and squirmed and wriggled constantly. She crawled and walked early and was always into something—much to her mother's dismay. She delighted in pulling the vacuum cleaner attachments apart, and emptied the kitchen cabinets time and time again. The dainty dresses were a nuisance; the baby seemed to have a gift for tearing and staining them.

Things only got more difficult as she grew. She preferred to be called Casey rather than Katy; she thought dresses were silly. She had no patience with dolls, and tossed them into the darkest corner of her closet or undressed and scribbled on them with ink. She insisted on "borrowing" her older brother's trucks

and skateboard, and as soon as she was able, she joined the older boys (despite their howls of protest) in their games, showing an astounding talent for playing street hockey and climbing trees. She even liked lizards and snakes. Janice tried offering ballet lessons and even gymnastics, but to no avail: Casey refused to be Katy. (It is interesting to note that when Casey had a little girl of her own, her daughter didn't follow in her mom's footsteps either. Little Diana delighted her Grandma Janice by loving dolls, dresses, and makeup, even as a toddler.)

Does Janice love her child? Undoubtedly she does. But one of the most beautiful ways of expressing love for a child is learning to love *that* child—not the child you wish you had.

THE POWER OF UNCONDITIONAL LOVE AND ACCEPTANCE

> ### Effective Methods for Building Self-Worth
>
> - Accept your child as he is.
> - Be patient with your child's development.
> - Provide opportunities for success.
> - Teach your child skills.
> - Be aware of self-fulfilling prophecies.

All parents have dreams for their children, and dreaming is not a bad thing. But we must love our children unconditionally in order for them to feel the acceptance and self-worth that leads to resilience and confidence. If you want to encourage your child and help him develop a sense of belonging and self-worth, you should keep several ideas in mind.

Accept Your Child As He Is
Children have their own unique temperaments. They have abilities you may not have expected and dreams of their own that don't match yours, and sometimes their behavior is a real disappointment.

It is all too easy to compare your offspring with the child down the street, his cousins, or even his own siblings, and to find him lacking in some way.

We humans are not good at unconditional love, yet children need to be loved unconditionally. You must remember that even the youngest child has an amazing ability to sense her parents' true feelings and attitudes. If she knows she is loved and accepted—if she feels the sense of worth and belonging she craves—she will thrive. If she senses that she doesn't belong, that she is a disappointment or a nuisance, her budding sense of self will wither, and you may never get to know the person she could have been. Encourage your child to be the best person she can be, not to be someone she is not.

Be Patient with Your Child's Development

Developmental charts are a wonderful way to keep track of the average time span during which children do certain things. The problem is that there are no average children! Each human being is a work of art. Look at the variety we see in appearance alone: skin color, hair color and texture, shape of the nose, color of the eyes, height, weight, shape—each one of us is unique. And physical characteristics are only the beginning of our uniqueness. Temperament, as we have discovered, is as individual as a fingerprint. So is the rate at which we develop and grow.

Children develop—crawl, walk, talk—at their own pace, and many early childhood conflicts stem from parental impatience. Your child will walk and use the toilet when he's ready; after all, have you ever seen a child crawl off to first grade in diapers? If you have serious concerns about your child's development, a word with your pediatrician may set your mind at rest and save both you and your child a great deal of discouragement.

Provide Opportunities for Success

Far more powerful than even the most loving and appreciative words are experiences that teach children they are capable, competent people.

Begin early to look for your child's special gifts and talents, his abilities and strengths, the things that make him bubble inside. Then give him chances to try those things.

Provide opportunities, too, for him to help you and to take on the little responsibilities he can handle. Early successes and experiences that say "I can do this!" are powerful builders of self-worth.

Teach Your Child Skills

Real self-worth grows when children have "competency experiences"— that is, when they learn skills and develop confidence in their ability to accomplish a task "all by myself." Yes, toddlers are young, but you

might be surprised at how much your little one can do. Your child can place napkins on the table, rinse lettuce leaves in the sink, and mop up spills with a sponge. She can place slices of cheese on hamburger buns, learn to dress herself, and pour her own juice. Will she do these tasks perfectly? Of course not—which is a good reason for you to have realistic expectations, lots of patience, and the willingness to teach these skills more than once. Still, skills are the foundation of healthy self-worth and self-confidence. When you teach your little one, you help her become a more responsible, self-reliant person.

Be Aware of Self-Fulfilling Prophecies

It is interesting to wonder just how terrible the twos would be if parents weren't forever reminding each other—and their children—just how terrible they are. Children have an uncanny ability to live up (or down) to their parents' expectations. If you call your rambunctious toddler a "little monster," don't be surprised if he does his best to be what you expect. In the same way, you can build self-confidence in your child by letting him know you love and accept him and believe in his ability to succeed.

Is your child always going to live out your predictions and expectations? No, of course not. But remember how powerful your words and opinions are to your child. If you tell your child that he's bad, or lazy, or stupid, or clumsy, don't be surprised if you reinforce the very behavior you dislike. By the same token, if you look for what's positive in your children, you can choose to encourage those positives. One of the most powerful tools a parent has for helping children develop a healthy sense of self-worth is looking for the positive.

When you focus on what is positive, positive behavior increases. Encouragement means noticing progress, not just achievement. It means thanking your small son for picking up most of his cars, even though he missed a few in the corner. It means giving a hug for an attempt on the potty seat, whether or not there was a result. It means smiling with a child who has put on her shoes, even though they're on the wrong feet. Encouragement says to a child, "I see you trying and I have faith in you. Keep it up!"

Looking for the positive in your child and encouraging it is a skill that will serve you throughout her childhood and adolescence, and it will help her to value herself. (You can use the activity at the end of this chapter to explore this concept further.)

FIRST STEPS

Children take many first steps—and only a few of them involve walking. Your child needs your unqualified support; he needs to know you have faith in him. He needs opportunities to practice new skills and take all his first steps, no matter how wobbly. He needs to know he can make mistakes without risking the loss of your love. When children live in an environment rich with encouragement, are allowed to learn from their mistakes, and experience kind and firm support, they will learn to believe in themselves and to bounce back when they experience frustration or defeat. Self-worth is inherent within each human soul, and, like any young seedling, it needs nurturing, warmth, and encouragement to thrive.

QUESTIONS TO PONDER

1. Take a moment sometime soon to make a list of everything you really like about your child.

2. Hang the list someplace where you can see it (the refrigerator or the bathroom mirror work well) and add to it when you think of something new.

3. Find an opportunity each day to appreciate your child for something on the list. Children often bloom amazingly in the steady light of love and encouragement. (Tip: Place a handful of pennies in one pocket. Every time you notice yourself naming a positive attribute of your child, transfer a penny to the opposite pocket. Aim to empty one pocket and fill the other each day.)

12

PERSPECTIVE AND PLANNING AHEAD

Confidence for You and Your Child

Most parents want their child to develop confidence, self-assurance, and the willingness to cooperate. Encouragement is an important step, but there is more you can do to nurture these important traits in your little one. When you let your child know how to deal with new situations by preparing him for what will happen and teaching him what he needs to know, it not only makes the experience more pleasant for all concerned, it gives him the opportunity to learn valuable skills and beliefs.

Patsy was on her way home from picking up her two-year-old son, Eric, when she decided to stop in at the jewelry shop to get her watch, which had been repaired. She hurried in with Eric tagging along behind her and went straight to the counter to present her claim check.

Eric stood clinging to his mother's coat. He had never been in a shop like this before, and there was a lot to look at. He was gazing around him when suddenly an open display shelf near a window caught his eye and utterly dazzled him.

The late afternoon sunlight was glinting off a collection of the most fascinating objects Eric had ever seen. They were small crystal figures—little animals and people, and even a perfect, tiny castle atop its own crystal mountain, exactly like the one in Eric's favorite storybook—and every movement of Eric's head created rainbows of bright light.

Before Patsy had time to realize what was happening, Eric was off toward the shelf as fast as his short, round legs could carry him. He reached for the wonderful castle, but his small fingers were only strong enough to drag the castle off its shelf and onto the tile floor, where it splintered into pieces.

Eric howled in fright. Patsy was embarrassed, apologetic, and angry—the crystal castle turned out to be shockingly expensive.

What are Patsy's options? Unfortunately, at this point she doesn't have many. She can pay for the broken castle and whisk her small son out to the car, vowing never to take him anywhere again. She can explore with Eric what happened and hope he remembers next time. (Notice that we haven't mentioned punishing Eric; it is doubtful a slap or a punitive time-out would make things any better, especially since Eric had received no guidelines beforehand.)

However, Patsy could have thought things through before entering the store, and taken the time to teach. She could have gotten down on Eric's level, perhaps placing her hands gently on his shoulders or taking his hands in hers, and explained that there would be many pretty things in the store but that touching and holding them might break them. Eric could look but not touch. She probably should have planned on holding his hand anyway, because it is too much to expect that a child will not want to explore at that age, or that he will be able to control his impulsivity, no matter how much teaching takes place. Patsy could also have made sure that Eric had something to occupy him while she was busy with the clerk. Or she could have decided that discretion was the better part of valor and picked up the watch at a time when Eric could be elsewhere.

Because avoidance is not always an option, though, your child will need to know how to behave in public places. **Taking a moment to teach, to talk quietly about behavior, and to prepare by packing a few small, quiet toys will help your child develop skills and confidence**—and will earn you the gratitude of your fellow diners, shoppers, and travel companions.

MAINTAINING DIGNITY AND RESPECT

Wait a minute, you may be thinking. *This sounds great, but how can I plan ahead and encourage confidence and resilience in a toddler who is constantly telling me no?* There are two beliefs that most parents share—beliefs that must be changed before you can work effectively with your little one. Do you recognize either of them?

- The belief that you can control toddlers and make them do what you tell them to do

- The belief that children are intentionally trying to defeat you

Because infants and toddlers are small and adults can easily pick them up and move them around, you may be seduced into believing that you can control their behavior. Think about this for a moment, though: Can any of us truly control another person's behavior? Feelings? Beliefs? It is often difficult enough for us to control our own! Instead of expecting to control young children, consider learning to invite cooperation. Abandoning the mistaken notion of control and working toward cooperation may save your dignity and sanity—and those of your child.

The cooperative child you envision living with five years from now is being shaped and encouraged each moment of every day. By contrast, the toddler you swat and scold when she pulls books out of the bookcase is likely to become the six-year-old who refuses to do anything you ask—or the teenager who slips out the bedroom window after you've grounded her for a month. The toddler who is gently redirected to the pots-and-pans cupboard without punishment is learning to cooperate. Hopefully, she will also become the six-year-old willing to help empty the dishwasher, or the teenage who can negotiate a reasonable curfew and then honor it.

You will know that children aren't trying to defeat you when you understand developmental stages and age-appropriate behavior. An  eighteen-month-old who heads for your new smartphone has no intention of defying you. He sees something new, colorful, and inviting, something that you are obviously interested in as well. He wants to touch and explore it. Previous experience may have taught him to glance at you as he reaches for it, but his wired-in need to explore is much stronger than your warnings. His behavior isn't defiance—it's curiosity. Once you realize this, it becomes far easier to respond without anger or punishment. Let's take another look at this as we explore every toddler's favorite word: "No!"

WHAT DOES YOUR TODDLER REALLY "KNOW" ABOUT "NO"?

Children under the age of three do not understand "no" in the way most parents think they do (and a full understanding of "no" doesn't occur magically when the child turns three or four; it is a developmental process). "No" is an abstract concept that is in direct opposition to the developmental need of young children to explore their world and to develop their sense of autonomy and initiative. Oh, your child may "know" you don't want her to do something. She may even know she will get an angry reaction from you if she does it. However, her behavior is not yet truly intentional.

Knowing things as a toddler means something far different from internalizing that knowledge as an adult. A child's version of knowing lacks the internal controls necessary to halt her roving fingers. Researchers including Jean Piaget discovered long ago that toddlers lack the ability to understand cause and effect in the same way adults do (an excellent reason not to try to lecture or argue a toddler into doing what you want). In fact, higher-order thinking like understanding

---

Cognitive Development—and Why Children Don't Understand "No" the Way You Think They Should

- Take two balls of clay that are the same size. Ask a three-year-old if they are the same. She will probably say yes. Then, right in front of her, smash one ball of clay. Then ask her if they are still the same. She will say no and will tell you which one she thinks is bigger. A five-year-old will tell you they are the same, and can tell you why.

- Find four glasses: two of the same size, one that is taller and thinner, and one that is shorter and fatter. Fill the two identical glasses with water and ask a three-year-old if they have the same amount. She will probably say yes. Then, right in front of her, pour the water from one into the short, fat glass and the other into the tall, thin glass. Then ask her if they still hold the same amount of water. Again, she will say no and will tell you which glass she thinks contains more water. A five-year-old will tell you they contain the same amount, and can tell you why.

Both of these examples demonstrate thinking abilities identified by Piaget. When you understand that perceiving, interpreting, and comprehending an event are different for young children, your expectations will change.

---

consequences and ethics may not develop fully until children are as old as ten. In the meantime, children need kind, firm limits, patient teaching—and supervision.

AT ANOTHER LEVEL: THE "CHILD POWER" OF "NO"

Toddlers are learning to see themselves as separate, independent beings. (This "individuation process" escalates when they become teenagers.) It's a natural and healthy part of development, but one that is frequently trying for parents and teachers. It doesn't take long for a young child to learn the power of the word "no" or that by using it he can provoke all sorts of interesting reactions. Adults can't always avoid these confrontations, but changing your own behavior and expectations can lessen their impact. There are actually three types of "no": the ones you can avoid saying, the ones you can avoid hearing, and the ones that you just learn to live with.

HOW NOT TO SAY "NO"

"Sometimes I listen to myself talking to my two-year-old," one mom confided to a group of friends, "and all I hear myself saying is 'no' and 'don't.' I sound so negative, but I don't know what else to do." There are actually a number of ways adults can avoid saying the "no" word themselves:

- **Say what you *do* want.** Hannah, who is three years old, is delightedly throwing blocks across the room. Her teacher walks in and immediately says, "No throwing blocks!" Now, Hannah hears what not to do, but she may have a hard time figuring out what she *can* do. It might be more effective if her teacher says, "Blocks are for using on the floor" or "You look like you want to do some throwing. Would you like me to help you find a ball you can throw?" *The next time you start to tell your child no, ask yourself what you want to have happen. Then tell your child what you want.*

- **Say "yes" instead.** Many parents are programmed to respond with an automatic no. When you are about to say no, try asking yourself, "Why not?" Take a look at sixteen-month-old Cindy. She is playing in the bathroom sink, splashing water everywhere, and having a wonderful time. When Mom enters the room, her first response is to grab Cindy and say, "Stop that!"

  But why? Cindy's eyes are sparkling; she is absorbed in the feel of the water and the magic of the droplets flying around. Her clothes can be changed, and she'll probably think it's a terrific game to help Mom mop the floor afterward. In other words, there may be no reason to say no this time. Mom and Cindy may be better off if they forget the "no" and simply enjoy themselves.

- **Try distraction and redirection.** Firmly and calmly remove a child from the forbidden item. Instead of scolding her about what she shouldn't be doing, refocus attention: "Let's see how many birds are at the bird feeder this morning."

- **Offer limited choices.** When your toddler demands apple juice instead of orange juice, hold up the cup of apple juice you gave her or offer to put the juice away until later. (Remember, toddlers may use their whole bodies to object, as in a tantrum. Just because little Sophie throws a tantrum doesn't mean that your handling of the situation was inappropriate.) Next time, try offering a choice of juice before pouring it, thereby giving her an opportunity to exercise appropriate power instead of demanding special service or engaging in a power struggle.

WHEN YOU MUST SAY "NO"

Where do children learn the word "no"? Well, probably from hearing their parents and caregivers say it so often. Try to say no only when necessary during these first three years of life. If you say no too frequently, you may be hampering normal development and creating unnecessary power struggles.

Remember, you must be willing to *teach* many times before comprehension occurs. We talk to children before they comprehend words, we remove them from things they can't do before they comprehend why, we hug and cuddle before they are able to hug back.

Real understanding—the ability to use a skill without consciously thinking about it—takes time. Providing kind and firm discipline and teaching developmentally appropriate boundaries are the goals, but you will make many mistakes along the way. Because infants and toddlers do not always comprehend, saying no is effective only when used with other methods, such as kind and firm action.

TEACH WITH YOUR ACTIONS

With children from birth to age three, it is best to say no with actions instead of words. As Rudolf Dreikurs used to say, "Shut your mouth and act."

Two-year-old Oliver loved books, but when Cynthia, his caregiver, found him ripping out pages in the book she had just read for story time, she gently took it away and led Oliver to the book corner. There, she helped Oliver choose a more rugged board book. Oliver was content with this new book, and further damage to a school library book was prevented.

When two-and-a-half-year-old Michael started a temper tantrum in the supermarket, his mother picked him up and took him to the car. She calmly held him on her lap until he stopped screaming and writhing. They then went into the store and tried again. They made three trips to the car that day; fortunately, Michael's mom took care not to load perishables like frozen peas or milk into her cart until just before they checked out! A few days later, they went to the supermarket again, and made only one trip to the car. The following week, Michael stopped crying as soon as his mother picked him up to head for the car. That's planning ahead (and kind and firm follow-through) in practice!

It was easier for these adults to act kindly and firmly because they knew it was normal for children to test their autonomy and initiative, sometimes in socially unacceptable or dangerous ways. Was Michael's mom embarrassed when the other shoppers stared at them or suggested that her child needed "a good spanking"? Perhaps. She also knew that it is a parent's job to build a sense of capability and resilience, to provide constant supervision, and to redirect misbehavior through kind and firm action. Parenting requires both patience and courage, and raising active, curious, energetic toddlers merits a medal of special honor. It is an awesome task.

Instead of expecting your child to comprehend and obey when you say no, follow through with action. You might say "No biting" while gently cupping your hand over the child's mouth and removing her from biting range. You might say "No hitting" while removing him

---

A Hugging "No"

There is a delightful cartoon that depicts a mother shouting "No!" to her toddler. The child shouts back, "Yes!" The mother shouts louder, "No!" The child screams, "Yes!" Then the mother remembers the importance of being kind and firm at the same time. She kneels down, gives her child a hug, and softly says, "No." The little boy says, "Okay."

Saying no is fine when you are aware of what your child does and does not understand. The frustration occurs when parents think the word "no" by itself is enough to create obedience.

and showing him what he can do: "Touch nicely." The "no" may be more for your benefit than the child's—it helps you create the energy you need for kind and firm action.

THE "NO" YOU WANT CHILDREN TO SAY

Believe it or not, children need to learn to say no. Saying no is a valuable life skill. Toddlers will one day grow into teenagers who will be faced with offers of drugs, alcohol, and other dangerous options. When these choices loom, you undoubtedly want your young adult to say no. Right now, when his entire vocabulary seems to consist of that one word, you may not be so thrilled.

Give children chances to say no in appropriate ways. "Do you want some juice?" A "no" response to juice is perfectly acceptable. Or you might ask, "May Auntie give you a hug before she leaves?" Because children need to have some control over their bodies, the answer of "no" ought to be an option, one that hopefully Auntie can accept without offense.

KIND AND FIRM

Another possibility is to use kind *and* firm statements that don't include the word "no." Notice how the "and" puts kindness and firmness together. Here are some examples:

- **Validate feelings:** "I know it is hard to stop playing, *and* it is time for dinner."

- **Show understanding:** "I understand why you would rather play than go to bed, *and* it is bedtime."

- **Redirect behavior:** "You don't want to brush your teeth, *and* I don't want your teeth to be icky. I'll race you to the bathroom."

- **Provide a choice:** "You don't want to take a nap, *and* it is naptime. Is it your turn to choose a book, or mine?"

- Offer a choice and then follow through by deciding what you will do: "I know you want to run around in the store, *and* that is not acceptable. You can stay close to me or we can go sit in the car until you are ready to try again."

PROCESS VERSUS PRODUCT

Few things in the world of parenting come in only black or white. This book is all about choices and possibilities. Understanding your child's individual progress—his development of trust, autonomy, and initiative, his temperament, his physical and cognitive development—will help you make the best choices for him and for you. Let's take a look at one way developmental stages influence your child's perceptions and behavior.

It's a busy Friday evening, and you're off on a quick trip to the grocery store with your toddler. You have a definite goal in mind—namely, to grab the necessary ingredients for dinner in time to get home, prepare and eat it, and still be on time for your older son's soccer game. For you, going to the store means obtaining the desired product. For your toddler, however, the product just isn't the point. **Children are firmly rooted in the here and now; they think and experience life differently than adults do.** A trip to the store is all about the process—the smells, the colors, the feelings, the experience. Being sandwiched into a busy schedule just doesn't allow time to enjoy the process.

Children do not share our goal-oriented expectations. It isn't always possible to go along with a child's relaxed approach, either. Sometimes you really do need to run in, grab the chicken, and run home again. But being aware of your child's tendency to focus on process rather than product can help you provide a balance. There may be times when you can browse slowly through the store, enjoying the flowers in the floral department and the magazines in the rack, or smelling the fragrant peaches and naming colors together. Children are miniature Zen masters, able to focus on the moment and enjoy it—an ability many adults would do well to learn.

When you must hurry, take time to explain to your child why you must shop quickly this time. You can explain that you want him to hold your hand and that you will have to walk past the toys and other interesting things. You can offer to let him help you find the chicken and carry it to the checkout stand. Then you will walk back to the car and drive home. Helping a child understand clearly what is expected and what will happen makes it more likely he will cooperate with you.

THE IMPORTANCE OF HUMOR AND HOPE

The ability to laugh and the ability to hope and dream are among the greatest gifts parents can bestow upon their children. There is no better way to prevent problems (or to deal with those that have already happened) than to change your perspective and see the humor in a situa-

tion. From the earliest games of peekaboo with your infant, laughter creates one of the closest bonds between you and your child. When your toddler's attempt to fill the dog's water dish results in a stream from the sink to the back door, try to smile and appreciate the effort. (We promise it will make a great story to share with his children someday!) Learning to share a smile, to make funny faces, or to find the humor in situations can carry your family through many tough times.

Rules and limits have their place, and we couldn't function well without them. But try the following experiment sometime: *Notice how often you reprimand your child, make a demand, or warn against danger or an infraction of the rules. Then count how many times you admire his skills, encourage his explorations, or chuckle together over some amusing incident. Which do you do more often?*

Hopefully, an awareness of the impact of negative statements will encourage you to be more encouraging to your children. Focus on the positive. Prevent problems when possible. Allow time for relaxing a bit, for giving a child an extra hug or a few extra minutes of talk before bed. There are times when the best medicine truly is laughter—with a healthy dose of perspective.

QUESTIONS TO PONDER

1. It is easy to focus on what's wrong. We have no trouble making long lists of what we dislike about ourselves, our spouses, our jobs—and our children. Think for a moment about how you'd feel if your boss at work never did anything but point out your errors and shortcomings. How motivated would you feel to try harder? For one day, count how many times you say no to your child.

2. If your list seems long and you are feeling discouraged, your child might be, too. Catch yourself saying "no" and see if you can turn it into a "yes" instead. See how many times you can manage this switch. You will both feel more encouraged.

3. Consider an errand that you frequently do with your child. Is there a way to engage her in the process? How can you plan and teach before leaving home so your time together goes more smoothly? If mistakes happen (and they often do when you're learning a new skill), think about what you can learn from the mistake to improve the process next time.

13

SLEEPING

You Can't Make 'Em Do It

Gather any group of parents with very young children together and, inevitably, the conversation will turn in one of three directions. "I can't get my little girl to take a nap," one mom complains. "She's up all day, then she falls asleep early in the evening. That would be great if she stayed asleep—but she wakes up at three in the morning and wants to play. How can I get her to sleep when we do?"

"We practice the family bed, and our children sleep fine, although sometimes *we* don't sleep very well," one parent reports. Another says, "We also practice the family bed, but not because we want to. We just can't get our kids to sleep in their *own* beds."

"My son sleeps fine," a dad says, "but he absolutely refuses to have anything to do with his potty seat. He's almost three. My mother says *her* kids were all trained by the age of two. We're starting to panic."

"Well, we're still on the basics," another mom adds sadly. "My little boy thinks he can live on hot dogs and SpaghettiOs, with an occasional cookie thrown in. I've bribed and coaxed and argued, but he just clamps his lips together when I offer him anything else. I dread mealtimes."

Most of us can relate to these beleaguered parents; in fact, you may be nodding your head as you read this. The next three chapters will deal with those perennial power struggles: sleeping, eating, and toileting. Who starts these wars? And why?

We believe that like any other parenting battle, the sleeping, eating, and toileting wars are based on a lack of knowledge, a lack of skills, a lack of faith, and a lack of confidence in yourself and your little one.

Understanding developmental and age-appropriateness will give you needed perspective as your child learns to master his body. Focusing on cooperation skills—especially when you face the reality that sleeping, eating, and toileting are three areas where your child is in complete control—will bring relief to both of you. It is, after all, his body!

Remember, it takes two to have a power struggle. You can't make your child sleep; you can't make her eat; and you can't make her use the toilet. Only she can perform these functions. There *are* ways to invite cooperation, however, using respectful and developmentally appropriate methods.

All humans must sleep and eat to survive. Toileting is a bodily function with strong (to say the least) social significance. None of these areas becomes a battleground unless it becomes more important for a child (or a parent) to "win" than to do what comes naturally. The key is for parents to learn to invite cooperation instead of engage in power struggles.

SLEEPING: "BUT I'M NOT TIRED!"

Most babies spend more time asleep than awake during the first few months of their lives, although their sleep schedules may be topsy-turvy for a while. Many power struggles over sleeping can be avoided if you help your child learn to fall asleep by herself as early in her life as possible. One of the most helpful strategies is to put her in her crib just before she falls asleep. Some parents are afraid to lay down a drowsy or sleeping baby for fear of waking her, but waking up and being allowed to go back to sleep after a little fussing is fine. It may help to add a gentle pat on the back to soothe her back to sleep.

With time and practice, you will learn what works best for your child. You can explore the relative virtues of darkness versus night-lights, music versus silence, warm rooms versus cool ones. Still, *sleeping is the baby's job.* You will invite a battle if you try to make his sleep your responsibility.

Sleep patterns are different, too. Some babies are born with more active temperaments, while others may have colic or other physical problems. These infants may require more holding and comforting during the first three to six months until you (and your doctor) know your baby well enough to know if the problems are physical or not. Establish good sleeping habits as soon as you feel confident that your child does not have any physical problems.

SLEEPING SINGLE

Q: My two daughters (twelve months and almost three years old) will not fall asleep by themselves. I have to lie down with them until they fall asleep. Usually I fall asleep, too, and the whole evening is shot. Actually, the whole bedtime routine is a battle. They scream about having a bath, getting into their jammies, and going to bed. My older daughter tells me she isn't tired. I try to convince her that she is. When I finally get them to bed and read a story, they cry for more. I'm a stay-at-home mom, so my children get plenty of attention—but it never seems to be enough. Help!

A: Parents usually suffer more than their children do when they wait too long to help children learn they can go to sleep by themselves (and in the process, can learn "I am capable"). In truth, your child's resistance may be much harder on you than it is on her! You chose to help her get to sleep when she was younger (an acceptable choice made by most caring parents). Are you willing to suffer a bit more to help your child now?

Your daughters probably will cry for three to five nights until they accept that you know what is best for them and that you are going to stick to your resolve with confidence. Use your intuition to decide if you want to help them learn cold turkey or in stages. If your child continues to cry, you can go in to offer a word or a touch after five minutes, then ten minutes, then fifteen minutes, and so on without lying down, cuddling, or coddling. (You may question whether a young child knows the difference between five minutes and fifty, but the important thing is that she experiences consistency in finding you when she wakes up.)

This may be the only way some parents can handle this adjustment; others see this as a way of teasing the baby and making separation more painful for both parent and child. In either case, parents who go cold turkey and parents who go in for a few seconds of comfort generally find that it takes three to five days for children to learn to fall asleep by themselves.

There are two main ingredients for success in helping your children learn to go to sleep by themselves:

1. Your understanding that this is the most loving thing you can do for your children, who have experienced secure attachment up until now. It is not helpful to teach them, even inadvertently, that their only power is to demand "undue service" from others.
2. Your confidence. They will feel this from your energy and from your body language. Remember mirror neurons? Your emotional state is very readable. Children feel safe and trusting when parents are confident. When you are confident, it will be easier for

you to be kind and firm. Conversely, if you feel unsure or give up and go in after several minutes of crying, your child may learn to cry longer, and you will both feel discouraged.

Your children receive plenty of love during the day, and they see you every morning. We do not believe they will feel unloved or abandoned if they cry a little as they learn to fall asleep by themselves. It is actually empowering and loving to teach children the skills they will need to become healthy, responsible people.

If you decide you just can't stand to allow your child to cry, that is a choice you can make—but you must recognize that you may be setting the stage for a child who will demand undue service from you for many years. In the end, sleep will triumph. (Believe it or not, the day may come when you have trouble getting her to wake up and get out of her bed.)

Crying or resistance does not mean that you have made the wrong choice. Your job as a parent is to make choices that are in your child's best interest—but that does not mean those choices will always be popular. How will children learn that they can solve problems or develop resilience if they aren't allowed opportunities to try?

CREATING A MORE PEACEFUL BEDTIME

Most parents and children will wrestle with bedtime at some point during their journey together. Here are some ideas that may help you make bedtime a soothing—instead of seething—time of day:

- **Establish a bedtime routine.** The predictability of the night's bath, toothbrushing, and bedtime stories will ease the transition from day to night. Consistency creates a feeling of safety and reassurance—the ideal atmosphere for a restful night's sleep. Many busy families report that bedtime is seldom the same from one day to the next. While older children may be more flexible, consistent bedtime routines are essential for little ones.

- **Create a comfortable sleep environment.** Like their parents, children have different preferences for how they sleep. Some children like a night-light, while others prefer pitch darkness; some like to hear the sounds of their parents and families, while others want silence; some like lightweight pajamas while others want cuddly, footed sleepers. These details aren't worth arguing about. Help your child find the formula that works best for her, then let her relax and fall asleep in her cozy nest.

- **Create a bedtime routine chart together.** As children grow older, the night's routine can be made into a visual chart. Invite your child to tell you all the things he needs to do before going to bed, while you write them down. (If your child

is too young to have this conversation, he may be too young to benefit from a chart.) If he skips something, you can ask questions such as, "What about choosing your clothes for the morning?" Then ask your child to tell you in what order these tasks need to be done while you put numbers on his list.

Now comes the fun part. Let your child pose while you take a picture of him doing each task. Print the photos and let your child paste them on a chart in the agreed-upon order (or let him staple them, in order, on a long ribbon), and ask him where you should hang it so he can see it. Now it is his. If he forgets, all you need to do is ask, "What is next on your bedtime-routine chart?" This puts him in charge and encourages feelings of capability.

- **Encourage your child to take an active role in bedtime preparations.** If he is old enough to manage, don't put his jammies on for him. (Remember, two- and three-year-olds are working on autonomy and initiative.) You might want to let him set a timer to see how quickly he can get his jammies on. Do this in a spirit of fun, not as a means of pressuring or hurrying your child. Encouragement is the key element whenever we promote independence and autonomy in young children.

- **Practice bedtime behaviors at other times of the day.** You may want to play "Let's Pretend" to prepare your child for what is going to happen. Try role-playing going to bed crying and then going to bed happy. You may want to play the part of your child, while he is the "parent." You can also use puppets or stuffed animals to act out a bedtime routine. Remember, this exercise is intended to teach, not lecture. (Children love this, especially when the adult "child" misbehaves.) This gives her the opportunity to show how much she really understands about appropriate bedtime behavior. Model cooperation and do remember to have fun. (No one ever said parenting had to be boring!)

- **Avoid power struggles.** If your child says, "I don't want to go to bed," don't argue the point. You might say, "You'd really like to stay up later, *and* it is time for bed," or "You don't want to go to bed yet, *and* your chart says it is story time now." These statements acknowledge her demands and help her to feel listened to, even though it is still bedtime. Be kind and firm at the same time. Trying to convince her that she is tired or telling her that she is cranky is not helpful. This only invites argument, and is a surefire recipe for a power struggle. Hang on to your sense of humor and playfulness. Many little ones resist a command to put jammies on, but few can resist a race to see who can get them on first—Dad or child!

Normally, whenever there's a power struggle, one participant wins and the other loses. In this case, though, you *both* lose because you will both be exhausted and frustrated by the time she finally falls asleep. It is your job to step out of the power struggle and create a win/win solution. Be kind but firm. Continue with the routine. Ask, "What is next on your chart?"

- **Decide whether bedtimes are the same.** If you have more than one child, do you want them to go to bed at the same time or at separate times? It probably won't take as long as you fear to do two routines if you combine part of the routines for both children. For instance, you may decide to have bath time and playtime together. One partner can play with an older child while the other gets the baby dressed. Or an older child can help by entertaining baby brother while he gets his diaper changed. This contributing role will help the older child feel involved instead of ignored, and will promote her cooperation when it is her own bedtime.

- **Decide what you will do—then do it.** Agree to read one book or two, then stick to the agreement. Don't get involved in a debate. Children learn best from actions that are kind and firm. If she keeps begging for one more story, give her a kiss good night and leave the room. Yes, she may cry, but your kind, respectful action will teach her that manipulation is not an option.

- **Make bedtime a time of sharing.** When your child has acquired language, you might say, "Tell me the happiest and saddest thing that happened to you today." You can also share your own happy and sad moments. This is a wonderful way to develop closeness. (Remember: today, yesterday, and last week are measures of time that children under four or five do not fully understand. Her happy moment might be something that took place months ago. Don't argue the details; simply enjoy the sharing.)

- **Give a big hug—and leave.** Remember, the more confident you are, the easier it will be for your children.

Trust yourself to modify these suggestions to fit your style; you may want to add prayers, a song, or some other special item to your routine chart. Bedtime may be difficult sometimes, but you can feel confident that you are helping your child learn to go to sleep by himself, to get the rest he needs—and building his confidence and self-esteem in the process.

Does It Work?

Tara tried one more time to stuff her small son's arm into his pajama sleeve, and gave up in frustration as he wailed and wriggled free again. Ever since baby Sean had arrived, bedtime had meant a battle with two-year-old Tyler. Tara knew that children sometimes struggled with the addition of a new sibling to the family, and had thought that she and Miles, her husband, had prepared Tyler well.

Ever since Sean had come home from the hospital, however, Tyler had refused to fall asleep without a parent in his bed. He woke up several times a night, and he resisted the whole bedtime process. Tara sighed and picked up the pajama top again. Tomorrow, she resolved, she would dig out the notes from her parenting class. It was time to declare a cease-fire in the bedtime wars.

The next morning was Saturday. Tara waited until Sean was napping, and then called Tyler to her side. "I have an idea," she said with a smile. "I need some help remembering how to do bedtime with you. Could you help me make a chart so we can remember everything we're supposed to do?" Tyler liked being consulted by his mom and agreed to help, watching with curiosity as Tara gathered poster board, markers, the camera, and stickers.

"Now," she said, uncapping a marker, "what's the first thing we do at bedtime?"

Working together, Tara and her small son listed the bedtime tasks and illustrated each one with a picture. When the chart was complete, Tara wrote "TYLER'S BEDTIME ROUTINE" in big letters and helped him sprinkle glitter on squiggly lines of glue. Tyler dashed off to show his creation to his dad.

Miles admired the bright chart, amused by his son's enthusiasm, but he looked dubiously at Tara. "I don't know," he said. "How can that make a difference?" But that night, Miles and Tara were both surprised by how well Tyler responded when they said, "What is next on your routine chart?"

Later that week, Tara shared the results with her parenting group. "Tyler still doesn't want to go to bed sometimes," she said. "But when he knows I mean it he immediately asks, 'Where's my chart?' We have to follow every step in order and he corrects me if I make a mistake. I tried to read him only one book last night and Tyler reminded me that the chart says he gets two. He's been falling asleep without a whimper and sleeping through the night almost every night. His grandpa was so charmed by the bedtime chart that he asked if he could keep it as a memento after Tyler has outgrown it!"

It is wise to remember that nothing will work all the time for all children, but as you will see, most toddlers thrive on routine, consistency, and encouragement.

SLEEPING WITH PARENTS

Many parents wonder whether or not they should let their children sleep with them. There are differing opinions on this issue. Books have been written about the "family bed" and the benefits of allowing children to sleep with their parents. Some people believe children feel

Beware of Bedtime Videos

Q: My two-year-old wants to watch her favorite video every night at bedtime. If we don't let her watch it, she puts up a terrible fight about going to bed. Sometimes we just give up and let her fall asleep on the floor in front of the TV. Even when we let her watch her video, she is a restless sleeper and often wakes up cranky and irritable in the morning. What should we do?

A: A significant amount of research has found that screen time just before bedtime can disrupt a child's sleep patterns—and sound sleep is important for growth, health, and consolidating learning. It may be a difficult transition for all of you, but it is best if you turn off all screens at least an hour before you plan to put your child to bed. Create a routine chart with her and let her know—kindly but firmly—that her video will not be part of her routine. Then follow the chart until her new bedtime routine has become the norm.

more loved and secure when they sleep in their parents' bed. Other experts believe children become demanding and dependent when they sleep with their parents, and that they have more opportunity to learn cooperation, self-confidence, and autonomy when they sleep in their own beds. *Positive Discipline A–Z** states, "If your children are in your bed by choice, that is one thing . . . However, most parents allow their children to sleep with them not by choice but by default and they

---

* Jane Nelsen and Lynn Lott (New York: Three Rivers Press, 2007).

are not happy about it. When this is the case, it is disrespectful to let your children sleep in your bed with you." This raises an important distinction, one that can help you sort out what is really going on in your situation.

The first thing to consider is what works for you. Follow your heart *and* your head. Do you find it difficult to sleep with your children in your bed? If you are a single parent, it is vital to consider the implications of a potential new partner entering the picture; ask yourself how committed you might be to sharing your bed with an infant, toddler, or preschooler in such an eventuality. Some couples find it hampers their relationship (emotional and sexual), and don't want to give up time for adult conversation after slipping under the covers, a quiet moment to read a book, and/or the chance to make love before going to sleep. (We purposely left out watching television, which can create a bigger wedge in a relationship than children in the bed.)

On the other hand, if you believe that sharing the family bed fosters emotional closeness, then do so with safety considerations in mind. (The American Association of Pediatrics advises against infants sleeping in an adult's bed, due to the risk of suffocation and an increased risk of SIDS, though not all experts agree with this advice.)

Aside from philosophical, emotional, and safety concerns, remember that each child and family is unique. How does sharing a family bed work for your children? Does it help or hinder their development of autonomy, self-confidence, and self-reliance? Each family must find its own answers to these questions. We don't claim to have "the" answer, but we do believe that parents will be able to sense when their child becomes overly demanding or is developing excessive dependence (instead of healthy independence).

Rudolf Dreikurs believed that there is a strong connection between daytime misbehavior and nighttime misbehavior. In other words, children who create difficulties during the day also tend to create bedtime challenges. Dreikurs told the following story about a woman who came to him with a "problem" child. After hearing the woman's complaints about her problems with the child during the day, Dreikurs asked, "How does the child behave at bedtime?" The woman replied, "I don't have any problems at night." This surprised Dreikurs, because his theory was that daytime and nighttime behavior are related. After a bit more discussion, Dreikurs asked again, "Are you sure you don't have any bedtime problems?" The woman assured him, "Oh no, I don't have any problems at night." Finally Dreikurs guessed what might be happening at night. He asked, "Where does the child sleep?" The woman replied, "Why, she sleeps with me, of course."

Dreikurs explained to the woman that the sleeping arrangement was part of the problem. The child was not creating any problems at night because in bed she had her mother's undivided attention. The child was only trying to get the same level of attention during the day that she received at night, and she created problems when her mother did not cater to her as she did at night. This child may have decided, "I'm loved only when I receive constant attention."

If your child is sleeping in your bed and seems overly demanding and dependent during the day, you might want to consider weaning her from the family bed. This decision can be difficult. As H. Stephen Glenn and Jane Nelsen point out in their book *Raising Self-Reliant Children in a Self-Indulgent World,* "Weaning has never been easy for the weanor or the weanee, but it is necessary for the healthy personal growth of both."

Some parents don't allow their children to sleep with them during the night but welcome them into their bed on weekend mornings for "morning snuggles." Other parents have a routine of lying down on their children's beds for story time. They make it clear to their children that they will leave when the story is over, avoiding the habit many children quickly adopt of insisting their parents stay in their bed until after they fall asleep.

Again, use your wisdom to decide what works best for you and your children. If you are part of a couple, listening and respecting one another as you make parenting choices will strengthen your relationship. Weigh your own needs against the skills your child will eventually need to develop, and chances are excellent that you'll make the choice that is best for all of you.

A WORD ABOUT BEDS

As if there wasn't enough to consider, there are many choices of beds for children today. Should a child sleep in a parent's room or in his own room? Should he be in a crib or on a mattress on the floor? Proponents of each of these styles have strong opinions and reasons to back them. Monitors make it easier if you prefer your child to be in a separate room, providing reassurance of your child's safety. Remember, the key is balance. What works for your family?

Speaking of balance, one unique sleeping choice is a rocking hammock that fans claim is especially helpful for babies who have colic. Even without colic, this choice appears to be very comfortable and makes it easy to keep a baby on her back, a position that the American Association of Pediatrics* recommends to reduce the risk of Sudden Infant Death Syndrome (SIDS).

WEANING

"What if it is too late?" you may be asking. "I have already allowed some bad habits to develop and my child is now very demanding. She won't go to sleep at all unless I lie down with her or let her sleep with us. When I try to break her of the habit, she screams—and I always give in. It has created all the problems you have discussed, but I can't stand to listen to her cry."

Here are some tips to help you survive the weaning process:

- **Give up your "guilt button."** Children know when they can push that button; they also know when it is gone. (Don't ask us how they know—they just do!) Guilt is rarely a positive, helpful feeling.

---

* www.aap.org/en-us/about-the-aap/aap-press-room/pages/AAP-Expands-Guidelines-for-Infant-Sleep-Safety-and-SIDS-Risk-Reduction.aspx.

Back Sleeping

Most parents have heard about SIDS, which is the leading cause of death in infants up to the age of one year, and know that a baby should be placed on his back to sleep (at home and at childcare) to reduce the risk of SIDS. But parents may also have concerns about back sleeping. Here is some useful information from the American Association of Pediatrics:

- **Spitting up or vomiting.** Parents sometimes worry that a baby will choke if he spits up while on his back. Reassuring research shows, however, that healthy infants are able to turn their heads if they spit up, and are no more likely to have breathing or digestive problems than infants who sleep on their tummies.

- **Flat head.** Parents also may feel concern that a baby who sleeps on her back will develop a flat head. While a baby's skull is indeed malleable early in life, the shape tends to fill out over time. You can also put your baby down for "tummy time" while she is awake, which will help strengthen her neck muscles and improve her coordination— and reduce the time she spends on her back.

- **Delayed motor skills.** Some parents are told that babies who sleep on their backs won't learn to roll over quickly and may even have delayed motor development. Again, if your baby gets lots of tummy time while he's awake, this will not be a problem. Be sure your little one gets lots of opportunities to stretch, reach, and move, and he will develop strength and coordination smoothly. (You can learn more about these issues at www.healthychild.org.)

Knowing why you are doing something will help you do what is necessary for the ultimate good of your child.

- **Tell your child what you are going to do.** Even if your child is preverbal, he or she will understand the energy behind the words. A little warning and time to prepare will help both of you avoid unpleasant surprises.

- **Follow through.** If you say it, mean it; and if you mean it, follow through with action that is kind and firm.

- **Take time during the day for lots of hugs and other special time with your child.** Make sure this isn't "guilt penance" (your child will "feel" the difference), but time for reassurance and enjoyment of your love for each other.

- **Hang in there.** If you've followed the above steps, it usually takes at least three days for your child to believe that you mean what you say—and it may take longer. This means that she will try very hard to get you to maintain the old habit. Decide beforehand how you will handle such resistance. Some mothers find it so painful to listen to their little one cry that they put their heads under the covers and cry themselves. (The crying time will probably get shorter each night—even though every minute might still feel like an eternity.)

Allowing a child to "cry it out" is always a dilemma for parents. Remember, crying is a form of communication. Of course, you must respond to your child's cries. The challenge is to be able to discern whether the cry is communicating a need or a want. Children need to be fed, diapered, and given love. They also need sleep. On the other hand, a child may want to stay awake, even if his body is exhausted. When this is the case, a bit of crying to express disappointment, to release excess energy, or to manage his sense of being overwhelmed by fatigue may be necessary for him to settle down and sleep.

Sometimes parents worry that letting a baby cry is traumatic and will scar him for life. When a baby experiences plenty of love and attachment during the day, trauma is unlikely for a child who is six months old or older. Certainly, it is unwise to allow a baby to cry for long periods of time without responding, but it is not helpful when a child develops the belief "I'm not capable," which may happen if she doesn't learn self-reliance in small doses.

Sometimes adults don't get what they want—and sometimes they, too, have temper tantrums! When anyone, child or adult, learns to deal with disappointment and setbacks, that person is more likely to develop resilience. The more confidence you have in your decision, whatever that decision may be, the easier it will be for your child to recover from the disappointment of not getting her way.

It is important to remember that **children do not always know what is best for them. The baby bird does not enjoy being pushed out of the nest, but the mother bird knows it is essential.** Bedtime struggles are common. Families do survive them,

Bedtime ABC's

Acceptance. Accept your child's limitations and your own.

- Have faith in your child and confidence in yourself.
- Accept that a child's resistance does not make an adult's choice wrong.
- Be aware of a child's developmental abilities; be sure your expectations are reasonable.
- Concede that you cannot make your child sleep—that's his responsibility.

Balance. Maintain a balance between your child's needs and the needs of the rest of the family.

- Provide plenty of love and attachment opportunities during the day to balance the need for independence and sleep at night.
- Acknowledge your fears and needs, including your need for rest.
- Balance your child's needs with the needs of all family members.
- Create a restful environment that is comfortable, safe, and secure.

Consistency. Yours will lead to your child's.

- Allow time for each child to prepare for the transition to bedtime.
- Be consistent: maintain routines and follow through on agreements.
- Create a bedtime routine that progresses toward that final tuck-in time.

however. Bedtime brings up difficult issues for many reasons, but we are confident that with a little thought and planning, you can discover a process that works for you and for your child.

QUESTIONS TO PONDER

1. Do you know what sort of environment helps your child feel comfortable enough to fall asleep? If not, give some thought to what might help him feel safe, secure, and cozy, whether or not it's what you would choose.
2. What are your typical challenges in getting your child to sleep? Can you resolve them by setting a consistent bedtime and by establishing a bedtime routine? What would "kind and firm" look like in putting your child to bed?
3. Create a bedtime routine chart with your child. Does your child respond well to the routine? Does the routine need some "tweaking" in order to work more smoothly?

14

"OPEN WIDE . . . PLEASE?"

Your Toddler and Eating

Food is not only something we humans need to survive, but something most of us enjoy. (In fact, some of us enjoy it a bit too much!) So why do mealtimes become such a struggle for the parents of so many toddlers?

Eating is a process entirely controlled by the person doing it. Even if you manage to squeeze, poke, or slide a bit of unwanted food between your child's lips, can you make him chew it? Swallow it? If you've ever tried, you undoubtedly know the answer. Let's explore when and why the battles begin.

Eating begins when you offer an infant a bottle or the breast. Adults often argue over which is better. We encourage every mother to get information about the advantages and/or disadvantages of both methods and then to choose the one with which she feels more comfortable. Your confidence is the key. A confident mother is better able to foster a sense of trust in her baby. Either choice, bottle or breast, can supply the nurturing (and nutrition) an infant needs.

Babies are programmed by nature and their own reflexes to suck for nourishment and comfort, and they usually want to eat frequently. The ongoing debate about feeding in the first months of life centers on breast-feeding, bottles, and formula. Not too many years ago, many doctors discouraged breast-feeding because formula, the product of science, was believed to be better. Now we understand that babies benefit in many ways from their mother's milk. Whichever choice you make, however, adapting to your baby's needs can be challenging.

LISTENING TO YOUR OWN HEART

You may remember Jane's story about nursing from Chapter 1. Another mom tells this story—with a very different nursing outcome. She, too, had to listen to her heart:

> *Barbara had nursed her first child for three months but the experience had been difficult, not because of the nursing itself (which Barbara loved) but because of its inadvertent effect on her own health. Barbara had taken a daily medication for years, one that helped her to maintain her health, but she had discontinued it during the months of pregnancy and nursing. The result was that her health began to deteriorate, making it even more stressful to take care of her young baby.*
>
> *When Barbara became pregnant with her second child, she made the decision to nurse him only a week or two before switching him to formula. Barbara then was able to resume her medication sooner, ensuring her own health needs were met. She felt healthier and had more energy to care for her newborn son as well as her older child, who was now a toddler.*

As Barbara's story illustrates, each parent must weigh the needs of all family members, including his or her own. Barbara was able to go

Pulling Hair While Nursing

Q: I know my eight-month-old daughter is too young for much active discipline, but I'm concerned that her roughness will become a habit and I won't be able to alter it in the future. She's extremely active, energetic, and highly sensitive. She has been tugging and yanking my hair for a few weeks now, usually when nursing. I've tried taking hold of her arm and demonstrating how to be "gentle" (while reinforcing the idea with words) over and over, but I don't seem to be making any progress. Our poor cats are at their wits' end, as she yanks on them, too! Do you have any ideas or is it too early to worry about this sort of thing?

A: Young children don't understand "no" the way you think they should. Knowing this will help you understand why supervision and distraction (over and over) are about the only things that are effective at this age. If your cats are nearby, you need to supervise to protect them, and to prevent scratches and bites. When she pulls your hair while nursing, immediately (kindly and firmly) remove her from your breast and wait about a minute before nursing again. She may cry for that minute, but children at this age learn more from kind and firm action than from words. If she is hungry, she will learn that you will stop nursing when she pulls your hair. An even simpler solution might be to tie your hair back while you nurse.

several months without her medication, but others may not have this option. There are lots of possibilities, but no "right" choice that will work for all. Although we encourage breast-feeding for its many nutritional and emotional benefits, it is not mandatory. Many emotionally and physically healthy babies have been raised on formula and baby food. When you have knowledge about and have considered all of the choices with care, you will feel confident in whatever you decide.

INTRODUCING SOLID FOODS AND
SUPPLEMENTAL BOTTLES

Eventually, all children are ready to be weaned from the bottle or breast and to move on to other foods. Jane continues with her own experience:

> *Introducing solid foods to Lisa was easy. When she was seven months old, we occasionally offered her some mashed banana or mashed potato. I might blend other fruits or vegetables in a blender with some liquid. I say "might" because sometimes we did and sometimes we didn't. We didn't feel any pressure, because we knew she was getting all she needed from breast milk during the first year. We saved a fortune (at least, it seemed like a fortune to us) on formula and baby food. By the time she was one year old, she could eat many of the foods we cooked for our own meals if we mashed, chopped, or blended them for her to eat.*

Babies often thrive on nursing for the first year. If you plan to be away from your baby, however (and an occasional night away is good for your own mental and emotional health, as well as your partner's), it is easier if she is comfortable taking a bottle.

Lactation specialists often suggest expressing (that is, pumping) breast milk into a bottle and freezing it so it is available when a mother needs to be away from her baby. This can allow Dad the opportunity to take turns with night feedings or other much-needed "mommy breaks." Expressing breast milk also makes it possible for nursing to continue when a mother returns to work and must place her child with a caregiver. With time and practice, parents will learn to gauge the needs of their baby. Some babies do well on a combination of nursing, formula, and solids; some babies never need anything but breast milk. Babies, like adults, are unique individuals. Patience and a bit of trial and error will help you learn your baby's requirements.

WEANING

Somewhere between the tenth and twelfth months, many babies lose interest in nursing (or in taking a bottle). Some mothers ignore the signs and push the bottle or breast at the baby until they give in and start taking it again. Mothers do this for one of several reasons: (1) They are not aware that a loss of interest during this window of time may be a natural phenomenon that indicates a readiness for weaning; (2) They sometimes want their babies to continue nursing or to keep taking a bottle to prolong this special time of closeness; or (3) It is an easy way to calm them when they are fussy, or to help them to go to sleep.

Many mothers believe weaning can't be that easy, but it can be if they are willing to watch for the signs of readiness in their babies. Keeping babies on the bottle or breast after they are ready to stop may squelch the first blossoming of their sense of autonomy. It is important to realize that once the window of readiness to wean passes, nursing or taking a bottle may become a habit instead of a need, making weaning harder in the long run. (This distinction between habit and need can help adults determine timing in many areas of development, not just nursing.) Still, missing this opportunity for weaning isn't a traumatic, life-damaging experience.

It is important to note that some cultures deliberately extend nursing to promote values different than those of independence or autonomy. In other cultures, nursing provides the only reliable source of nutrition. Some people advocate nursing children for five or more years. This may feel right for some, but we also want to encourage parents who are miserable with extended nursing to do what is right for them.

Become educated and aware before you decide what works for you and your baby, then follow your heart. La Leche League and other groups encourage nursing for as long as it feels right for the mother and her child. If you decide you want to nurse for an extended period of time, La Leche League offers classes and support.

WEANING IS DIFFICULT

Weaning is part of the larger, lifelong process of letting go, and is vital to helping children develop their full potential. Weaning (and letting go) should not be confused with abandonment. Children need a lot of loving support during the weaning process. When parents let go with love at developmentally appropriate times, children are encouraged to trust, to learn confidence, and to develop a sense of healthy self-worth.

Betty's son, Ben, began preschool at age two and a half. He proudly carried his own lunch box to school with him. But his bravado turned to dismay when snack time came. He wanted his bottle, while everyone else was using a cup. Ben's teacher soon realized the cause of his tearful whimpering. That afternoon, she spent some time discussing the situation with Betty. They agreed to allow Ben to use a bottle when he sat at the snack table and when he was lying down for his nap, but the rest of the time the bottle would be kept in the refrigerator. Also, the bottle would contain only water. This plan was relayed to Ben. At the same time, Betty decided to limit the contents of Ben's bottles at home to water. She chose not to reduce their availability, allowing him to use the bottle with fewer restrictions at home.

Several times over the next week, Ben tested his teacher to see if she would give him his bottle at other times of the day. The teacher was sympathetic, offered to hold or hug Ben if he wished, and reassured him that he could have his bottle at snack or rest time but held firm to the plan she had made with Betty. By the second week, Ben stopped asking for his bottle throughout the day. Within the month, he had lost interest in the bottle at other times as well.

Ben continued to use his bottle at home. When Betty saw how successfully the plan at school had worked, she set similar

limits at home. After another week or two, she happily gath-
ered up the forgotten bottles and packed them off to a commu-
nity welfare program serving infants.

Betty and Ben's teacher used a gradual approach to weaning. Betty
could have just refused to bring in any bottles, but Ben, his teacher,
and his classmates might have had a much more stressful few weeks.
In the end, Ben would have given up his bottle either way. Being firm
does not mean that "cold turkey" is the only way to break lingering
habits.

AVOIDING FOOD FIGHTS

"If you don't eat your vegetables, you won't get any dessert!" "If you
don't eat your oatmeal for breakfast, you'll get it for lunch!" "You
are going to sit there and eat until you finish your dinner if it takes all
night!"

These phrases are familiar to many parents, who seem to believe
they can make a child eat, but we have seen just as many kids demonstrate that you *can't* make them eat. We've known children to throw
up, sneak food to the dog, glare at the oatmeal through breakfast,
lunch, and dinner, and sit there all night (as one of the authors did
with her lima beans)—or at least until the parent gives up in despair.

As you've seen, insisting on a particular course of action or behavior
is an invitation for most toddlers to engage in a power struggle. It may
also be helpful to realize that it isn't usually necessary to force exact
quantities of healthy foods down your child's throat. Unless he suffers from a metabolic disorder or requires a special medical diet, many
pediatricians believe a young child will tend to choose, over time, the
foods his body requires, although this may not happen in one meal
or even one day. A parent's task is to prepare and present healthy,
nutritious foods; it is a child's task to chew and swallow. Of course, it
doesn't hurt to include foods you know your child likes as well.

INVITING COOPERATION AT MEALTIMES

People who live anywhere food is scarce are unlikely to battle about menu choices or complain about picky eaters. A family with six mouths to feed does not have time or energy to worry about what color cup  Angie's milk is served in, or whether little Yelena ate enough mashed carrots. The bigger worry is if there is enough food to go around. When children don't get any mileage out of being picky or resistant, they eat what is available or go hungry. (And, we suspect, "hungry" is relative: few children whose parents are reading this book are likely to starve anytime soon.)

For many of us, the challenge is not too little food but too much. Snacks abound, portion sizes are far larger than necessary for health, and sugar and fat content reach unhealthy levels. It is easy to lose sight of the simplicity of eating. Some parents have been so thoroughly hooked by their demanding children that they prepare two or three different meals for dinner.

Have children really gotten pickier? No; children do what "works." If refusing to eat what Dad puts on the table gets them the meal of their choice (and the feeling of power or sustained attention that goes along with it), they'll continue to refuse family meals, harried parents will continue to prepare alternatives, and no one will enjoy mealtimes. There are, however, any number of ways to invite cooperation and harmony at the table. As with so many other issues in early childhood, parents can decide what they will do, give up the notion of control, remain kind and firm—and teach children to be responsible, cooperative, and capable.

"Sounds too good to be true," you may be thinking, "but he won't get enough nutrients." There is no one magic answer to mealtime hassles. Children (like adults) sometimes just aren't hungry. Their food preferences change over time (and may not match yours), and they may not always want to eat on your schedule. Still, some of the following suggestions and ideas may help you keep food from becoming a fight in your family.

- **Don't force-feed.** Insisting that children eat particular foods in particular quantities at particular times will only create power struggles—and most parents of toddlers find they have lots of those already! If your baby spits food at you, it may be a clue that she's had enough. Don't insist on feeding more; get a sponge and let her help mop up the mess.

- **Presentation counts, even for little ones.** Good nutrition is important, but distasteful foods can sometimes be offered in tasty ways. Rather than forcing your child to stare at the soft-boiled egg congealing on his plate, serve eggs by including them in a slice of French toast or a cheese-filled omelet. Include extra fruits and vegetables by pureeing and adding them to milk or yogurt, or blend and strain soups so that they can be sipped from cups. Serve healthy meals. Include a variety of new foods as well as familiar ones you know your toddler likes, and then relax with the reassurance that even if he doesn't eat everything, whatever he does eat will be nourishing. (Tip: One easy way to ensure you are offering a balanced variety is to serve foods that are different in color, such as slices of red-skinned apples, bright green peas, and sunny-orange sweet potatoes and carrot sticks.)

- **Learn your child's needs and preferences.** Your little one may have no trouble eating on a regular schedule, but some children do better eating small amounts of food throughout the day. You and your toddler may feel better about her eating if you allow her to do what feels natural. If your child is a snacker, make healthy snacks available. One family set aside a kitchen drawer for their little snacker. Whenever Patrick felt hungry, he could go to "Patrick's drawer" and eat anything he found there. Patrick's mother kept the drawer stocked with crackers, pretzels, raisins

225

or other dried fruits, and small bags of granola. Patrick loved to see what turned up each day in his drawer, and his mother enjoyed not arguing about meals. As long as your child is gaining the appropriate amount of weight and growing (well-child checkups are a must), he is probably doing just fine.

- **Pay attention to the labels on foods.** There are a surprising number of hidden sugars and fats in the prepared foods young children love (breakfast cereals are a prime example), and too much sugar can wreak havoc with a child's appetite for nutritious food. Balance is the key. Your child needs a certain amount of fat to grow and be healthy, so the low-fat, low-sodium diet you may be following yourself is not a good idea for her; nor is it necessary to always substitute carrot sticks for holiday candies and treats. Don't be afraid to serve the same favorites over and over again; children aren't usually as fond of variety as their parents are. But do continue to offer new foods as well. In fact, one way to get a suspicious eater to try new foods is to serve the "strange" item often. The food becomes familiar and children may be more willing to sample it. Your pediatrician can answer your questions about specific foods, and help you feel confident that your child is healthy and growing.

- **Use mealtimes to invite contribution.** While toddlers may resist force, they usually enjoy being invited to help in the kitchen. Even young children can place napkins on the table, rinse lettuce 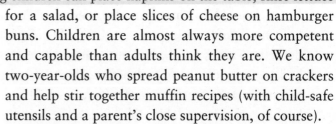 for a salad, or place slices of cheese on hamburger buns. Children are almost always more competent and capable than adults think they are. We know two-year-olds who spread peanut butter on crackers and help stir together muffin recipes (with child-safe utensils and a parent's close supervision, of course).

Teach children how to make simple sandwiches or spread beans and cheese on a tortilla. Include them in the planning and preparation of meals. If an older toddler doesn't want to eat what is on the table or complains about a meal, simply ask, "What can you do about that?" Then, without making a fuss, sighing, or rolling your eyes, let him choose to prepare the crackers, sandwich, or tortilla he has learned how to make.

Inviting your child to help plan meals, choose ingredients at the grocery store ("Can you find the yellow bananas we need for your pudding?"), dish up servings, and help in the kitchen will not only take some of the struggle out of eating but will help you create a more resourceful, confident child.

- **Be patient.** Most children change their eating habits over time, and the toddler who turns up his nose at broccoli today may well love it next month. This miracle usually happens a great deal sooner if parents aren't shouting, lecturing, and pushing.* Be patient; offer new foods occasionally, but don't insist. Enjoy mealtimes as an opportunity to gather your family together and share one another's company. In other words, relax a bit. This, too, shall pass!

SPECIAL DIETS

Over the years, food-related allergies have increased worldwide. Some attribute this to the ways in which food and farming methods have been modified, others to environmental changes. Whatever the cause, helping a child maintain a restricted diet without feeling restricted is challenging. The cooperative focus of Positive Discipline is especially helpful for challenges with eating. Allowing a child to feel empowered and to participate in meeting his own needs is helpful, and can even enhance his developing sense of capability.

---

* *Bread and Jam for Frances,* by Russell Hoban (New York: HarperColllins, 1993), is a fun book to read with your child. Use it to begin conversations about food, as well as to remind yourself to avoid turning mealtime into fight time.

A child who cannot eat gluten can still go to a birthday party with a gluten-free cupcake, frosted in the yellow frosting she chose and helped to stir. When the party cake is cut, she has her own satisfying treat. Carrying a supply of cut-up veggies or suitable crackers for a child unable to eat nuts or soy products reduces the number of times she must be told that she can't have the treats others are having. Explaining to her that her tummy needs special foods to help her grow will help gain her cooperation and make the process easier. Instead of saying, "No, you can't have those cookies," you can say, "Here is your special snack." Over time, this kind of advance planning will come to feel automatic for both of you. Supplying an egg-free pumpkin pie at the family's Thanksgiving meal makes it possible for a child to eat his food alongside others, without feeling left out or deprived.

THE MEDIA AND THE BATTLE AGAINST UNHEALTHY FOODS

One of the real challenges parents face is that of advertising targeted toward children, in particular the promotion of foods that are either unhealthy or low in nutritional value. The Institute of Medicine, a well-regarded scientific advisory body, has linked television advertising to obesity in children under the age of twelve.[*] The simplest way for parents to prevent unhealthy media influence is to shield a child from such advertising by simply turning off the television.

You can also resist buying unhealthy foods, especially when they are associated with a cartoon or media character. Nutrition, even for a "picky" eater, will be of less concern if all of the foods available to him are nutritious and food doesn't become a way to acquire toys or satisfy a playtime urge. Fast-food chains advertise to children for a reason: they want to create a "need" for the high-fat, high-salt, and high-sugar products they sell. However, such foods are not *needs,* and you should

[*] www.iom.edu/Reports/2011/Early-Childhood-Obesity-Prevention-Policies/Recommendations.aspx.

consider the long-term consequences carefully before beginning a habit you may later regret.

Here are some additional suggestions for ways to protect your child and encourage the development of healthy eating habits. First, model healthy eating yourself. It is hard to convince your child that she shouldn't eat high-fat chips or sugar-laden candy when she sees you polishing off a bag of nacho cheese crisps or eating chocolate bars. She will want to eat what you do, especially if it's sweet or salty.

You can also contact manufacturers by sending letters and e-mail when you disapprove of inappropriate foods being marketed to young children or identified with popular entertainment figures. Complain to the manager of the restaurant that offers only high-fat choices such as french fries or macaroni and cheese on the "children's menu," with no healthy alternatives available. Businesses want to sell their products and when customers question those products, they listen.

Positive Discipline includes encouraging the self-discipline you want your children to develop, and food and eating habits play a large role in this. Sadly, today's children may have shorter life spans than their parents, at least in part because of their eating habits. Prevention of poor eating habits and future obesity are important goals with long-term consequences for your child's health, ones that you can promote through your actions, awareness, and thoughtful consumer choices. *Don't forget to encourage healthy exercise, even for toddlers. Today's children are far more sedentary than earlier generations, which does not improve their health—or their appetite.*

Learning that you "can't make 'em do it" takes most parents until their children are well into adolescence—and sometimes even beyond. Eventually, children will have to manage their own eating habits. They will need to know what constitutes a healthy diet, how much to eat and at what time, and when to stop. Parents can allow their children to explore these concepts right from the beginning by inviting them to participate in the process of meal planning, shopping, and cooking, acting as guides and teachers rather than enforcers. Mistakes, as we have said so often, are opportunities to learn—for parents and for children. Life with energetic young children will hold lots of challenges; mealtimes don't have to be among them.

MORE THAN FOOD

Meals are much more than food. They provide a time and place for families to connect, and can introduce the important cultural or family traditions you hope to pass along to your children. One of the best ways to prevent behavior problems, especially as children grow older, is by having regular family meals where there is time to talk together, to listen, and to connect with those you love. Because of these vital larger roles, making mealtimes pleasant is important. Your special rituals and traditions—holding hands before eating, offering a prayer, or sharing something you are grateful for—will enrich your time together.

When you make mealtime an opportunity to come together, not just to share food but to share your lives as a family, you will feed both bodies and spirits.

QUESTIONS TO PONDER

1. Keep a chart of what your toddler eats over the course of a day or several days. What do you notice? Are you surprised at how balanced his diet really is? Is he getting a good part of his daily nutrition between meals, through healthy snacks?
2. Identify which nutrients seem to be missing from your list. If snacks are a major source of nutrition, make sure snacks are as nutritious as possible.
3. What snack foods are not providing important nutrients? What might replace them? Add healthy choices and reduce the unhealthy

options. Make this transition gradual. (Tip: Offer cut-up carrots or unsweetened dried fruit as snacks, instead of sugary gummy bears or high-fat chips.) Decide on two or three ways to incorporate missing nutrients into your child's diet without fighting over specific foods. (Tip: To add vegetables, consider adding mashed carrots or sweet potato to spaghetti sauce, or stirring them into a macaroni and cheese dish.)

4. Make a list of your ideas and try a different one each week. Keep the list in the kitchen for quick and easy reference.

5. Relax. Feel confident that what your child is eating will provide appropriate and adequate nourishment, no matter when she eats it. Focus on making mealtimes opportunities for connection and enjoyment.

15

TOILETING

"It's My Job, Not Yours"

The struggles parents encounter with sleeping and eating pale in significance when we move to a discussion of toileting. No other topic in the world of raising young children arouses such strong emotions, it seems, as potty training.

The issue of toilet training has been blown out of proportion in our society. It can be the origin of feelings of guilt and shame, power struggles, and competition between parents. But here's the truth: *Even if parents didn't worry about it at all, children would still become toilet trained in due time just because they would eventually want to do what everyone else does.* It is adults who create the power struggles that sometimes make it more important for children to "win" than to "cooperate" (which may feel like losing to them).

Paula took a great deal of pride in the fact that her first child was using the toilet at the age of eighteen months. She was so pleased, in fact, that she thought about writing a book about toilet training to help other, less fortunate families. Before she could get around to it, however, her second child was born. Much to Paula's surprise, this child wanted nothing to do with her prizewinning toilet training techniques. In fact, despite being placed on the potty for long periods of time, this child was almost three years old before the "training" worked.

So much for genius. The reality is that **children will use the toilet when they are ready to do so.** You can cheer, beg, and threaten, but hang on to your diapers. Each child has his or her own unique schedule—and absolute control. What can parents do to set the stage for this important developmental milestone?

READINESS

Perhaps the real question is *who* is ready for toilet training. Is it you? Are you ready to be done with diapers? Are you feeling pressure from the neighbors who claim their eighteen-month-old is already potty trained? And who is actually training whom?

If you could observe closely in most homes where parents claim their toddlers are trained, you might notice that it is the parents who are trained. They watch the clock and take their little ones to the potty chair—usually offering candy bribes and stars on charts for a tinkle or poop in the potty. They monitor how much their children can drink—especially before bedtime. Many wake their toddlers up in the middle of the night and prop them, half asleep, in front of the toilet and turn on the sink faucet in hopes that the sound of running water will coax some fluid from their sleepy ones.

So, when *are* toddlers ready for toilet training? **There is no precise age at which children are ready to use the potty. Few children master control before eighteen months, while most do so by age four.** Complete nighttime success can take slightly longer and still be within the typical developmental range. When children are truly ready, the process often takes only a few days or weeks. Physical readiness, emotional readiness, and environmental opportunities set children up for success.

PHYSICAL READINESS

Children give us a number of clues when they are physically ready to begin toilet training. Observe your child's behavior and ask yourself the following questions: Do long periods elapse between your child's diaper changes? Is her diaper dry after naptime? Does she stop what she is doing and get a look of concentration on her face when she wets herself? Does she demonstrate discomfort when her diaper is wet?

These things indicate increasing bladder capacity and awareness, and mean that your child is becoming more able to connect her physical sensations with the need to use the toilet. As children acquire language and become more self-aware, they often show increased interest in their own bodies—especially the "private parts" responsible for elimination. You can talk comfortably with them while changing diapers or dressing about what these parts do, and how eventually they will use the toilet rather than diapers.

Children with regular bowel movements experience early success when their parents or caregivers tune in to those rhythms. As we have mentioned, however, adults are often more "trained" than the child. Many parents know their child's patterns or facial clues and train themselves to put the child on the potty in time to catch the droppings in the toilet. This is one approach that helps a child become aware of her behavior and know what to do in response. After all, nothing succeeds like success.

Remember that every child is different. In one family, Mom and Dad became very familiar with the different physical capacities of their three children. When driving in the car, Mom and Dad knew they had about twenty minutes to find a place to stop when Kenny said he needed to use the bathroom. If Lisa needed the bathroom, they had about ten minutes. If Brad said he needed to "go," they immediately pulled off the road and hoped a bush was nearby.

EMOTIONAL READINESS

Q: I have a son who needs to be potty trained. He turned three years old two months ago. He does not like to use the potty. He does not show me signs when he has to go, but he will tell me when to change him. Please, I need some advice!

A: It does not take great intuition to recognize your desperation. It is hard to keep changing diapers as children grow older. Your son's reasons for not using the potty are probably magnified by your own discouragement. Take heart. He will succeed, but it may take more patience than you think you have. (Does it help to know that he probably won't still be wearing diapers when he goes to college?)

Here are some ideas to keep in mind:

- Try to de-emphasize the whole issue. When parents *in*sist on a certain behavior, children (who are hard at work developing a sense of autonomy) may *re*sist. Power struggles usually ensue. Remaining calm and kind and refusing to argue over using the toilet will ease the process for everyone concerned.

- Sometimes a discussion of safety regarding the flushing toilet eases a child's mind. Help him see that he is too big to fall through the toilet seat; allow him to flush the toilet to reassure himself that he is in control of this powerful, gulping monster; and reassure him that nothing scary will happen to him. Of course, using a small potty chair avoids this problem altogether for a while.

- Don't become so focused on the bathroom that you lose your ability to enjoy the other parts of your lives together. Express your confidence in him; tell him that you know he will manage using the potty successfully one day. He, too, needs encouragement.

- There are many ways to set the stage emotionally for successful potty training. Toddlers often dislike having to lie still while being changed. Use this time to talk to your child, engaging her interest and thereby distracting her attention. Consider hanging a toy above the changing area, using a strip of elastic. Your child can swat, reach for, and handle the toy while she is being changed. This sort of distraction creates a more cooperative atmosphere, avoiding emotional resistance later on when potty training begins. Hang a musical mobile above the area or tape a fun picture on the ceiling. Changing these items every so often sustains children's interest. Another possibility is to change diapers while your child stands up. We have watched mothers do this with amazing skill and swiftness—even for poopy diapers.

- As your child matures, invite him to help with the job by handing you supplies, holding the clean diaper in readiness, or laying out the changing mat. This increases opportunities to develop autonomy and sends the message that you believe your child is competent and capable. When he needs to be changed, show him ways he can help out. He can wash or wipe himself off, help empty the stool into the toilet bowl, and practice washing his own hands afterward. Encouraging his participation also invites cooperation, an important ingredient for success.

- Lighten up and make toilet training fun. One parent emptied the toilet bowl and painted a target in the bowl. His son could hardly wait to try to hit the bull's-eye.

- Avoid rewards and praise like stars on a chart or candy treats. ***Rewards can become more important to your child than learning socially appropriate behavior, and may give him unexpected ways to manipulate you.*** Allow your child to feel capable within himself instead of getting hooked on outside validation.

Kevin had always suspected that offering candy as a reward for cooperation might backfire one day, but he was still surprised at how quickly his two-and-a-half-year-old son Braden learned to work the system. One night at dinner, Braden stubbornly refused to eat any of his dinner, turning up his nose at the meat loaf and peas Kevin had placed before him. "Fine," Kevin said, annoyance clear in his voice. "No treat for you for eating your dinner."

Braden gave this announcement careful thought, then said, "Potty, Daddy?"

"Potty" was the magic word in this household, and Kevin was quick to respond. "Do you have to go, Braden?" he asked.

"Yes, potty," Braden said with a nod of his head, and scampered off to his potty chair, where he promptly produced a result. Without hesitation—and with a wicked gleam of victory in his eye—Braden looked up at his father and held out his small hand. "Braden pooped. Treat, Daddy." Kevin realized he had been expertly maneuvered into supplying candy after all, and resolved to get rid of the treats the very next day.

Here is another suggestion on toilet training from *Positive Discipline A–Z*:

If your child is still not toilet trained by the time she is three years old, be sure to get a doctor's evaluation to see if there is a physical problem. If there is not a physical problem, you may be involved in a power struggle. Guess who will win! One thing you can't control is a child's elimination functions. It takes two to engage in a power struggle. Stop. Allow your child to experience the consequences of his choice with dignity and respect. Teach your child to change his own clothes during a calm time. When the pants get wet or soiled, kindly and firmly take your child to his bedroom to find new clothes. Then lead him to the bathroom and ask if he would like to change alone or with you there to keep him company.

Action Please

Toilet training usually coincides with another toddler milestone: the ability to say no. What will most toddlers say when asked, "Do you need to use the potty?" "No" is a pretty safe guess. A better plan might be to pay attention to your child's facial expression and body language, or to set a reasonable schedule and say, "It's time to go potty," then act. Take his hand and walk to the bathroom, then help him to sit on the toilet or potty seat. Consider letting him sit on his potty while you sit on the big one nearby. This might be too much togetherness, but if you are comfortable with it, your little one will probably love the chance to be "just like Mommy or Daddy."

(Do not do it for him.) It is unlikely that he will refuse if you are kind and firm, and if you have truly dropped the power struggle. If it still feels like a power struggle, offer help by handing him the washcloth or wipes, holding the diaper pail lid open for him, or providing a bag for him to place his soiled clothes in. Be empathetic; help him in appropriate ways (without doing it for him).

ENVIRONMENTAL OPPORTUNITIES

Some of today's diapers make it difficult for children to respond to their own natural clues. Disposable diapers do such a good job of absorbing moisture that some children do not notice when they are wet, or do not feel enough discomfort to react. Give children opportunities to notice what happens when they "go." You can also use training diapers that provide less complete absorption, or cloth training pants—with lots of clothing changes nearby.

Allowing a child to go diaperless in the backyard on a warm day often provides an eye-opening experience. You can almost read her

mind: "Wow! Look what I can do." The awareness of what happens physically often leads to mastery. Some parents have found it helpful to wait until the summer after their child reaches two-and-a-half years old, and then spend some time in the backyard with a naked child and a potty chair, making it a game to pee and poop in the potty. One family found that their son became potty trained during the week of their family's camping vacation. Urinating in the woods with his older brother beat diapers any day!

Make the process as easy as possible. Switching to training pants or pull-ups eases the transition from diapers. Small potty seats or conversion rings for adult toilets with a small stool for climbing are helpful modifications. Be sure your child is wearing clothing that helps rather than hinders; elastic waistbands and loose articles are easier for small fingers to manage than snaps, buttons, and bows. The easier the on-and-off process, the more successful your little one will be.

WHEN ACCIDENTS HAPPEN

As with most skills, there will be accidents or mistakes during the process of mastering bladder and bowel control. Some children may have accidents for up to six months after toilet training, or when they are feeling stressed by changes in the family or home. **Treating toilet accidents calmly and respectfully makes it less likely that power struggles, resistance, and lack of cooperation will result.** Don't humiliate or shame your child when he has an accident; don't put him back in diapers. Scolding, lecturing, or punishing won't help, and may damage the sense of trust and caring between you and your little one.

Instead, be empathetic. After all, accidents are just that: *accidents.*

Help your child clean up. Say, "It's okay. You can keep trying. I know you'll get it soon." You can also be sure your child knows where the bathroom is when you travel, and be sure to take along clean clothes. With time and patience the skill will be mastered.

Again, a parent's patient confidence makes a difference. Take young Andrew, for instance:

> By the age of three or so, Andrew was ready to give up his diapers. Because he'd decided it was time, his mom and dad found the process delightfully easy. In just one day and two nights, Andrew was completely trained and accident-free.
>
> Imagine, then, how surprised Andrew's mom and dad were when he demanded his diapers back after just one week. In checking out their son's request, his parents learned that Andrew had observed an interesting fact. Going to the bathroom, undoing his clothes, sitting down, cleaning up, and dressing again took more time away from important play than he was willing to spend. Andrew had discovered that diapers were simply easier, and he wanted to go back to them. When Andrew found that his parents weren't willing to provide any more diapers, he sighed—and remained in his "big boy pants," entering the grown-up world of bladder-regulated inconvenience.

If your little one wants to change his mind after the training process has been completed and celebrated, don't despair. Remain kind and firm, and the situation will undoubtedly resolve itself. And remember, each child eventually masters toilet training—on his own timetable.

QUESTIONS TO PONDER

1. Toileting can cause stress and feelings of inadequacy—for you and your child. Take a moment to consider: How sensitive are you to what other adults say about your child's progress in toileting? Why is it important to you that she be out of diapers?

2. Consider the elements of physical and emotional readiness discussed in this chapter. Name two things that will help you know when your child is truly ready for toilet training. Does your child meet these criteria? If not, is it worth beginning the process now?

3. How can you encourage your child's sense of healthy autonomy during the process of toilet training? What can you do to set the stage for success?

16

GETTING ALONG IN THE GREAT BIG WORLD

Development of Sharing and Other Social Skills

Did you know that a crying baby is practicing social skills? In the first months of a baby's life, crying brings adults, who provide food, comfort, and entertainment. Before long he's smiling, and by five to eight months of age he is giggling, cooing, and otherwise enchanting his grown-up companions.

Understanding child development can help adults comprehend how primitive a child's social interactions will be for a while. When adults understand that most social skills don't develop naturally but must be taught, they may be less dismayed when children hit, bite, push, or fight as they discover how to get along with others.

Social skills like sharing and playing develop through training, practice, and mistakes—especially mistakes. The road is not smooth; emotional bumps and scrapes, with an occasional real bite and scratch, mark the way.

SOCIAL SKILLS IN THE FIRST THREE YEARS

Time passes and a child grows. Eventually he will need social skills: to know how to get along with others, to communicate, and to choose behaviors that help his progress in life. In fact, most researchers now understand that social and emotional learning deeply influences all other aspects of a child's early development, as well as his academic progress later on. When a child is learning to play and share, he is actually hard at work!

PARALLEL PLAY

Parents usually have questions about this stage of life—lots of them. Many parents find their toddler's behavior frustrating, irritating, and downright defeating at times. Let's look at how children's interactions develop.

When toddlers play together, most of their play is "parallel play." They play near other children rather than with them. Jeffrey, for instance, is fourteen months old. At the childcare center, the caregivers feed him, carry him, comfort him, and change him. There are other children present, but they are more like mysterious new toys. Jeffrey has begun to be curious about them and to explore them; he knows they cry when he pokes them, and when he tried to put one child's hair in his mouth it created quite a commotion. For now, Jeffrey is content to do his own thing while other children do theirs—at least most of the time.

As Jeffrey grows, he will begin to interact directly with the children around him, mimicking their play, laughing when they laugh, learning their names, and beginning the process of making friends. Play is the laboratory in which young children experiment with connection, relationship, and social skills. Your child's ability to connect with others begins with her connection with *you*. Taking time to play with your child is one of the best ways to create a solid foundation for social and life skills.

SHARING VERSUS "MINE"

Sharing is a big issue in the world of young children. Parents often expect children to take turns, to be happy with equal portions, or to give up playing with a favorite toy. But children under the age of two are egocentric; that is, they are the center of their own world, and everything else exists only as it relates to them. This is not selfishness—it's natural human development.

> *Mary was the first to raise her hand during the question-and-answer session at her parenting class. "My little girl, Jetta, is eighteen months old. I'm trying to teach her that everything does not belong to her," Mary said with an exasperated sigh. "She grabs my purse and says, 'Mine purse.' I try to reason with her and tell her, 'No, this is Mommy's purse,' but she just hangs on, repeating, 'Mine purse.' She does the same thing with the cereal box, the telephone, and even the dog."*

Guess what? As Mary will learn from her parenting class facilitator, in Jetta's world everything *is* "mine." Jetta looks out at the world from its hub: herself. If you believe that the world begins and ends with you (and toddlers believe exactly that), it follows that everything in the world belongs to you. No amount of logic will change Jetta's perspective, because it is simply the way she sees her place on the planet right now.

During the "mine" stage of development, do not waste energy on debates. Try saying, "You like Mommy's purse. Want to help me carry it?" Without arguing with her and inviting a power struggle, you are giving her accurate information, offering her a way to make her own small contribution to help you, and making space for her view of the world. Until her development moves forward, this makes far more sense than holding endless arguments over ownership. If you try to correct her thinking, you will almost certainly create a power struggle, perhaps setting a pattern for the future. Cooperation promises a much healthier future for both of you.

A survey conducted by the Zero to Three National Center for Infants, Toddlers, and Families asked, "Should a fifteen-month-old be expected to share her toys with other children, or is this too young of an age to expect a child to share?"

They found that 51 percent of parents of children ages birth to three years believe a fifteen-month-old should be expected to share. However, research shows that developmentally, fifteen months is too young to expect a toddler to share. Parents may mistakenly believe that if a child acts "selfish" now, he will be a selfish adult.

Zero to Three offers some sound advice: ***Children this age need guidance and teaching rather than "discipline" if they are having trouble sharing.*** Providing solutions such as finding another toy they can offer a friend, using a timer to cue taking turns, giving them something else to do while they wait their turn, or suggesting (and demonstrating) ways they can play with the toy together may be helpful. After lots of practice (and with your help), by the time they are two to two-and-a-half they can begin to do it on their own (but don't expect consistency!).

SHARING IN THE REAL WORLD OF TODDLERS

When twenty-month-old Susie grabs another child's toy, an adult can step in, remove the toy gently from Susie, return it to the other child, and carry Susie away to find some other interesting object to play with, saying, "Tommy is playing with that toy right now" or "Let's find a toy that Susie enjoys."

When Susie is two and a half, things change a bit. She no longer merely plays next to her companions but enjoys running around the

Successful Strategies for Teaching Toddlers to Share

Possessiveness and ownership are normal steps before the ability to share truly begins around the age of three or four. Meanwhile, teach the process of sharing while your child's ability to do so is still under developmental construction.

- **Demonstrate sharing.** Give your child bites or half of a special treat. Offer to let him hold something that is yours. Play trading games with him. "What do you want to share with me while I share this with you?" Kindly and firmly remove an item that belongs to someone else or that she can't have, without lecturing or shaming.
- **Create opportunities to share.** Hand your child two crayons and ask him to pick one for his playmate to use. Thank him for sharing.
- **Avoid judgment and show compassion.** Support your child's need to possess. (Don't you have some possessions you don't want to share?) Help older children find another toy to play with, or provide more than one of the same toy. When a child is upset, offer whatever comfort you can, but don't try to shield him from experiencing disappointment—after all, disappointment and frustration are a part of life that your child needs to learn to cope with. You might say, "It is hard to share. You really wanted that." Empathy eases the pain and paves the way to later acceptance of sharing.

playground *with* them. When Susie grabs a toy now, adults can respond differently from the way they did earlier. Susie is ready to learn and practice the social skill of sharing. A more appropriate response now is to take the toy and explore with her ways of learning to share with another child.

Susie and Tommy are playing in the block area when Susie grabs the toy car that Tommy has just picked up. Both children begin to yell, "Mine! Give it to me!" Naturally, the uproar

draws the attention of Mrs. McGee, the children's teacher. She walks over and gently takes the car.

"Susie," she asks, "do you want to play with this car?" "I want it," Susie agrees. Mrs. McGee turns to Tommy. "Are you playing with the car, Tommy?" Tommy's lower lip juts out a bit as he says, "Mine."

Mrs. McGee places the car in Tommy's hands and turns to Susie. "Susie, what do you think you could say to Tommy if you want to play with the car?" "I want to play with it?" Susie offers (with only a little sulk in her voice). Mrs. McGee agrees that's one way to ask. She suggests that Susie could also try saying, "May I play with the car?"

Tommy has been watching this exchange with interest. When his teacher asks him what he might say to Susie when she asks for the car, he responds right away. "Here, you can have it," he replies, offering the car to Susie. Mrs. McGee smiles. "It's nice of you to share, Tommy. What might you say if you weren't finished with the car?"

This is a new thought for Tommy. The teacher has made it clear that just asking may not be enough. She is helping Tommy learn that he has some options and can assert his own needs, but Tommy is momentarily baffled.

Mrs. McGee turns to Susie. "Can you think of something Tommy can say, Susie?" Susie has just the answer. "He could say, 'In a minute.'" Mrs. McGee nods. "That's a good idea. Perhaps he could say that he will give it to you in five minutes. Would that work, Tommy?" Tommy nods, and Mrs. McGee encourages him to practice saying, "I'm not done yet" to Susie.

Throughout this conversation, both children were invited to explore the possibilities available to them. Sharing is a skill that must be taught and practiced (even by adults). How will a child know what to do if no demonstrations are given? This is also a period of intense language development. Providing the necessary words and ways to use them is part of the training process. Teaching and encouraging young children to "use their words" (if they know which words to use, of course) is a wonderful way to nurture social skills. But it is important to remember that training is a process that must be repeated over and over as the developmental clock keeps ticking. It is the adults' job to guide continuously—not to expect that children will learn and remember after one experience, or even a hundred.

PUPPET PRETEND

Playing "Let's Pretend" with dolls or puppets is another way sharing can be modeled and practiced. An adult can act out a conflict between two children, showing what happened as well as other, more appropriate responses. Then children can practice, holding the puppets and exploring both the inappropriate and appropriate behavior. This invites children to recognize inappropriate behavior in others and, eventually, to notice and take responsibility for their own. Puppets, dolls, and similar pretend play provide an important buffer. If Johnny says, "No—it's mine!" little Alice believes him and starts to cry. But when the puppet says it, neither child feels threatened or gets upset.

SHARING AND CULTURAL VALUES

Attitudes toward many social skills vary by culture. The idea of personal property is not seen in the same way by all people. Many Asian cultures, for example, believe that the needs of the group are more important than those of any one individual. In New Zealand, a Maori child is deliberately given the last serving of a special treat and told to share it, because placing the needs of the community first is an ideal that her culture values. Your values (and your own social behavior) will influence the social skills your child masters. Ultimately, a child's sense of belonging will to some degree be tied to feeling connected to the values of her culture.

HITTING AND AGGRESSION

Toddlers are short on both language and social skills, and when they play together they can easily become frustrated. When they lack the ability to express their feelings in words, hitting and other types of aggression sometimes result. When you set one toddler down to "play" with another, neither is particularly sure of what the other is all about. Watch them eyeing each other and you can guess what they might be thinking. "What is this creature? Does it break? Can I taste it? What

happens if I poke my finger in its eye?" Walking up and hitting another child is sometimes just a primitive form of saying hello.

Still, children under the age of two need to learn that pulling hair, poking eyes, and hitting are actions that hurt people and cannot be allowed. Firmness, coupled with removing the child temporarily and redirecting his attention to something else, works best. You can say, "It is not okay to hit Rebecca or pull her hair. Let's go find another toy to play with. When you are ready to be kind, you and Rebecca may play together." It does not help to scold or punish. How might we feel if someone scolded and punished us when we practiced a foreign language for a month but failed to speak it fluently? Social skills are a language that must be practiced, integrated, and learned at deeper levels when children are developmentally ready.

LITTLE "MUNCH"KINS—WHAT TO DO ABOUT BITING

One type of toddler aggression—biting—really sets off alarms for parents and caregivers. Most biting incidents happen from about fourteen months to three years of age, which coincides with the development of spoken language. Biting often indicates frustration or anger, especially when a child isn't able to make herself understood with words.

Developmentally, children master control of their hands before speech. A baby as young as eight months can learn simple signs to ask for food, to say she wants more of something, or to indicate that she is thirsty as opposed to hungry. Proponents of teaching children to communicate their needs and thoughts through signing contend that a child who can sign is less likely to resort to aggressive behavior. This simplified version of signing can be available to a young child when words are not, and is an option that you may want to consider.*

Both teething and the need to "chew" can also play developmental roles in biting. Providing carrot sticks or apple slices to crunch, raisins to chew, and orange wedges or frozen juice bars to suck on will offer stimulation and may satisfy the urge to bite in more appropriate ways. Biting may even be the result of a vivid imagination. Twenty-month-old Teddy spent two weeks biting the ankle of anyone who wandered by, before an observant adult realized he was imitating the nipping actions of his aunt's new puppy.

The most consistent explanation for biting is its connection to impulse control. Young children lack effective impulse control (remember, the prefrontal cortex of toddlers is still "under construction"), making their response to frustration immediate—and usually beyond their conscious control. Impulse control develops gradually; by about the age of three, the combination of language development and a maturing nervous system will combine to reduce or eliminate most early biting. In the meantime, regardless of the reasons it happens, biting is very disturbing (not to mention painful) for the biter, the bitee (the person who was bitten), and all adults involved. We're not sure which is worse: to be the parents of the biter or the bitee. The parent of the bitee feels angry and protective. The parent of the biter feels embarrassed and protective. Both will feel a little better if they understand child development.

---

* For more information, see *Sign with Your Baby* by Joseph Garcia (Mukilteo, WA: Northlight Communications, 2002), or visit www.sign2me.com.

Biting that occurs because a child lacks the words to express feelings and frustrations will diminish as he learns the verbal skills to express himself in more appropriate ways. And no, biting the child back, washing out his mouth with soap, or placing Tabasco sauce on his tongue doesn't help; such responses are far more likely to escalate conflict than resolve it, and may be considered abusive.

There are no magic remedies for biting. The most helpful responses begin with one essential element: supervision. Children who bite must be watched carefully. Look for patterns. Does your child bite at a certain time of day, perhaps when she is hungry or tired or when too much is going on around her? If you spot a pattern, use your knowledge to be especially watchful during those times.

Despite the most diligent supervision, biting often continues. Once biting occurs, there are three essential steps: preventing further injury, involving both children in healing, and showing compassion to both children.

1. **Prevent further injury.** Act at once. Separate the children and check the seriousness of the injury. Your actions should be firm and decisive, but kind. Try to remain calm, not letting your own frustration or feelings of anger fuel your response. Realize that time usually solves the problem, and know that you are doing all you can to deal with it. Keep words to a minimum, such as a calm "No biting."

2. **Involve both children in healing: Tend the wound and hurt feelings.** Biting is particularly worrisome to parents because of the possibility of blood-borne disease. Adults and children tending the wound should wear plastic gloves, which provide protection and teach everyone concerned to avoid contact with blood. The child most at risk is the biter, who may have ingested blood, rather than the child who was bitten (this information—along with generous helpings of compassion and calm—may be useful when dealing with the bitten child's distraught family). In addi-

tion to the physical wound, there are also feelings that have been wounded. Healing feelings requires compassion.

3. **Show compassion for both children.** Both children, the child who did the biting and the bitee, may feel hurt, distressed, and discouraged; both need to be shown compassion. Even the biter needs to know that you still care about him. Emotions run high after a biting incident, and the child who bites often finds himself villainized. Teachers march him to time-out and tell him to stay there all morning. Parents yell, send him to his room, and shun him. They frequently demand that preschools expel children who bite. (Please, remember to maintain confidentiality for both children when biting occurs in a caregiving setting.)

It may be difficult in all the tumult to remember that this tiny person probably bit out of frustration and immaturity, not evil intent. He cannot manage his impulses and probably can barely speak. What he really might need is a hug, as well as continued supervision. The child who was bitten suffers hurt feelings as well as hurt skin. Both need tender care.

A bite happens in a nanosecond. Even a child holding his mother's hand might manage to chomp down on the child in the next stroller before his mom can stop him. In cases where biting becomes unmanageable, it may be necessary to give a youngster time to develop communication skills (perhaps including signing) while reducing time spent with other children. If a child must be in continued contact with others, such as in a childcare setting, try having him carry a "bite-able" object. A small teething ring clipped to his shirt offers a temporary solution. Keep a close watch on the child while helping him learn he can always bite on his ring, but may not bite a person.

Reinforce gentle touches by saying, "We touch our friends like

Biting and Hitting

Q: I have twenty-one-month-old twin boys. I know that hitting and biting can happen at this age, but one of my boys hits and bites more than the other. When he hits me, I leave the room, but he still has his brother for entertainment. What would happen if I give the one who is behaving himself lots of attention and ignore the boy who hits?

A: Dealing with two toddlers at once can certainly be challenging. Our suggestions may be shocking to people who don't understand Positive Discipline concepts: Consider paying more attention to the twin who is biting and hitting, and be sure to invite him to help you comfort his brother. No, this does not "reward" the misbehavior.

Giving a child the means to contribute to the well-being of another provides an experience of compassionate action. Your little one is frustrated about something and doesn't have the skills to express his feelings. You can comfort him and teach him skills at the same time, but don't expect your lessons to "stick" without supervision. Give the hitter or biter a hug for just a few seconds. Then say, "Look. Your brother is crying. Let's go give him a hug." (You are modeling hugging instead of hitting.) You are also helping him see the effects of his actions on others, a key step in developing empathy. After hugging for a few seconds, teach him a skill. Take his hand and show him how to "touch nicely." If he has already bitten his brother, after a few seconds say, "Let's go get some ice and help your brother feel better." Then let him hold the ice on his brother's bite.

Understanding development will help you recognize why this is helpful. Toddlers can't understand abstract concepts, but they do develop a "sense of" feelings and ideas, and will begin to learn. For example, the child you rescue may develop a sense of being a victim and believe, "I need other people to take care of me. I am helpless." Or, "Being a victim helps me get a sense of connection." If you scold or punish the aggressor, this child may develop a sense of doubt and shame. His discouragement may actually motivate more "misbehavior." When you show compassion for the needs of both children, you provide reassurance that you are there to help a child who cannot stop himself (remember, young children lack impulse control), and that you can be trusted to provide comfort when needed (for both the injured child and the aggressor).

this," as you model the action. If a child continues to bite after the age of three, it may be helpful to get a speech and hearing evaluation to ensure that language skills are developing appropriately.

SOCIAL INTEREST AND COMPASSION

In this chapter we have focused on some of the skills that children need when they interact with others. There is another social aspect of development as well: that of "social interest," which is a blend of empathy and compassion. Alfred Adler, a pioneer in the field of families and children's behavior, described "social interest" as concern for others and a sincere desire to make a contribution to society.

A big developmental leap occurs when a child begins to understand that the same emotions he feels and is learning to name—sadness, fear, or joy—are also felt by others. This is the beginning of empathy, and parallels his shift away from egocentricity toward the end of the toddler years. When a child brings a bandage for a child who has fallen and scraped her elbow, or shares lunch with a child who forgot hers, this developmental doorway begins to open. You can name and acknowledge a child's acts of kindness and caring, and thus encourage more of the same.

As children enter into the lives of their families and schools, they want very much to feel that they belong. One of the most powerful ways to achieve a sense of belonging is to make a meaningful contribution to the well-being of others in the family or group.

For young children, there really is no difference between play and work. When a baby strives over and over again to grab a toy that is just out of reach, we say she is "playing" but actually she is hard at work, growing and developing new skills. Young children are usually eager to participate in whatever they see us doing, and the time to invite children to participate in the family is when they want to—not when they can do a task perfectly. Once you begin to see your youngster as an asset, he won't seem to be "underfoot" so much.

COMPASSIONATE ROOTS

Compassion lies at the heart of social skills. Feeling capable and able to contribute to others is important. An eight-month-old hands her clean diaper to her dad when he is ready for it. A fifteen-month-old helps pile the bath toys into the tub. A two-year-old energetically helps

mop up spills in the kitchen. These tasks are fun for youngsters and form the basic patterns for future learning. The next time your toddler picks up a precious vase or fragile flower, ask her to hand it to you instead of trying to take the item out of her hand. The transformation will be almost magical as she switches from resistance to willing compliance. Her response makes sense when you remember that children like to be helpful.

In fact, one study discovered that toddlers appear to have an inborn desire to help others. When a researcher on a ladder accidently "dropped" clothespins, every toddler in the study rushed to pick them up and hand them to the researcher. (The toddlers also picked up books and other items.) When the researcher *threw* items on the floor, however, he was on his own. The children only picked up the fallen objects when they sensed that the adult needed their help.

More critically, we are planting the seeds for empathy and compassionate action when we allow children to contribute to the well-being of others. ***Children, even little ones, can do any number of things to contribute to their family's welfare.*** As you watch your little one during these first years of life, remember that he is watching you as well, and your example speaks more clearly than your words. Wise parents and caregivers will use a child's natural desire to imitate adult behavior by modeling desired skills and welcoming a child's involvement and help.

What will your child learn if you tell him to treat animals gently, but he then sees you angrily toss the cat outside after it claws the furniture? Will he learn compassion for others if he watches you sit comfortably on the bus while an elderly passenger stands nearby? Will he learn to speak respectfully if you holler across the room, admonishing him and his squabbling sisters to "quit yelling"? Which lessons will a child remember? Your words or your actions?

Remember those mirror neurons you read about in Chapter 3? Those neurons transmit their message as soon as a child sees an action performed. That means that **if you want your child to be gentle, kind, and thoughtful, you must be a parent who hugs instead of hits, who demonstrates compassion and comforting actions instead of impatience or retribution, and who listens instead of lashing out in anger. Your skills will become her skills.**

QUESTIONS TO PONDER

1. Over the next week, notice ways in which your child demonstrates empathy, compassion, or other positive social skills. Perhaps she patted your cheek when you seemed upset, offered an apple slice to her sister, or brought a tissue when she saw a classmate crying. Write down what you noticed. Acknowledge and name the child's behavior to him:

   "It is very kind of you to give Mommy a gentle touch."
   "Thank you for sharing with your sister."
   "Bringing a tissue to your friend was thoughtful, and helped him feel better."

2. Give your child an opportunity to empathize with another's suffering or to act compassionately. Some ideas are:

   Read a book about a child or animal struggling with something difficult, such as feeling hurt when she is excluded by friends, feeling sad about moving from her home, or worrying about a new situation—a new school or a different babysitter, for example. Ask how that child might be feeling. Name the feelings. Ask your child if he has ever felt like that.

Talk about the needs of others, such as people who are hungry or who cannot buy presents for a coming holiday. Invite your child to help in some way, perhaps by selecting canned foods to bring to a food bank or choosing toys she no longer uses to give to a child in need. How does your child feel when she experiences generosity?

SECTION FOUR

THE WORLD OUTSIDE YOUR HOME

17

NURTURED BY NATURE

As you explore what it means to be a parent or caregiver, it is wise (and important in ways that may surprise you) to consider another mother, the one we all share: Mother Nature. Mother Nature's wisdom is that of the natural world that surrounds us. This book focuses on ways to encourage your toddler's healthy development and to prevent problems. Interestingly, contact with nature can prevent or alleviate many common struggles while re-energizing us to deal with the rest. Mother Nature is always ready to impart her wisdom and experience. Nature silently surrounds us, in the quality of the air we breathe, as the source of the water flowing from our taps, and even in a piece of ripened fruit pollinated by unseen insects. It is easy to forget that you must consciously include nature in your life and the life of your child.

Sadly, nature and her gifts have all but disappeared from the lives of many families. Anxiety is a constant presence for parents and children; the world can seem dangerous and complex, and most parents struggle with finding the balance between explorations of the world "outside" and keeping children safe. In fact, anxiety is epidemic in twenty-first-century life—and most children catch anxiety from over-protective parents or the media. Life also has become increasingly busy. Parents work; children are rushed to and from childcare, and from one well-intentioned activity to another. There simply isn't time (or so parents may believe) to get messy, to slow down, and to breathe in the world of nature.

All over the world, children go from carpeted floors to paved roads to plastic-covered play yards and never feel the soft sponginess of grass, the slick glide of moss, or the shifting grittiness of sand against bare toes. Hard shoes separate them from the earth beneath their feet. While shoes are necessary to protect tender skin, it is all too easy to keep those wiggling toes from ever experiencing the wonderful textures of the world. From the very earliest moments of life, there is a grand planet waiting to be explored, and it is through this natural world that we learn about life itself. Connection with nature is essential for more than sentimental reasons. Research tells us that *contact with the natural world stimulates early learning and may actually help prevent problems such as obesity, depression, and anxiety.*

FROM HANDS TO HEARTS

Mother Nature tends to our needs in many ways. Bodies thrive from exposure to fresh air, receive doses of oxygen thanks to hardworking green plants, and are nourished by clean, clear water. The food we eat comes from her rich soil—or would, if we ate fewer processed foods. She helps brains develop through the experiences of the senses—what we see, hear, smell, touch, and feel.

Nature also tends to our emotional health. Exposure to nature can soothe our souls, drain away the stress of our days, and help us heal both emotionally and physically. Sunlight provides essential vitamins and alleviates depression. Time spent with this other mother improves our ability to focus, solve problems, and tap into creativity. And the more we learn from her, the more we come to care about her needs, too. As the planet's environment is increasingly stressed and the climate shifts, we will need the active engagement and problem-solving abilities of our youngest citizens. When you involve your child in the natural world, you increase the chance that she will care deeply about the planet she inhabits and will want to contribute to its well-being.

EXPERIENCE + BRAIN = LEARNING

Throughout our lives, but especially during the early years of life, much of what we experience comes through our senses. The natural world is rich in such experiences.

Little Nadine learns through touch that a kitten's fur is soft, that water can be cold, warm, or even hot, and that rain feels different than sunshine on her face. But she cannot learn these things if she never gets to stroke a kitten, wiggle her fingers in water, or have her face exposed to the weather.

Sam learns that bright sun makes him squint, that a delicate daisy petal feels different than a rough pinecone, and that a sparrow looks very small flying above him in the sky but much larger when it is picking up crumbs along the sidewalk. Each of these experiences provides lessons in how the world works and helps to wire his brain with new information. Smell alerts him to the presence of newly turned earth in a garden, causes his nose to tingle from the saltiness of an ocean mist, and makes him turn his head toward a blooming lilac bush.

When Miss Barbara's preschool class walks past an open field, a loud "caw" invites them to look at the crow flying overhead, while a mooing cow or barking dog alerts them to the presence of very different creatures. As their outdoor adventures continue, they learn that a rose is pretty but its thorns are sharp, and that snow is soft but makes your hands cold. Rocks are shiny and tempting—but they taste yucky!

The human brain uses these experiences to create memories and to wire the brain. Even language is affected. How will your child make sense of a word like "squishy" if his toes have never mushed through a mud puddle?

WONDER AND CREATIVITY

Newton came up with the theory of gravity after sitting beneath a tree and having an apple fall on him, or so the story goes. Fortunately, nature does not need to hit one over the head to stimulate creativity. Have you ever stopped working on a difficult task and gone for a walk through a garden, and found yourself better able to solve a vexing problem afterward? Nature can do that! One study of adults showed that in an office with green plants the creative suggestions of the participants increased by at least 15 percent.

Beauty and wonder are linked to creativity. The purples and pinks of a sunset, the yellows, oranges, and golds of autumn leaves, and the silky softness of a puppy's nose fill us with wonder. Isn't that sense of wonder something you want your child to know? Mother Nature is the world champion of wonder. She offers this gift to us every single day, if only we take the time to look.

Walk out your own front door* with your child. Notice that cardinal perched on the edge of a rainspout. Blink and you might miss the sparkle of water droplets when it splashes in its morning bath. Look at your baby's eyes as she watches a tiny crab scuttle across the sand. Observe your toddler trying to lick a raindrop from a leaf. These are

---

* For a book detailing a toddler's year of discovery and wonder, read Ann Pelo's *The Goodness of Rain* (Redmond, WA: Exchange Press, 2013).

moments of wonder. Children instinctively dig in beach sand. As their skills develop, their eager fingers create intricate structures laced with rivulets. Nature flows through them as creativity.

LIFE LESSONS

Nature's lessons are often effortless—true examples of "natural consequences." No one needs to tell a child to slow down when walking along a sandy beach. The sand takes care of that lesson. Watch a picky eater's appetite soar after a day outdoors. A hat that isn't tied down or buttoned up will soon be snatched by the wind, a better lesson than endless parental reminders.

What other lessons might your toddler learn from nature? Plant a radish seed and watch it grow from a tiny brown bead to little green leaves to a huge red bulb that she can eat. What a wonderful lesson in patience! The silence of a desert landscape invites tranquillity, as does the sound of waves whispering over the sand along a beach. Mother Nature offers solace and respite, and encourages a child to listen to her own inner voice.

Unless there is a dark sky, stars cannot be seen. For much of the world, finding a place of true darkness requires deliberate effort; in fact, in many urban communities it is rarely possible to see stars, let alone the Milky Way, because of the light from streets and buildings. If you want your child to understand trust and security, you can teach her that the stars are always there (even when she cannot see them), just like when Mommy leaves for work and comes back day after day.

Nature brings bigger lessons, too, about both life and death. Nurturing a tiny kitten or puppy, watching it grow, and learning to care for it with gentleness teaches a child responsibility and kindness. The loss of a beloved pet is often the first experience children have with death, a sad but inescapable part of life. Nature helps us learn to deal with life in all its aspects.

PHYSICAL BENEFITS

Isn't it amazing how even a tiny toddler will walk through piles of leaves or along a grassy trail without complaint, but beg to be carried even the short distance from a car in the parking lot to a nearby store, whining about it being "too far" or claiming to be "too tired"? Time spent in the natural world develops endurance. When in the presence of nature we slow down, even though time may seem to pass more quickly.

If getting your child to sleep is a problem, try spending time outside together before bedtime. A few minutes exploring the plants in a garden, or even a walk around the block, taking time to notice the sky and the trees or birds overhead, will make calming down for sleep much easier for both of you.

EMOTIONAL HEALTH, STRESS REDUCTION, AND HEALING

Mother Nature provides a ready means of finding calm in busy lives. The silence of a walk in the woods or the sound of ocean waves brings a sense of peace unmatched by any lullaby. Because few of us have access to woods and beaches on a daily basis, you may need to actively seek out such experiences in your life.

The exciting news is that both you and your tired little one may face a less cranky evening after a long day at work or in childcare with the addition of a touch of nature. A few moments spent outdoors, or a tour of the houseplants while checking to see if they need water, and caring for them together, can restore both of you.

It is well known that stress plays a role in illness. Fortunately, if you reduce stress, healing may follow. For instance, patients able to see trees from their hospital windows actually need less pain medication and their hospital stays are shortened. Children playing in natural settings on a regular basis show improvement in coordination and agility; they also tend to get sick less often.

INVITING "MOTHER" IN

There is so much our other mother has to offer. You need only open your eyes and her gifts surround you. Your task as a parent or caregiver is to be sure that these gifts remain accessible for your child. A playground covered in shock-absorbing rubber mats can still have planters filled with evergreen bamboo or local shrubs. You can create a "nature table" where children can bring in treasured finds to share: a smooth seashell, a shiny pebble, or a juicy honeycomb.

Here are some suggestions for bringing nature into your home:

- Start a garden or give a child a houseplant to care for. Even growing sprouts in a jar from tiny alfalfa seeds will do. Watching a seed turn into tiny sprouts that can be tossed into the evening salad puts children in touch with the miracle of how food grows.

- If you don't have garden space, make time to visit a farm or nearby garden. Even better, get permission to harvest a carrot, snip a few leaves of mint to add to water glasses, or gather a bouquet of daisies and sweet peas to place on the dinner table. Each of these activities brings nature into our lives and hearts.

- Place a bird feeder where you and your child can watch as birds flit in and out, twitch their heads alertly, snatch seeds, and then fly off to crack them open. Make time to watch together. Listen to the different sounds the birds make. Can you tell them apart? Match the birds you see or hear to pictures.

One childcare program in Australia decided to remove all man-made play equipment in its preschool classroom and replace it with items from nature. They talked about Aboriginal children, and what they might have played with when only natural items were available to them. There were logs to build with, baskets of shells and twigs, and containers of sand and pebbles on all the shelves. The children discovered ways to draw using soft rocks on tree bark. They created amazing mandalas, composed of shells, pebbles, and twigs. These took up large sections of the floor, and they spent long periods of time working with incredible focus. The teachers had planned to try this program for a week, but the children loved it so much that they continued on for several months.

Another event, International Mud Day,* was started by the early childhood community in Nepal, and encourages people around the world to simply (yes, you guessed it) play in mud. Centers or communities create mud, and children arrive dressed in washable clothing or swimsuits, and spend the day slithering through silky mud. They experience its slip, slosh, and smooth or gritty textures. They get wonderfully, washably dirty. Will your child ever know the feel of mud? Have you had that experience yourself? Why not?

SUSTAINABILITY

Mother Earth benefits from all this interaction, too. Just as we are interconnected through our relationships with others, **giving children opportunities to connect with the natural world helps them develop a sense of stewardship and caring.** What we learn to love, we treasure and will care for. That translates into adults who value, take care of, and preserve the natural world.

Experiences with nature and a sense of connection to the natural world are among the greatest gifts we can offer children. They are preventive parenting at its best, meeting a child's physical, cognitive, and emotional needs in ways that are infinitely sustainable as lifelong skills. How have you invited nature into your home, childcare setting, or life? Have you made room for her or blocked her out? She is a polite mother and prefers an invitation. Perhaps you are overdue for a family visit.

QUESTIONS TO PONDER

1. Inspire creativity by visiting a petting zoo, walking through the woods or along a beach, or watching a sunrise or sunset together.

---

* www.worldforumfoundation.org/working-groups/nature/international-mud-day.

Afterward, supply your child with art materials such as crayons, colored pens, or paints. Join him and simply create together. What happens? What colors are used? Were they the ones in that sunset? Do the spots of the goats you stroked appear? Is the green of the trees or the blue of the ocean in the picture? Even if there is no noticeable relationship, the energy of the experience will feed it. Repeat often.

2. Go for a silent stroll with your little one. Explain that for a few minutes, you will both listen to only the sounds that surround you. Even though a tiny baby may not understand the words, she will feel your body language as you become still and listen. Take this walk in as natural a setting as possible. Even a city street can teach you to listen with attention. What do you hear?

> *The scrunch of gravel underfoot?*
> *The sounds of cars rattling past?*
> *The caw of a crow perched on a wire or tree limb overhead?*

With luck, you may even hear . . .

> *Silence.*

Silence has a way of filling us and expanding within us. Enjoy.

18

WIRED MINDS

The Impact of Technology

igital natives. Mobile-born. Touch-screen generation. Remote-controlled child. These phrases, used in the media to describe children today, didn't even exist a few short years ago. Neither did the term "Googling" (or the company it refers to, for that matter), yet many parents now routinely use a Google search to decide on a name for their child. After all, who wants to give a child a name that turns up thousands of references to an infamous criminal?

From television to smartphones to tablets to computers (and whatever is still to come), technology, screen time, and social media are today's reality. Most adults can't imagine life without social media or texting, and are rarely far from their device of choice. It is not only the devices that are thought-provoking; the rate at which change is happening is increasing rapidly. Like the technology itself, the use of mobile devices by children is galloping ahead at an unprecedented pace.

At the time of writing, nearly four out of every ten toddlers and infants have used a mobile device, as compared to only one out of ten two years previously. A 2013 SquareTrade study found that

85 percent of American children use mobile devices every day, averaging more than three hours each day of "screen time." Believe it or not, toddlers two years old and younger are connected to a screen an average of 1.5 hours each day. Parents may laughingly call their tablet computers "pacifiers"—but what is the real long-term impact on a child's developing brain?

There is no question that healthy connections with parents and caregivers are critically important to a child's development, but recommendations about developmentally appropriate use of mobile devices are in flux. The American Medical Association's previous recommendation of no screen time for children under the age of two has softened to "Discourage screen media exposure for children under two." Despite the recommendations, it is all but impossible to go out for a meal these days without seeing a toddler entertaining herself with Dad's smartphone, and many parents brag about their child's precocious ability to operate digital devices. Like it or not, **today's children have become a living technological experiment about the effects of screen time.**

Psychologist Jerome Bruner uses the term "enactive representation" to describe the way in which a child's hands are connected to (and express) his thoughts. A thirsty child, for example, will pantomime drinking from a cup. It also explains what makes touch-screen devices such a game changer. When passing a finger over the screen makes a rainbow appear, what child wouldn't want to do it again? And again? But what does this teach? What does it do to brain circuitry? The sobering answer is that we don't yet know.

WIRED MINDS: THE SCREEN TIME / SOCIAL MEDIA DILEMMA

Changes in technology are now so rapid that it is all but impossible to predict long-range effects, let alone answer the questions each new advance poses. As you have learned, your child's brain is being wired for life in these first important years. Whatever your views or choices regarding technology, you must step back and make conscious, thoughtful decisions about what and how much exposure is appropriate for your child.

ATTITUDE IS THE BEST APP

Life in the twenty-first century is hectic. Parents are busy and rushed, and it is tempting to sit a child in front of the television or a game console while you hurry to prepare dinner, get laundry folded, or simply grab a few minutes of quiet for yourself. One parent said, "Those parents who are willing to restrict TV or computer time must work outside of the home. Those of us home all day with little ones need some kind of break!" The point is not whether parenting is demanding (it is) or exhausting (it can be) but that you must be conscious of your choices and attitudes, and the impact they have on your child's development and beliefs.

All parents need a break from time to time, and mobile devices may appear to be helpful "babysitters." Like junk food, a little bit may not be permanently damaging. Still, media use in the home can become a slippery slope when parents aren't paying attention. Instead of seeing your child as a distraction or a burden, what if your attitude changed? Is it possible to slow down enough to enjoy working alongside your child? She can learn valuable skills by doing tasks with you, and you will be strengthening your relationship.

Our goal is not to make parents feel guilty about their choices. We do not advocate raising either overprotected princesses or overindulged tyrants. We do encourage thinking and confident action—yours and your child's.

What Is Effective? The Tongue in Your Mouth or the One in Your Shoes?

Alfred Adler taught, "Watch the movement if you want to know what people have decided to do—even when they are not aware of their decision." In other words, watch the tongue in the shoes (what they do), not the tongue in the mouth (what they say).

Do you yell across the room, telling your child to put that phone or tablet down? Or do you walk across the room, remove the item, and put it away or turn it off yourself? Children do what they see others do. What does your child see? How much do you use technology around your child? What do you prefer to spend your time with, your device or your child? What does *she* believe you prefer?

CAREGIVERS AS ALLIES

With so many decisions to make, and so many unknown factors, it is easy to feel overwhelmed by rapidly changing technology. Many infants and toddlers are in the care of others while their parents are at work, exposed to whatever their caregivers decide is appropriate. **If your child is in care for all or part of his day, you should begin a conversation with his caregivers about technology and mobile devices.** What a child experiences at home influences his behavior at childcare—and the opposite is true as well.

Children are influenced by what they see on screens. Your child's caregiver may notice that your child is hitting or pushing more than usual. If the caregiver brings such issues to your attention, consider it an invitation to have a discussion about how what he views may be affecting your child and his behavior. Such discussions may help you be more conscious of the choices you are making. You can also make an agreement with your care provider about limits and expectations, and strengthen consistency between your home and childcare.

RELATIONSHIPS MATTER

One thing we know for certain is that relationships—how we interact with and learn to respond to others—are crucial to the life decisions we will make.

> *Two-year-old Esperanza decides whether or not others can be trusted based upon her experiences of consistency and predictability in everyday encounters with those around her. She decides whether she can expect kindness and respect, and learns to give both when she experiences these important qualities. If she is subjected to constant criticism, she may decide to retreat or quit trying. And if she is spanked, she will be more likely to hit or hurt others to get what she wants.*

Every decision in the life of a young child is an important decision. You undoubtedly want to be sure your child is given every opportunity to make the healthiest choices possible. Television and other media expose children to both content and values. Are the messages your child receives in line with your own values and beliefs? The decisions you make about screen time may have more of an impact on your child's beliefs than you realize.

Time matters, too. Does screen time replace or outweigh time spent with adults and other children? Whether the interaction takes place over bowls of cereal, between children at childcare or on a playdate, or during a walk to the park, time spent with others builds skills and strengthens relationships. Does watching colorful animals bop each other over the head, or pressing buttons to a cacophony of beeps and pings, do that? Probably not.

CONTENT AND LEARNING

Parents pay attention to what is in the books they offer to their children. No toddler is likely to find *War and Peace* interesting bedtime material, but most enjoy *Where the Wild Things Are*. Content matters when it comes to technology, too.

Much children's media content markets itself as "educational." Surely, if your child is learning the alphabet or how to count, this can't be a bad thing, right? Well, there is learning and then there is wiring the brain. What is happening inside that brain when a screen is placed in front of it? Researchers are currently looking for the answer to this question, but the truth is that no one knows.

Take a chubby finger and have it poke the belly of an on-screen kitten. The kitten wiggles its feet and meows. This toddler is learning that his behavior can elicit a predictable reaction (even though it may not be the same one a real cat might offer). Although this learning includes interaction, is it a valuable lesson? Research indicates that the mere light and action on a screen (rather than the content) has an impact on a child's brain. The flashing lights and rapidly changing colors and figures may be influencing attention span and the development of nonverbal learning skills, and the screen's light itself appears to affect sleep cycles. At the very least, be wary of offering your precious baby or toddler as a science experiment to the unknown world of technology. If you are unsure, unplug!

LOCATION, LOCATION, LOCATION

One thing we are sure of: A child's room does not need a screen of any kind. We can think of no reason for a child younger than three (or older, for that matter) to have a television, computer, or other screen in his room (in fact, older children score lower on tests at school when they have a screen in their rooms)—yet we know many do. *A young child does not yet have the ability to choose his own viewing material wisely—no matter how well he operates the remote or can swipe his finger across a screen.* Be sure that all screens are located where you can easily view them along with your child. Supervision is essential, at any age.

Is It Bookish?

A common verbal trick among young adults these days is the use of "ish" as a suffix. One teenager we know looked out the window at the falling sleet and said, "Look! It's snowish." This semantic trick may be useful when it comes to screen-time decisions as well.

Mobile devices have many uses. We have long understood that reading with young children is one of the best ways to encourage language development and school readiness. You may find it helpful to ask yourself, "Is this device used like a book? Can we call it 'bookish'"?

What are the properties of a book?

- The experience is in your control. (You turn the page.)
- Imaginations are activated; images are formed in the mind.
- Thinking is encouraged.

How does a book activate the imagination? Books invite us to create our own mental pictures. Books with pictures invite thinking through questions:

- "What do you think Little Bear will do next?"

or by tempting us to turn the page:

- "Moo," said the . . . (*Hmm. What could it be? Turn the page!*) . . . Cow!

Now, apply these same criteria to a program on TV, the game or app on a tablet, or the images on a computer screen. Does it qualify as "bookish"?

- Who is in control? (interactive versus passive)
- Is the imagination engaged?
- Is thinking encouraged?

Watching images float and explode across a screen (no matter how entertaining), or repetitively pushing buttons to get a result, may be great training to play video games or operate drones, but it is passive at best and robotic at worst. (Not bookish!) Reading a book on an e-reader with Grandma and getting to turn the "pages" is much more bookish. Think about and define your own criteria for a book, then ask if a given type of screen time can be called bookish. If yes, use it sparingly. If no, don't use it at all.

Screen time can be addictive (as many adults have discovered), and it is far too easy to spend long hours in front of a screen when access is uncontrolled. A television or other device located in a child's room encourages isolation instead of connection. When you combine addiction and isolation, you have a child who may be developing habits of "life numbness" instead of "life enjoyment." When media screens are in a common room (such as the family room), family members have the opportunity to negotiate what to watch or play, when, and for how long.

FUN OR FACTS

There is nothing wrong with having fun. Building a sand castle at the beach is fun—even if there are no architectural lessons involved. Running and playing tag are both fun and good exercise, even if they do not teach better writing skills. Sometimes playing a game on Mom's smartphone is just plain fun. If it makes you laugh, there is nothing wrong with that, either.

Still, are there better ways to have fun? Certainly. Playing peekaboo with Dad is more fun (and more helpful to learning and connection) than staring at a colorful screen game. Children need to learn how to engage with others, to be creative, and to enjoy interacting with other children and adults. As long as those remain priorities, the *occasional* use of a touch-screen game for fun is probably fine. Just be sure you can set reasonable limits and follow through with kindness and firmness—even when your child howls for more.

CONTENT VERSUS COMMERCIALISM

Much of children's programming is marketing in disguise. Young children do not take in enough information during a brief commercial to prefer a product, so entire programs have become, in essence, commercials for toys, food, and other products. This means that the characters and the products they inspire are inseparably entwined, and designed to make your child want them.

Parents must pay attention. First, watch what your child is watching, and watch *with* her. This allows you to know what values are being taught, what behaviors are being demonstrated, and what impact it has on your child. Watching programs together allows you to discuss with her what you are seeing, and influence the messages being sent. It is also an opportunity for your child to learn to think critically. Watching television or other programming is inherently passive; when you discuss what you're seeing with your child, you will engage her interest and encourage her to think for herself.

> *What do you think about the way that dinosaur grabbed the bone his friend was playing with?*
> *Is it a good idea to hit a friend who has a toy you want? How would your friend feel?*
> *What do you think the dinosaur could do instead?*

Watching together will also tell you what products a child is being encouraged to demand. If you, as a parent, feel that such marketing manipulates your child, you can use your pocketbook to make a statement by not purchasing these products. Better yet, turn off the program and do something creative and active instead.

ALTERNATIVES TO SCREEN TIME

Technology is enticing, and most parents want to provide wonderful things for their children. But are these devices really so wonderful? Should your baby be staring at the computer screen strapped to her car seat, or should she be looking out the window at the sky, the trees, or even at her older sister on the seat beside her? Believe it or not, you can purchase a potty seat that will hold a tablet computer. But does that mean you should? We don't think so.

Consider this issue carefully. Whatever you do, do it thoughtfully.

Do not leave your child's screen time to chance. Set reasonable limits; be kind, but be firm when necessary. Here are a few more ideas:

- The library remains a great resource. Many children's books are now available as e-books. Remember the "bookish" discussion? If there is one acceptable use for screens, this may be it. Reading a paperless book is still reading.

- Another option is for childcare programs or caregivers to develop a lending library of toys and interactive (non-technology) games.* Children will be excited about picking out counting blocks or puzzles to take home over the weekend, and families will get the benefit of these toys without the expense. The whole process encourages thoughtful play alternatives to screen time at home. (For more information on these topics, we have listed additional resources at the back of this book.)

ARE YOU THERE?

Conduct an experiment the next time you go to a playground, wait in an airport lounge, or go grocery shopping with your child. Look around. How many parents or caregivers are watching a child build his skill at pumping higher on a swing, marveling at the planes taking off and landing outside the window, or talking through their grocery list with a listening child? How many are talking on their phone, sending or reading text messages, or connecting more intimately with technology than with their child?

---

* See *Beyond Remote-Controlled Childhood: Teaching Young Children in the Media Age,* by Diane E. Levin (Washington, DC: National Association for the Education of Young Children, 2013).

Mobile devices are like money. They are not inherently good or bad; their value depends on how they are used. Your child is making important decisions in these early years about herself, about you, and about how the world around her works and what her place in it really is. What do you want her to decide? To believe? Do your best to be fully present for these precious moments of human connection and learning; make them a priority. You'll have lots of time for technology when your child has grown up.*

> ### Cheat Sheet: Questions to Ask Before Any Screen Use
>
> - Does it replace or overshadow interactions with real people?
> - Does it replace hands-on experiences?
> - Is it "bookish"?
> - How might it affect my child? What might he decide, learn, or believe as a result of this experience?
>
> Unsure? Unplug!

QUESTIONS TO PONDER

1. Make a commitment to switch off all devices, whatever they are, and try to be truly present the next time you and your child do something together. Whether it is time outdoors, shopping, or even waiting in a line, notice what is going on. Engage with your child; ask questions and invite questions from her. Practice listening carefully.

2. Do some journaling about this experience. Ask yourself:

   How did it feel?
   How was it different?
   What difference did it make for me? For my child?

3. Consider making family meals, or perhaps whole days, technology-free times. Turn off all your devices and focus on being truly present with your family members. What might happen if you did this regularly?

---

* For more information, see *Help! My Child Is Addicted to Screens (Yikes! So Am I.): Positive Discipline Tools for Managing Family Screen Time*, an e-book by Jane Nelsen and Kelly Bartlett (www.positivediscipline.com).

19

WHO'S WATCHING THE KIDS?

Choosing (and Living with) Childcare

No matter how capable and competent you are as a parent, it is unlikely you will care for your child entirely on your own. Most adults must work, either in or out of the home, and for most families childcare of some sort is a fact of life.

In thousands and thousands of homes across this nation, each working day begins with the ritual of packing lunches, gathering backpacks, precious stuffies, or jackets, and getting children to their childcare facility. Some children go to friends' or relatives' homes, some stay home with a nanny, while others spend the day in centers or home childcare programs. For thousands of such parents, childcare is a necessity, and choosing the best care for the available money is their main concern. Still other parents remain at home, believing that only a parent should care for a young child, and that childcare is a poor substitute. Each family has unique needs and often conflicting beliefs to reconcile. Listen for a moment to the voices of two different parents:

Q: I have read that you feel that mothers who work do not have a negative effect on their children. Could you please expand on this? Radio programs, newspaper articles, and magazines offer such conflicting advice that I feel really confused. At the present time it is not possible for me to quit my job, because my husband is bed-ridden with a back injury. My son spends about nine hours a day at childcare. Will this have a negative impact on him? I feel terribly guilty. I love my son more than anything and want to be with him, but I can't be. Thank you.

Q: My neighbor just came by for a visit. Her son Joseph attends childcare three days a week while she works at a part-time job. Joseph is two months younger than my son, and yet Joseph can count and write his name and knows all his colors, while my son does none of these things. I am a full-time mom at home with our son all day. I feel really inadequate whenever my neighbor and her son visit. I am worried that my son will be behind when it is time for him to begin school. Our money is tight, but should I look into putting him in a preschool?

A: Most people hold strong opinions about who should care for young children and the benefits of early education versus the value of being at home with a parent. We believe that where or from whom a child receives care matters less than the quality of the care itself. "Quality" childcare supports the development of healthy self-worth, emotional well-being, learning and brain growth, and the ability to form healthy relationships with other people. Children need healthy connections with their caregivers *and* parents. If a parent must be apart from her child, she needs to nurture strong connections during whatever time is available to do so. And there are numerous ways to enrich learning in the home, even with limited resources.

Many mothers seem to feel guilty whether they stay at home or not. Feeling guilty does not do anyone the least bit of good. Neither does being judgmental. Everyone makes choices based on his or her own situation and beliefs. Young children love to be with their parents, and we know that the bond of mother, father, and child is vital. But this bond does not thrive only in isolation. Children can learn and grow in many different settings.

IS CHILDCARE HARMFUL?

Roslyn, one of the authors and the mother of four, shares her experiences as a stay-at-home mom with her first two children, and then as a working mom with her two youngest children in childcare:

> I stayed home with our two oldest children throughout their first three years. When our second child turned three, our family opened the Learning Tree, a Montessori childcare center. In many ways, our two youngest children had the best of both worlds. They were with their parents, since both their dad and I worked at the childcare center, and they also took part in a wonderful childcare program each day.
>
> All four of our children are thriving today. The center is, too; it's still operating more than thirty-five years later and even our grandchildren have attended it. Many of the children our center has cared for are now young adults; some are parents themselves and some have brought their own children back to attend our center. Former students frequently stop by to visit and reminisce with us, and more than one has told us that their time at our center helped them experience subsequent successes in their lives. They are loving, capable, and responsible people, and we are grateful our family played an important role in so many young lives.

There are all kinds of conflicting studies, attitudes, and theories about childcare. Roslyn's experience offers a long-term perspective, one that includes raising children both in the home and out of the home. You may be thinking, *It isn't working outside the home when you are able to take your children with you.* That is not the point. Roslyn's children still had challenges to deal with, such as sharing their parents with other children and being separated from them even when they were in the center's care, often for long hours each day. Some parents work at home and must deal with constant interruptions. The point is that every life situation presents challenges that can be dealt with successfully if you have effective attitudes and skills.

Being a stay-at-home parent offers many rewards for both parents and their youngsters. So do the experiences available in quality childcare programs. Neither scenario guarantees magical outcomes, positive or negative.

WORK AND CHILDCARE: WHAT ARE THEY?

Parents work in the home and out of the home all the time. Brian is an editor for a local newspaper and brings two-year-old Jason to a childcare center near his office. Mary Beth puts together the weekly church newsletter, spending two mornings a week at the church office while her son plays with other children during the women's Bible study playgroup. Both of these parents work. (Volunteers are working parents, too.)

Childcare refers to more than just home- or center-based programs. Grandma takes care of baby Lori while Mom volunteers as a reading tutor at her oldest daughter's elementary school. Every morning when Eli leaves for his job as a clerk at the city courthouse, he takes his infant son to the neighbor's house, where his neighbor watches her own infant, Eli's son, and several older children who arrive after school every day. Jean entertains her younger brother after returning home from high school each afternoon so their father can process tax returns in his home-based accountant's office upstairs. Childcare has many faces.

The definition of "working parent" refers to more than those who are paid for work outside the home, who use providers other than family members, or who work for more than a few hours each week.

In fact, moms and dads do all kinds of work, and their children experience all kinds of childcare.

CHILDCARE: A GLOBAL PERSPECTIVE

Over the course of time, few cultures have expected mothers to stay home all alone to care for tiny children. Most often, children have been cared for by older siblings, aunts, and nearby or resident grandparents.

The popular phrase "It takes a village to raise a child" comes from rural Africa. In this context, the "village" is a child's blood relatives, neighbors, and community or tribal members. East Indian families typically contain several generations in one household. In many Asian countries, a woman moves in with their husband's family when they marry. In Native American culture, it is traditional for children to be raised by many "aunties," some not related by blood at all. In all these cultures, children receive care from an extended family of friends and relatives. They might view our belief that mothers and fathers should raise children without outside advice or help as a form of insanity!

CHOICES

Take a moment to read the stories of some of the parents who bring their children to childcare facilities.

Stephanie is grateful that a childcare facility is located in the hospital where she works. Her son will be six months old next week and the proximity of the childcare center makes it possible for Stephanie to continue nursing him, something that is very important to her. She hurries downstairs on her breaks and lunch hour, eager to cuddle with her son. Stephanie was not married when she became pregnant, and the baby's father does not support her or their son, but Stephanie chose to continue her pregnancy and raise her son as a single parent. Divorce, single parenthood, and even military deployment may leave few options for a man or woman raising a child without a partner, but Stephanie is devoted to her son and works hard to provide him with a loving home.

Roger and Jennifer both work at the same hospital as Stephanie does. Jennifer tried staying home with three-year-old Todd but found she missed the stimulation of her job. The harder she tried to be a stay-at-home mom, the more discouraged she felt—and the angrier she became when Todd misbehaved. Perhaps, she worried, she just wasn't meant to be a full-time mom. She and Roger love Todd dearly; Jennifer discovered, however, that she became a much better parent when she wasn't cranky and irritable from being isolated all day with an active toddler. She struggles with guilt, but she and Roger truly believe that Todd is happier and healthier at the childcare center, climbing on the equipment and playing with his many friends. Jennifer thrives at her job and is enjoying being Todd's mother far more than she used to.

Tyneesha, on the other hand, has two children who do not go to childcare. The children share a bedroom so that the spare room can be rented to a college student. The rental income makes it possible for Tyneesha to stay at home with four-month-old Erica and three-year-old Micah. Tyneesha's husband works at the shipyard in town. His commute takes an hour each day, but homes located closer to the harbor are out of their price range. The long days wear Tyneesha out and sometimes the demands of her two youngsters make her want to scream. On other days, her heart melts just looking at them and she offers prayers of thanksgiving for this time she gets to spend with them.

Stay-at-home parents find that one-on-one daily contact with an infant, toddler, or preschooler includes magical moments of discovery, tender times of sharing, and precious memories for both parent and child. Staying home also means moments of despair when toilets overflow from being fed whole rolls of toilet paper by a curious toddler, episodes of hysterics when a preschooler's screeching wakes up his sleeping baby sister, or feeling helpless when a defiant toddler throws his blocks across the room after refusing to pick them up. Working parents experience these same moments. In fact, these aspects of early childhood will happen no matter what shape your life takes.

Many parents want nothing more than to stay at home with their babies. In a perfect world, that choice would be possible for everyone—but in the real world, harsh reality intervenes. Parents who choose to stay at home to raise a child, to forgo career and financial rewards, or to accept a simpler lifestyle, deserve recognition, respect, and support. Those who work deserve the same. **The issue is not whether you agree with your neighbor's choice but whether you have made the best choice for yourself and for your children.** Choosing to work or stay home is a complicated decision, and there is rarely a simple "right" or "wrong" answer. You must face your own reality and make the best decisions you can.

THE NEW EXTENDED FAMILY

For many of us, it has become increasingly rare to live near extended family who are willing and able to care for our children. Today's childcare programs may take on the role of the historic extended family, including such events as potluck dinners where parents can get to know one another and share stories. When this happens, childcare supports both connection and community.

Families need the support of many people when raising young

children, and the staff of a quality childcare program can provide knowledge, experience, and information.

When Ellen's daughter was diagnosed with asthma, the teacher at her daughter's center provided reassurance and recommended a support group for families whose children had similar problems.

Janell has few friends with young children. Her own daughter, Hanna, arrived only a few weeks ago after more than a year of paperwork, delays, and waiting lists; Hanna turned four months old on her adoption day. Janell is a single parent who needs to work, and the childcare center has proven invaluable as a source of support for her newly formed family. Other families at the childcare center provide the sense of community, sibling-like relationships, and social gatherings that Janell and Hanna need. Several other children at the center were adopted, and one of them comes from the same country as Hanna. This child's family quickly formed a close bond with Janell and Hanna, with the two families planning get-togethers and supporting each other as they and their new infants get to know one another.

Stay-at-home parents also need support. The absence of a nearby extended family may create isolation for those at home. Even if they have family nearby, parents need encouragement, social contact, and support.

BENEFITS OF CHILDCARE: EARLY INTERVENTION AND CONSISTENCY

Quality childcare goes beyond simply providing a place for children to be cared for in a parent's absence. Screening and early intervention, consistency during times of change, and the extended family support previously mentioned are wonderful ways in which childcare programs can enhance the quality of children's lives.

Bailey gets bussed every afternoon to childcare. Each morning, he participates in a special program for youngsters with a variety of developmental delays. Bailey's mom, Shirley, had wondered why he seemed to have such a hard time learning new skills. Being a first-time mom, Shirley assumed her own lack of experience caused her to worry needlessly about Bailey, but only a few weeks after Bailey began attending his childcare, the director asked to meet with Shirley. The program's initial screening raised concerns about Bailey's development. Together, the center and Shirley sought outside help. Shirley and the staff were right to feel concerned. Bailey was delayed in motor, speech, and other communication skills. Specific problems were identified, and a few months later Bailey was admitted to a special morning program at the university. Without the center's experienced staff, caring support, and knowledge, Shirley might not have gotten Bailey the early intervention he needed.

Early intervention is more effective in helping children with delays "catch up" than intervention provided when children are older. (See the Resources section for a link to the free CDC milestones checklists.) Screening and assessment, along with the experience and training of skilled caregivers, offer opportunities to identify children and families in need of special assistance. Not all care providers offer such screenings. Still, if your child's teacher or caregiver expresses concerns about any aspect of your child's development, it may be wise to pursue the matter. Consistency and stability are also crucial.

Kyle's parents have filed for divorce. He now sees his dad only on weekends. He and his mom have moved into an apartment, and she has to work longer hours than before. The only thing that remains unchanged in Kyle's life is his childcare center. Kyle sees the same faces every morning, recognizes the circle songs, and knows that snack time comes just after story time. With everything else in his life shifting like quicksand, he feels safe, secure, and reassured at his childcare center.

Even when family circumstances change—a new sibling, or the illness of a family member—the routines and familiarity of childcare can provide stability, support, and consistency in a child's life.

FINDING QUALITY CHILDCARE

We've talked about parents who work, by choice or necessity, and those who stay at home. But no matter their situation and choices, for almost all parents some form of outside care, even babysitting or time spent in a nursery during church services, is a fact of life. We've dis-

cussed the benefits of quality childcare, but what about care that is less than ideal? Obviously, not all childcare is created equal—and not all of it benefits children. How can parents know that they're leaving their little ones in competent, qualified hands? What makes for *quality* childcare?

First, be sure that the person you leave your child with can be trusted. A new boyfriend or girlfriend may not be the person you want to care for your child, no matter how much in love you may be. A babysitter should supply references so parents can talk to people who know her well. Even in group settings, having at least two people in charge provides a measure of accountability.

If you are one of the many parents who need to find regular care for their child, you need to consider a number of factors. Don't be in a rush to choose; take time to visit different childcare programs. What do you see? Are the children happy? Do they move around the center confidently? Does a caregiver get down on the child's eye level to talk with him? Is the artwork displayed low enough for children to see it, or only at adult eye level? Is the building clean? Are there visible safety hazards? Do the caregivers look cheerful or frazzled? (Do remember that even the best teachers can have tough days!) Is there enough equipment to offer a variety of activities for art projects, role-playing, building, outdoor climbing, sand and water play? Does the equipment provided allow children to play freely, to come in contact with nature, and to be physically active? Or are children expected to be quiet, stay indoors, and "be good"? Are they confined to infant seats or parked in front of a television?

Find out if the program is licensed, and by whom. Does the center pass city licensing requirements, health department codes, and fire safety requirements? Some areas have local childcare resource and referral agencies to aid in this process. Affordability is a factor for most parents, but choosing childcare should not involve bargain hunting. Children—all children—are worth our investment.

WHY CARE ABOUT QUALITY CARE?

If you are a parent in a family that doesn't need outside care, you may feel that issues of establishing and funding quality childcare programs are not relevant to you. The truth is that the type of care, quality or otherwise, that any child receives affects everyone.

The historic *High/Scope Perry Preschool Study Through Age 40* found that adults who had participated in "quality" early care programs went on to achieve higher school test scores and had higher rates of high school graduation than those children who had not received "quality" early care experiences. The children in the programs identified as "quality" care were also less likely to be involved in crime as adults, and averaged far more in annual earnings. Many other studies have also verified benefits of quality childcare, ranging from social and emotional learning to academic advantages.

Findings such as these remind us of how deep the roots of our early experiences are. What happens to children in and out of childcare affects the type of society and world all our children will someday share.

293

QUALITY CHILDCARE: HOW CAN I TELL?

Looking at lists of characteristics and requirements for quality childcare can feel overwhelming. You may be wondering how you will ever know if the facility you are considering meets these standards. There is a relatively simple solution: *ask*. Childcare is an important decision, and your confidence as a parent will influence your child's comfort with and response to her new setting. Don't hesitate to ask for all the information you need to make an educated decision. If a center or provider seems reluctant to answer your questions or to allow you to observe personnel in action, it's wise to look elsewhere.

CHILDCARE CHECKLIST

Identify quality childcare using the following indicators.

1. The center or home has:

   - Current licenses displayed

   - A low rate of staff turnover

   - Local, state, and/or national accreditation

2. The staff is:

   - Well-trained in early childhood development and care

   - Working as a team

   - Staying up-to-date through training programs

   - Adequately paid

3. The curriculum emphasizes:

   - A balance of age-appropriate academics and play (and an understanding that in early childhood, play and social skills are the most important lessons a child will learn)

   - Social skills—lots of interaction with children and staff

- Exploring through the senses, with access to nature

- Problem solving (with equipment and with other children)

4. Discipline is:

- Nonpunitive

- Kind and firm at the same time

- Designed to help children learn important life skills

5. Consistency shows:

- In the curriculum

- In the way problems are handled

- In routines the children can count on

- In day-to-day center management

6. Safety is demonstrated by the:

- Physical setting

- Program health policies

- Preparedness for emergencies

Copy this checklist and take it with you when you visit prospective childcare facilities. It contains the information you'll need to know in order to make an educated choice for your child.

THE FACILITY

Most states or cities require centers and homes to meet a variety of licensing requirements. Many also have a Quality Rating System with a score assigned to centers to help families judge quality. Seeing licenses posted tells you the requirements have been met. You may want to ask if a center uses an assessment system such as CLASS Toddler,* which measures the emotional climate in a classroom, the teacher's sensitivity, and the appropriateness of learning and language. (The CLASS tool was researched for more than ten years. It is used by Head Start as well as many teacher-training programs around the country. You can learn more at http://teachstone.com/the-class-system/.)

Centers with low staff turnover indicate that staff members are well-treated, receive fair compensation, enjoy their work, and feel supported by the center's administration. When staff members do not receive a living wage, they go elsewhere, which creates inconsistency in the center and hampers your child's ability to form a supportive attachment to her caregivers.

Look for special licensing. These will vary by state. There are also national licensing organizations, such as NAEYC (National Association for the Education of Young Children) and NAC (National Accreditation Commission for Early Care and Education Programs). The fact that a center obtains licensing and/or accreditation demonstrates a commitment to accountability.

THE STAFF

Training and experience make it more likely that caregivers understand the needs of young children, provide activities that meet those needs, and have developmentally appropriate expectations. Educated, experienced caregivers plus low turnover create a winning situation for everyone involved.

Look for the types of training that staff members receive. Doctors, stock market analysts, childcare teachers—all must stay knowledgeable about current information in their fields. Do staff members at the center you're considering attend workshops? Are there in-house training programs, or are employees encouraged to take part in additional

---

* See *Classroom Assessment Scoring System (Toddler)* by Karen LaParo, Bridget Hamre, and Robert Pianta (Baltimore: Brookes Publishing, 2012).

educational programs? Is there a statewide registry that tracks continuing education and verifies that teachers are staying current with information about what toddlers need? Teachers deserve the opportunity to learn about new research, get inspired by and reminded of basic concepts, and feel encouraged when they hear others share solutions to common dilemmas. Are there special training requirements? Montessori, Reggio Emilia, and Waldorf programs have specialized training curricula for their teachers. Community college, undergraduate, and master's level degree programs in early childhood studies exist in most states.

Look for harmony. When there is discord at a center, the children feel it. Remember, young children can read the energy of the adults around them, and they respond to what they sense. Centers that encourage cooperation—between children and staff members—model the value of teamwork. Look for regularly scheduled staff meetings, in-house communication tools, and camaraderie among staff members.*

Is there a written discipline policy? In what manner are problems handled? Are there texts on discipline recommended by the center? Are regular parenting classes or programs available? Ask what teachers do about a child who hits, bites, or grabs toys. Find out if teachers receive training in how to deal with problems that arise.

Does the center condone spanking? Many states still allow corporal punishment or exempt some programs, especially church-based ones, from bans on corporal punishment. This is extremely important, especially in these vulnerable early years. Even if you approve of spanking (and by now you know we do not), please be aware of the extra fragility of very young children. Shaking a baby can lead to death, and an adult's strength can turn an intended swat from mild to bone-cracking in a heartbeat.

---

* For more information on childcare, staff, and discipline, see *Positive Discipline for Childcare Providers,* by Jane Nelsen and Cheryl Erwin (Harmony, 2010).

Is the attitude at the center positive or punitive? Are children being shown what to do, or repeatedly reprimanded about what not to do? It is important to find childcare where discipline is neither punitive nor permissive. Trained childcare staff know how to deal with problems in a kind and firm manner that also teaches valuable life skills such as cooperation, problem solving, and language. (Remember, children do not yet know *which* words they need, so the willingness to coach children in verbalizing and resolving problems is important.)

Watch how teachers talk with children:

- Does the teacher get down to the child's eye level when talking to him, or do teachers yell instructions across the room?

- Do teachers speak to children in a respectful way? Do they engage in conversation with the children, or are their comments merely functional ("Put away the toys," "Sit down," or "Clean up your snack mess")?

- Are boundaries made clear, or does a teacher giggle uncomfortably when children run up and slam into her?

- Do teachers follow through? For instance, does a teacher call out to a child "Put down that stick!" and then proceed to chat with a coworker while the child brandishes the stick overhead? Or does the teacher walk over and calmly remove the stick after giving the child a moment or two to put it down himself?

- Are the teachers focused on the children, or do they spend their time talking with each other?

The best childcare emphasizes respect, kindness and firmness, and encouragement—just as you do at home.

CURRICULUM

There is a growing tendency for parents to seek childcare centers that offer academics such as reading, writing, and arithmetic. This is of concern to many early childhood experts, and you should know why.

Kathryn Hirsh-Pasek, Ph.D., director of the Temple University Infant Language Laboratory and coauthor of *Einstein Never Used Flash Cards: How Children Really Learn—and Why They Need to Play More and Memorize Less,* conducted a research project in which 120 four-year-olds in a middle-class Philadelphia suburb were followed as they progressed through kindergarten and first grade. The research confirmed that the children who attended academic preschools did know more numbers and letters than the children who went to play-oriented preschools. By age five, however, the kids from the play-oriented preschools had caught up, while those who had attended academic preschools felt less positive about school.

It is wise to pay attention to the presence of screens in any home or program you consider for your child's care. Children need unhurried, child-directed time to play and talk with caring adults. Rows of computers and televisions may prompt you to ask whether this setting favors screen time over human interaction. You can then decide based on what you believe is most important.

Be wary of pushing your child to learn academic and technological skills too early. The key is to follow your child's interests. It is unlikely that you are pushing if your child is asking to learn. Some three-year-olds find counting or using a pencil interesting. Some may teach themselves to read, or beg to play the violin.

Regardless of the setting or curriculum, be sure there are lots of hands-on experiences. Look for children pouring equal amounts of water into two matching cups rather than coloring a graph of a circle divided in two. Make sure children have lots of objects to count, instead of merely tracing numbers on worksheets. And, of course, look for ways that nature is included in the curriculum and environment.

CONSISTENCY

Consistency in the curriculum means that certain activities are provided regularly. Show-and-tell, daily story time, and singing are examples. Children thrive on routine at their care facility as well as at home. Consistency also means that learning objectives exist and are implemented. Contrast a well-defined program to a place where children are given some old egg cartons to cut up, plopped down in front of the same container of blocks every morning, or left to watch endless videos and television programs. In the context of a clear curriculum, some of these activities may be fine. Just be sure that the program values hands-on learning, healthy activity, and developmental growth—not just silence and obedience.

Is there consistency from teacher to teacher or class to class in the way problems are handled? Does one teacher refuse to allow children to help prepare snacks while another turns snack time into a yogurt finger-painting free-for-all?

Centers with consistent programs encourage children to develop trust, initiative, and a healthy sense of autonomy. If these tasks are important at home, they must also be important where your child will spend so much of his time. Consistency begins with center management.

In addition, you should examine the way a childcare facility operates on a daily basis. Here are some questions to consider:

- Are expectations of the children, the staff, and the parents made clear?

- Are events well-organized?

- Do finances get handled in a businesslike manner?

SAFETY

Safety includes the physical setting, the program health policies, and the emergency preparedness of the center. A program with exposed electrical cords, unimpeded access to a laundry cupboard, or broken-down play equipment does not provide an environment safe for little ones. Leaving your child in the care of other people each day requires faith *and* vigilance.

Watching a teacher wipe down the changing table with bleach solution after every diaper change reassures Keith that his son will not be exposed to dangerous bacteria. Seeing the center staff load the blocks into the dishwasher each evening gives Marnie peace of mind when she sees her toddler handling those same blocks the following morning. Kenneth and Robert visit their daughter's center and see the staff and children participating in a fire drill. They are impressed with the level of competence shown at the center—and it gets them thinking about the need to develop their own emergency plan at home.

Find out if staff members have current CPR and first-aid training and HIV/AIDS training. Under what conditions will sick children be sent home? Look for fire safety procedures and earthquake or other emergency preparedness. (Like Kenneth and Robert, you may decide you want to acquire these skills yourself.) Ask how injuries are handled. Reassure yourself that the adults in this place know how to care for your child under a variety of circumstances.

TRUST YOURSELF—AND GET INVOLVED!

Only you can decide what your needs as a family really are. If you decide there is a need for outside care, use the guidelines listed above to find the best possible place to entrust with the care of your little one. Take time to visit a program. That is the only way you can see if they practice what they preach, and the only way you can observe how comfortable your child is in the environment. Give your child time to

make connections.* Of course, many children cling to their parents in a strange environment and do fine when their parents leave, but an extended visit lets you know how your child will be treated. Be sure to stay involved and tuned in; if at all possible, make occasional visits to the childcare center to reassure yourself that all is well.

No center or staff is ever perfect. If there are changes or improvements you would like to see made at your center, work toward bringing them about, support your program's efforts, and recognize the caregivers as a valuable extended family, part of your child-rearing team. You might even offer the director or caregiver a copy of this book, or volunteer to begin a Positive Discipline parenting group.

Above all, give up your guilt button. Whether you care for your infant or toddler at home or entrust her to a center, you are likely to have some mixed emotions. Pay attention, make choices as wisely as you can, then relax and trust your choices. All children will inherit this earth—no matter where they took their naps, got cuddled, or first discovered *Curious George*. Knowledge and awareness will help you give your children everything they need during their important first three years of life.

QUESTIONS TO PONDER

1. Make a copy of the Childcare Checklist provided in this chapter.
2. Bring it with you when you visit programs and use it to guide your questions and observations.
3. Come up with a similar checklist for finding caregivers for other group events, such as a church Sunday school, summer play-

---

* *Love, Longing, L'Inserimento,* a reprint from Roslyn Duffy's "From a Parent's Perspective" column, addresses this connection (www.childcareexchange.com).

group, or special event (birthday, wedding, or other party). Create a checklist for choosing a babysitter. Share these lists with your friends; offer feedback to one another and improve upon them as you see fit.

4. Do some journaling about your own feelings toward childcare or being a stay-at-home parent. Are you comfortable and confident about the decisions you've made? Do you feel guilty for leaving your child in care? For staying home and not working? How might resolving your own feelings improve your child's experience?

20

IF YOUR CHILD HAS
SPECIAL NEEDS

Every new parent counts toes and fingers, compares his child's development with others, and worries about anything that seems unexpected. **If you have concerns about your child's growth or development, you should take them seriously and ask your pediatrician or community health nurse to check them out.** Early identification and intervention are the best tools for supporting a child who has special needs.

Rosemary noticed that her four-month-old daughter, Angela, did not wave at her crib mobile the way her friend's son did. She also thought that Angela seemed to turn her eyes inward at times. At first Rosemary told herself she was imagining things. Then she decided to have Angela's eyes checked at the local clinic, just for her own peace of mind. Rosemary doubted that it was possible to treat an infant's eyes, but to her surprise, Angela was diagnosed with strabismus, or crossed eyes, and within two weeks was fitted with special, tiny eyeglasses.

This early intervention probably saved Angela's vision. Untreated crossed eyes can result in a loss of vision in one of the eyes, but early intervention solved the problem. Angela, now in grade school, sees beautifully and no longer needs glasses of any kind. Other parents have discovered (after having the courage to insist on more thorough medical checkups) that what might have been dismissed as "colic" was in fact severe pain in the ears that could be corrected. One mother found that her infant stopped crying when she stopped putting him to bed in "footed" pajamas. As he grew older, it became apparent that he had sensory processing disorder, a condition that interferes with the brain's ability to integrate information from the senses and often leads to communication and behavioral problems; he benefited a great deal from occupational therapy.

Sharing the Attention

Q: I have three boys. My oldest turns six in March, the next will be four in February, and my youngest just turned two. The oldest and youngest of my boys are profoundly deaf. My problem, however, lies with my middle child. He is a very bright child who has been sandwiched between two siblings who require special attention. As a result, he has taken on responsibilities beyond his age. In the last month, however, he has become defiant. He whines all the time when he doesn't get his way, and he has become somewhat withdrawn. I have racked my brain trying to find out what is different in our lives or daily routines, or anything that would account for this change. I know he receives a different type of attention than his brothers, but he does not receive any less attention. Is there something I'm missing? Do you have any suggestions? Or is this just a phase, and it, too, shall pass? Please, any ideas would be greatly appreciated.

A: It takes a great deal of patience and sensitivity to raise children with special needs, particularly when you have more than one. Children are wonderful perceivers (they notice everything) but they are not good interpreters, and often believe that the special therapies, doctor appointments, and treatment that their special-needs siblings receive indicate more parental love and attention. Attention isn't just a matter of quantity—it's a matter of the *beliefs* that children form about how much they (and their siblings) receive, and what that tells them about their own place in the family.

While children develop at different paces emotionally as well as physically, three- and four-year-olds are often experimenting with what we call "initiative"—forming their own plans, wanting to do things their own way, and, occasionally, practicing by becoming defiant or whining.

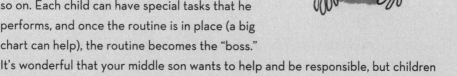

Some of this will indeed pass, but here are some suggestions to try in the meantime:

- **Routines.** If you don't already have them, create routines for morning, evening, off to school, and so on. Each child can have special tasks that he performs, and once the routine is in place (a big chart can help), the routine becomes the "boss." It's wonderful that your middle son wants to help and be responsible, but children sometimes make themselves overresponsible in an effort to earn love and belonging.

- **Relief.** Because your son is bright and all children are naturally egocentric at that age, he may feel responsible somehow for being the only hearing child in his family; he may actually feel guilty for being able to hear, without being able to understand or express that feeling. Make sure he knows it's okay just to be a kid, and that his brothers' deafness is not about him.

- **Connection.** It may help to set aside special time with each child, time that you spend just with him. This doesn't mean spending money or huge chunks of time—fifteen minutes to go for a walk, throw a ball, or read a story is usually all it takes. One dad used bath time as his chance to sit and visit with each of his twin sons, one at a time. During your special time, ask your middle son to share his happiest and saddest times of the day; be prepared to listen well and to share your own. The keys to his behavior lie in what he believes about himself and his place in the family. Let each child know how much you value this time with him, and be sure you set aside time in your busy week for special moments to happen.

Many special needs can be discovered by thorough medical exams or when parents ask questions about what they notice. (And sometimes babies *do* have colic that just takes time to outgrow.)*

Speech, hearing, and vision problems are all common in young children. These problems can and should be treated as soon as possible. A child with frequent ear infections does not hear sounds consistently and his developing speech patterns may suffer. If you are unable to understand a child at all by the age of two and a half, consider getting a speech evaluation from a qualified speech therapist. Early speech therapy often provides excellent results.

> *The teachers at Aaron's preschool were frustrated. He did not seem to listen to them at all. One day his teacher tried an experiment. She stood behind Aaron, out of sight, and rang a small bell. All the other children turned in her direction. Aaron did not. Then she whispered his name. Again there was no response. The teacher urged Aaron's mom to seek a hearing evaluation. As it turned out, Aaron had a partial hearing impairment. He received treatment, and his teachers learned to make eye contact before speaking to him. Not surprisingly, his behavior improved at once.*

Remember, an advantage of early education programs for young children is routine screenings by public health nurses or other community or school personnel. These can identify problems that might otherwise go unnoticed. Whatever the concern, parents need to trust their own instincts and seek help when worried about a child's health or development. The possibility of their child having special needs frightens most parents, but early diagnosis and intervention will give you confidence that you are doing everything your child needs to grow and learn.

---

* For more information, see *Positive Discipline for Children with Special Needs,* by Jane Nelsen, Steven Foster, and Arlene Raphael (New York: Three Rivers Press, 2012).

Abuse Awareness

Jennifer was three when she began having problems at childcare. She bit and hit children and adults, yelled and disrupted group times, and ran away instead of coming inside from the play yard when asked to do so. Her caregivers used positive time-outs, were kind and firm, and tried to gain her cooperation by allowing her to climb and run in the play yard for longer periods of time. They met with her mother and asked if the same problems were occurring at home. Her mother said they were. Jennifer's behavior continued to worsen, both at school and at home. It wasn't until her mother consulted a counselor that the possibility of sexual abuse by a family member surfaced. Child Protective Services was contacted, the person suspected of the abuse was identified, and contact with him stopped. Over time, with counseling and support, Jennifer became calmer and her behavior gradually improved.

Clearly, not every child who has behavior problems is a victim of abuse. As scary as the possibility of abuse is—and it is very scary—adults are the only ones who can protect vulnerable children. Be sure you stay connected to your child and take her behavior seriously. Always ask for help if you need it.

If your child has a special need, be aware that respectful, encouraging Positive Discipline skills will be extremely helpful in coping with the challenges you may face together. Eating, sleep, social skills, and the development of capability all can be quite different for a child with special needs. Build a strong support network, ask for help when you need it, trust your wisdom and common sense, and encourage your child to do as much for herself as she can. These tools will help you and your child develop a sense of capability and confidence.

CRISIS SITUATIONS

Crises and emergencies can come about at any time. Floods, fire, hurricanes, violence, terrorism, and even war strike unexpectedly and can cause anxiety and stress for adults and children alike. Still, even in terrible circumstances, children can find comfort if parents and caregivers focus on creating a sense of belonging, and on monitoring their environment. Establishing routines, limiting media exposure, and offering calm and loving reassurance can make all the difference.

MEETING THE NEEDS OF CAREGIVERS

In order to be calm and loving during difficult times, you must take care of yourself. Take whatever steps are needed to address the situation. Once you ensure that children are safe, seek help for yourself. Work on your own coping skills. Allow yourself time to process your

Caregiving in a Crisis

Caregivers are able to provide important support in crisis situations. Whether the trauma results from a medical procedure, family changes, or an outside event, here are some suggestions for parents or caregivers that may be helpful:

- **Hands On:** Providing art supplies for drawing or clay to shape and squeeze may offer a way for a child to process what has happened, and to release tension.
- **Empowerment:** It is important to give children the means to make a contribution, if possible. This can be as simple as helping to carry bottles of water or snacks to others or holding a packaged bandage to hand to a nurse. Doing something to help others diminishes a child's feelings of helplessness and increases coping skills and resilience.

feelings. Take time to cry. This is true for all caregivers, as well as for parents.

Accept a child's feelings, too. Do not try to reason these feelings away. Resilience develops as a result of dealing with adversity—not evading it. You can do what is required, find the strength and support you need, and increase the chances you and your child will survive this difficult time.

No matter what special circumstances your child may face, he will always need a sense of belonging and self-worth, the opportunity to make a contribution to those around him, and compassionate connection with caring adults.

QUESTIONS TO PONDER

1. If you have concerns about a child's development, write them down. Wait a week or two and look at what you have written. Do you still feel concerned about what you have written? If so, schedule an appointment with your pediatrician or childcare provider to discuss your concerns.
2. If your child has been diagnosed with a special need, how does that change the way you see your relationship with him? How will you care for yourself so you can provide the support and services your child will need?

GROWING AS A FAMILY

Finding Support, Resources, and Sanity

No matter how sweet-tempered your new baby, and no matter how delighted you are to be a parent, these first months and years can be challenging. Parents staying at home with a new baby often find that the job isn't exactly what they expected. Long nights punctuated by endless feedings and diaper changes can numb even the most devoted mom or dad. Your partner may find blow-by-blow descriptions of your baby's bowel movements enthralling, but many people will not. After a while, most parents long for a real adult conversation, a movie, or an hour or two of solitude.

Many parents of young children are tempted to blurt out, "Talk to me!" to anyone who wanders by, and with good reason. It is essential for new parents to seek out support through the early weeks and months of parenting. Connection with other adults nourishes new parents and, through them, their children and families.

LEARNING FROM THE WISDOM OF OTHERS

While people seldom agree on every detail of raising infants and children, building a support network—a circle of friends who've been there—provides an invaluable source of information about raising and living with children. Make an effort to build relationships with folks who have children the same age as yours, or who have recently experienced the stage your child is going through. Don't be afraid to ask lots of questions. Finding out that other people's children have done the same strange or appalling things that your child does can help you relax.

Options include church- or community-based parent and child groups, parenting classes, La Leche League, online support groups or other social media connections, and friendships with other parents.* One successful model is PEPS (the Program for Early Parent Support), a community-based program that began in the Pacific Northwest. PEPS groups form right after a baby's birth and consist of people whose babies are born within days or weeks of one another. These families meet regularly in each other's homes or in family centers. There is also a special program for teen parents. The goal is to reduce isolation and create a network of support, resources, and encouragement.† Another popular group is Mothers of Preschoolers,‡ which offers get-togethers and parenting support through neighborhood churches. You may be able to search online for similar programs in your area. If there are none, consider initiating one of your own. Consult your pediatrician, too. Family doctors see and hear a great deal as they go about the business of helping young patients and parents. They can often provide support as well as practical information and advice.

Some parents have started "book study groups," where they get together and take turns discussing the concepts in this and other

---

* Check out the Positive Discipline online community (www.positivediscipline.ning .com) for support, workshops in your area, and answers to your questions.

† PEPS can be contacted at www.pepsgroup.org.

‡ Mothers of Preschoolers: www.mops.org.

Positive Discipline books and work together on how to use Positive Discipline tools. Many parents and caregivers have also attended "Teaching Parenting the Positive Discipline Way" workshops so they could learn to facilitate parenting classes, knowing that teaching (and having the courage to be imperfect) is the best way to learn.* For caregivers, Exchange Press offers many excellent resources, including parenting and teaching support and international connections.†

Still, there's nothing like real, live people. If you can, find a parenting group for parents of young children. Perhaps your parenting group, with dinner out beforehand, can be part of a night out with your partner. However you arrange it, having a sympathetic group with whom to discuss problems, ask questions, and explore the mysteries of raising young children can make all the difference in the world.

No matter where you find support, however, remember that in the end you must decide what feels right for you and your child. ***Gather all the wisdom and advice you can, then listen to your heart before you choose what will work best for you.***

REFILLING THE PITCHER

Q: I am a young mother with three children who are younger than five years of age. They are my greatest joy and I dearly love being a mother! Lately, though, I'm really overwhelmed. My husband

---

* You can receive information about Positive Discipline directly at www.positive discipline.com or www.positivediscipline.org.

† You can also find a copy of Roslyn Duffy's *Top Ten Preschool Parenting Problems* book, a compilation of her long-running "From a Parent's Perspective" columns, on the Exchange Press website (www.childcareexchange.com).

works long hours and attends evening school. I do the housekeeping, work part-time, pay the bills, take care of business, and raise the children. They are nice, talented kids (I'm a little subjective, of course!), but they are all, more or less, what you call strong-willed children. I feel like I'm pulled in so many directions, and no matter what I do, it's never enough.

From the minute I wake up until late at night, I never get more than a minute to myself. I'm always tired and sick, and I get terrible headaches. The bottom line is that I've been losing my temper a lot lately. Then I'm even more upset because I feel so guilty. I've read so many books and magazines, and I understand and agree with Positive Discipline in theory. No offense, but usually the examples and ideas seem so far removed from my real life that it just makes me more depressed.

A: What's wrong with the picture you describe? You are not working part-time or even full-time, but overtime! The person you are not taking care of is *you*—and everyone suffers because of it. It is easy to get so busy with all of life's "shoulds" that your own needs get shoved not only to the back burner but completely off the stove. The best thing you can give to your family is a calm, rested *you*.

Consider getting a high school student to help with the housework. Be creative if money is short; perhaps you can barter something. Trade babysitting hours with someone else so you can go for a walk, take a yoga class, or get in a swim and sauna at the local Y once or twice a week. Your family will notice the difference, and of course, so will you.

Being a parent is a great deal like pouring water from a pitcher: You can only pour out so many glasses without refilling the pitcher. All too often, parents and other caregivers suddenly realize they've poured themselves dry for their children and the pitcher is empty. Effective,

Caring for Yourself

It is important to take care of yourself as well as you take care of your child. Consider the following ideas:

- Budget time wisely.
- Make lists.
- Make time for important relationships.
- Do the things you enjoy—regularly.
- Avoid overscheduling.

loving parenting takes a lot of time and energy. You can't do your best when your pitcher is empty, when you're tired, cranky, stressed-out, and overwhelmed.

How do you refill the pitcher? Taking care of yourself—filling up your pitcher before it runs dry—can take any form. If you find yourself daydreaming in a quiet moment about all the things you'd like to do, that may be a clue that you should consider ways to take care of yourself.

Budget Time Wisely

Most parents find that they must adjust their priorities after the arrival of a child. It can be extremely helpful (and quite a revelation) to keep track for a few days of exactly how you spend your time. Some activities, such as work, school, or tasks directly related to raising your children, can't be changed much. But many parents spend a great deal of time on activities that are not truly among their top priorities.

For instance, if you're often up during the night with an infant or young child, make an effort to nap when your child naps. It is tempting to fly around the house doing all that "should" get done, but cleaning the bathroom and dusting the furniture will wait for you; you'll be happier and more effective if you take a nap instead.

Time is precious and all too short when you share your life with young children; be sure you're spending the time you do have as wisely as you can.

Make Lists

In a quiet moment, list all the things you'd like to do (or wish you could get around to). Then, when your child is napping or with a caregiver, spend those precious hours working your way down your list. Be sure you include not just chores and duties but activities that nurture you, like curling up with a good book, soaking in the tub, or having a cozy telephone chat with a friend.

Another option is to make a list of no more than three or four tasks, and then do all of them. You will end the day feeling encouraged by your success. Everyone does better when they feel better.

Make Time for Important Relationships

It's amazing how therapeutic a simple cup of tea with a good friend can be, and sometimes a vigorous game of racquetball can restore a positive perspective on life. Conversation with caring adults can refresh you, especially when your world is populated with energetic little people. You and your partner may trade time watching the children so each of you has time for friends, or you may choose to

spend special time together with other couples whose company you enjoy. A "date night" out together should be on your list as well. Meeting friends at the park can give parents and children time to recharge and play together. Keeping your world wide enough to include people outside your family will help you retain your health and balance.

Do the Things You Enjoy—Regularly

It is important that you find time for the things that make you feel alive and happy, whether it's riding your bicycle, playing softball, singing with a choir, tinkering with machinery, working in the garden, or designing a quilt. Hobbies and exercise are important for your mental and emotional health, and you'll be a far more patient and effective parent if you're investing time and energy in your own well-being. Yes, finding time for these things can be a problem, and it is tempting to tell yourself, "I'll get around to that later." All too often, though, "later" never arrives. Even twenty minutes a day for something you love is a good beginning.

Here are some suggestions:

- Read a chapter of a book before getting out of bed.

- Spend fifteen minutes sketching or knitting while your child plays nearby, before beginning dinner cleanup or bedtime routines.

- Take a walk during your lunch hour or sit quietly beside a sunny window while your little one naps, rather than checking the day's e-mail.

- Take a relaxing bath before bed. Ask your partner to alternate your child's bedtime routine with you so you have time for this at least every other day.

Self-care really isn't optional, because without it, *everyone* suffers. Parents often see taking time for themselves as "selfish." Nothing could be less true. Trust us: Your children will survive without constant attention from you. In fact, they'll thrive all the more with healthy, well-supported parents. **Children sense emotional energy; exhaustion and resentment will not help your child grow, and may drain the joy out of family life for all of you.**

Avoid Overscheduling

Most parents do all they can to provide a rich and stimulating environment for their young children. After all, they're learning and developing important skills during these early years. Many young children find themselves enrolled in a surprising number of groups, often before the age of two or three. There are baby gymnastic groups and baby swim classes. There are preschools and playgroups. There are even music and educational classes for toddlers. Parents often discover that they are living in their vehicles, rushing their children from one activity to another. While these activities can be enjoyable and stimulating for a young child, it is wise to limit the number you sign up for. Researchers have noted that time for families to relax and just "hang out" together has become scarce; everyone is busy rushing off to the next important activity, and relationships suffer as a result. Mothers and fathers are irritable and tired; children have little or no time to exercise their creativity, learn to entertain themselves, or simply play. Remember, your child needs connection and time with you far more than she needs "stimulation." Time to cuddle, crawl and play on the floor together, or read a book is far more valuable than even the most exciting class.

LEARNING TO RECOGNIZE—AND MANAGE—STRESS

Clenched teeth and fists, tight muscles, headaches, a sudden desire to burst into tears or lock yourself in the bathroom—these are the symptoms of parental stress and overload, and it's important to pay attention to them. Most parents, especially first-time parents, occasionally feel overwhelmed and exhausted, and even angry or resentful. Because parents want so much to be "good" parents, they may find it difficult to discuss these troubling thoughts and feelings with others.

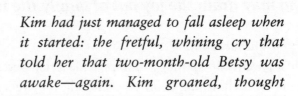

Kim had just managed to fall asleep when it started: the fretful, whining cry that told her that two-month-old Betsy was awake—again. Kim groaned, thought

briefly about burying her head under her pillow, then heaved herself out of bed. Her partner had been out of town on business for more than a week, and this was the second time tonight that Betsy had awakened. Kim was exhausted.

She stumbled into the baby's room and began her night routine without even bothering to turn on the light. Half an hour later, Betsy had been fed, changed, and burped, but she was crying more loudly than ever. Kim settled the baby in her arms and began rocking in the old rocking chair, fighting the urge to cry herself. She felt helpless, completely at the mercy of this little person who couldn't even tell her what was wrong. She hadn't had time to do the laundry in a week, the house was cluttered, and she would have given just about anything for a soothing massage. What had happened? This wasn't what she'd imagined when she was pregnant with Betsy.

Kim looked down at her daughter's face and suddenly saw not a beautiful, beloved baby, but a demanding, noisy monster who wouldn't even let her get a decent night's sleep. What Kim really wanted was to put the baby down and simply leave.

It took almost two hours, but Betsy, soothed by the steady rocking, eventually fell asleep. It took her horrified mother a lot longer to deal with the unexpectedly strong emotions the encounter had created in her.

There's a difference between a feeling and an action. It's not unusual for parents of infants and young children to be frustrated, overwhelmed, and exhausted, and most parents feel terribly guilty when they experience anger or resentment toward their children. The feelings are quite normal—but you need to be careful what you do with them.

If you find yourself wanting to snap or lash out at your child, accept those feelings as your cue to do something to care for yourself. Make sure your child is safely occupied, and take a few minutes of time-out. (It usually works better for parents than for kids anyway.) Better yet, arrange for some time to nurture yourself. Exhaustion and frustration can lead even the best parents to say and do things they later regret; it's far better to invest the time it takes to help yourself feel better. If these efforts aren't helping, or your despair deepens, seek help from a therapist or pastor. Finding help will improve life for you and your child.

EMERGENCY RELIEF

Even without depression or external crises, a parent may still feel unable to cope sometimes. Most communities offer a crisis line for immediate phone assistance. Some hospitals provide similar services; a few moments spent speaking to an understanding, reassuring adult may make a world of difference.

If you ever feel your child might be at risk, check to see if respite care is available in your community. It is not wrong or shameful to need help; it is true wisdom to ask for it.

REACH OUT AND TOUCH SOMEONE

Beth looked back at the front window, where her friend Caroline held fourteen-month-old Gregory up to wave good-bye. As she slipped behind the wheel of the minivan, Beth looked at the two good friends who shared the backseat.

"Boy, am I ready for this," she said.

Anne and Joleen laughed. "Us, too!" Joleen said. "And you'd better enjoy yourself—next week, the kids are all at your place."

Beth, Anne, Joleen, and Caroline had been sharing their "moms' day out" for about six months, and none could imagine how they'd survived without it. Each Saturday morning, one of the four women cared for the group's six children. Lunches were packed, activities were planned—and the three moms who had the day off had four blissful hours to shop, play tennis, take a walk, or just share conversation and a cup of coffee. All had felt a bit guilty at first, but they quickly learned to wave bye-bye and drive away, knowing their children were well cared for, and would be happy to have a calm, cheerful mother pick them up. Because the women were careful always to return at the designated time, no one felt taken advantage of.

Support comes packaged in different ways. Whatever works for you and wherever you find it, accept it with gratitude. **Parenting is too big a job to tackle alone.** Children and their families need a community of support. The face that community wears may be that of a familiar relative, a parenting class, good friends, or even words floating through cyberspace. The important thing is that it is there. Use it—for everyone's sake.

The truth is that parents need a sense of belonging, too—with partners, family, friends, and community. After all, you can't give your little one something you don't have. Time spent nurturing *you* will make a difference for everyone.

QUESTIONS TO PONDER

1. What do you love to do? Write down three things. Look over this list. If the list includes seemingly impossible things, such as *travel to Paris,* ask yourself what small piece of this might be possible in your current situation. Perhaps you could trade a couple of hours of babysitting with another parent, and use that time to visit a local art gallery.

2. If your list says *prepare a gourmet meal,* you might manage to make an exquisite salad dressing before bed and pour it over your box of salad bar veggies on your next lunch break. No matter

how small, finding ways to enjoy things that matter to you will help you feel better, and do better.

3. Many adults discover that it is difficult for them to seek help. If you want time to care for yourself or have a date night with your partner, whom could you ask for help? What might you offer in return?

CONCLUSION

It sometimes seems as though the first three years last forever. You live with your infant's endless parade of diapers and bottles—and, sometimes, the equally endless nights—and sometimes you can hardly wait to move on to the next stage of your child's life.

And so you enter the toddler years. You rush around childproofing your home, trying to remain calm and patient, doing your best to cope with this active, challenging little person and his occasional tantrums and misbehaviors. You collapse, exhausted, at the end of another hectic day—and you can hardly wait to get on to the next stage of your child's life.

And so it goes. Ask parents whose children are older, whose children are busy with school and friends, whose children are independent teenagers, or whose children have grown up and begun a family of their own, and they will tell you: The first three years go by too fast, far more quickly than you realize when you're in the midst of them.

In only an instant, the darling little outfits will have been outgrown, the binkies and blankies cast aside. The favorite toys will lie untouched in the closet while their formerly devoted owner busies himself with new activities and new friends. It may be incomprehensible now, but the day will come when you watch your confident, eager child run to meet his friends and find yourself longing for exactly what you have now: the sweet, cuddly baby who needs you so desperately, the busy toddler who can turn your world upside down and still capture your heart with a single glance, the child who tests your patience and perseverance one moment, then runs to hug you and plant a sticky kiss on your cheek the next.

There is a great deal to learn and remember when you're raising a young child; we've just spent an entire book exploring it all. But

if there's one lesson we (as authors, and as parents of children now well beyond their first three years) want to share with you, it is this: Cherish these moments while they are yours. Stop to wonder at the miracle of a sleeping infant, the marvel of a curious toddler, the infectious joy of an unrestrained giggle. Take a slow, deep breath and savor the joy of watching your child learn, grow, and discover his place in this world. Take lots of photographs; make time to laugh, to play, to simply enjoy. These first years will be gone before you know it.

It is our hope that in these pages you have found information you can use as you and your little one navigate these critical first months and years together. It is a vitally important time; both of you are learning a lot, and both of you will make lots of mistakes. Remember that mistakes are wonderful opportunities to learn and grow together, and that the hugs and tears that sometimes follow may actually draw you closer to those you love.

The best gifts you have to offer your children are not things they can touch, hold, or play with. In fact, they may not recognize or appreciate these gifts for years. They are, nonetheless, priceless. You can offer your children trust, dignity, and respect. You can believe in them, encourage them, and teach them. You can bestow on them the gifts of confidence, responsibility, and competence. And you can show them how to love and appreciate life by sharing it with them, every step of the way.

Learn as much as you can; ask for help when you need it. Forget about that fantasy child. Watch, listen, and learn to understand the child you have. Most important of all, have the courage to trust your own wisdom and knowledge of your child. There is no greater challenge than parenting—and no job more rewarding.

ACKNOWLEDGMENTS

WE ARE OFTEN asked, "Where do you get your stories?" We have had many opportunities to learn from parents in our parenting classes, parents and teachers attending our trainings and talks, and those we see in our counseling and coaching practices. Without them, this book could not have been written. We want to note that names and details throughout the book have been changed to protect the privacy of individuals. Some stories are composites of several children or families, which makes sense since adults and children everywhere experience common challenges. We all can learn from one another.

You might not think parenting has changed much in recent years, but we continue to learn new ways of understanding both our children and ourselves. Families, relationships, and the world around us continue to evolve, making us even more grateful for the opportunity to offer encouragement and support to new generations of parents.

We will always be grateful to Alfred Adler and Rudolf Dreikurs, the originators of the philosophy upon which Positive Discipline is based. These pioneers left a legacy that has changed the lives of thousands—including our own. We feel honored to continue their legacy by sharing their ideas with others. Much of the information in this book has been contributed to and enhanced by other Adlerian professionals as well as numerous early childhood educators and contemporary research insights. We are grateful for all of it.

We have had excellent editorial help and gratefully acknowledge Nathan Roberson, our project editor at Harmony Books. Nate is accessible, encouraging, and always open to our ideas. Our copy editor, Lawrence Krauser, did an awesome job. He made sure things were clear, made sense, and fit in context. He also brought a fresh generational eye, which is always helpful.

A special thanks to the Learning Tree Montessori Child Care for much of the background material for the chapter on finding quality childcare. Such insights helped bring deeper meaning to this work.

One extra hurrah goes to Paula Gray's artwork. Paula has devoted her talent, energy, and patience to this and several other *Positive Discipline* books, and we continue to be very grateful for her contributions.

And, oh, how we love our families. Instead of complaining about the time it takes for us to write books, they support and encourage us. They constantly demonstrate how capable they are of being self-sufficient instead of demanding. And we owe our biggest thanks to our children and grandchildren, who have provided us with personal family "laboratories." They have put up with our mistakes—and have helped us learn from those mistakes. We love them, appreciate them, and are grateful for them, always.

Although our children are grown now and busy living independent lives, we continue to love spending every moment we can with them and with the next generation, our grandchildren. May this book make the world a healthier and happier place for them, their peers, and the children they will one day care for and parent.

RESOURCES AND BIBLIOGRAPHY

SUGGESTED READING

Adler, Alfred. *Social Interest*, New Ed edition. Oxford, UK: Oneworld Pub. Ltd, 1998.

———. *What Life Could Mean to You*, New Ed edition. Oxford, UK: Oneworld Pub. Ltd, 1992.

Chess, Stella, M.D., and Alexander Thomas, M.D. *Know Your Child*. New York: Basic Books, 1987.

Dreikurs, Rudolf, and Vicki Soltz. *Children: The Challenge*. New York: Plume Books, 1991.

Duffy, Roslyn Ann. *The Top Ten Preschool Parenting Problems*. Redmond, WA: Exchange Press, 2008.

Erikson, Erik H. *Childhood and Society*. New York: Norton, 1993.

Erwin, Cheryl L. *The Everything Parent's Guide to Raising Boys: A Complete Handbook to Develop Confidence, Promote Self-Esteem, and Improve Communication*. New York: Adams Media, 2006.

Garcia, Joseph. *Sign with Your Baby: How to Communicate with Infants Before They Can Speak*. Seattle: Northlight Communications, 2002 (www.sign2me.com).

Gerber, Magda. *Dear Parent: Caring for Infants with Respect*. Los Angeles: Resources for Infant Educarers, 2002.

Gilbert, Susan. *A Field Guide to Boys and Girls*. New York: Harper Perennial, 2001.

Glenn, H. Stephen, and Michael L. Brock. *7 Strategies for Developing Capable Students*. New York: Three Rivers Press, 1998.

Glenn, H. Stephen, and Jane Nelsen. *Raising Self-Reliant Children in a Self-Indulgent World*. New York: Three Rivers Press, 2000.

Gopnik, Alison, Ph.D., Andrew N. Meltzoff, Ph.D., and Patricia K. Kuhl, Ph.D. *The Scientist in the Crib: What Early Learning Tells Us About the Mind*. New York: Harper Perennial, 2001.

Greenman, Jim, and Anne Stonehouse. *What Happened to the World: Helping Children Cope in Turbulent Times*. New South Wales, Australia: Pademelon Press, 2002.

Greenspan, Stanley I., M.D., and Serena Wieder, Ph.D. *The Child with Special Needs: Encouraging Intellectual and Emotional Growth*. Cambridge, MA: Perseus Publishing, 1998.

Harlow, Harry F. *Learning to Love*. New York, Ballantine, 1973.

Healy, Jane M. *Endangered Minds: Why Children Don't Think and What We Can Do About It*. New York: Simon & Schuster, 1990.

Hirsh-Pasek, Kathryn. *Einstein Never Used Flash Cards: How Children Really Learn— and Why They Need to Play More and Memorize Less*. New York: Rodale, 2003.

Hoban, Russell. *Bread and Jam for Frances*. New York: HarperCollins, 1993.

Kindlon, Dan, and Michael Thompson. *Raising Cain: Protecting the Emotional Life of Boys*. New York: Ballantine, 2000.

Kohn, Alfie. *Punished by Rewards*. New York: Houghton Mifflin, 1999.

Levin, Diane E. *Beyond Remote-Controlled Childhood: Teaching Young Children in the Media Age*. Washington, DC: National Association for the Education of Young Children, 2013.

Lipton, Bruce H. *The Biology of Belief*. Carlsbad, CA: Hay House, 2009.

Lott, Lynn, and Jane Nelsen. *Teaching Parenting the Positive Discipline Way: A Manual for Parent Education Groups*. Lehi, UT: Empowering People (www.empoweringpeople.com).

Nelsen, Jane. *Positive Time-Out and Over 50 Ways to Avoid Power Struggles in the Home and the Classroom*. New York: Three Rivers Press, 1999.

———. *Serenity: Eliminating Stress and Finding Joy and Peace in Life and Relationships*. Lehi, UT: Empowering People, 2005. E-book available at www.positivediscipline.com.

Nelsen, Jane, and Kelly Bartlett. *Help! My Child Is Addicted to Screens (Yikes! So Am I): Positive Discipline Tools for Managing Family Screen Time*. E-book available at www.positivediscipline.com.

Nelsen, Jane, and Cheryl Erwin. *Parents Who Love Too Much*. New York: Three Rivers Press, 2000.

———. *Positive Discipline for Childcare Providers*. New York: Three Rivers Press, 2002.

———. *Positive Discipline for Stepfamilies*. Lehi, UT: Empowering People, 2005. E-book available at www.positivediscipline.com.

Nelsen, Jane, Cheryl Erwin, and Carol Delzer. *Positive Discipline for Single Parents,* 2nd edition. New York: Three Rivers Press, 1999.

Nelsen, Jane, Cheryl Erwin, and Roslyn Duffy. *Positive Discipline for Preschoolers,* 3rd edition. New York: Three Rivers Press, 2006.

Nelsen, Jane, Linda Escobar, Kate Ortolano, Roslyn Duffy, and Deborah Owens-Sohocki. *Positive Discipline: A Teacher's A–Z Guide*. New York: Three Rivers Press, 2001.

Nelsen, Jane, Steven Foster, and Arlene Raphael. *Positive Discipline for Children with Special Needs*. New York: Three Rivers Press, 2012.

Nelsen, Jane, Mary L. Hughes, and Michael Brock. *Positive Discipline for Christian Families*. Lehi, UT: Positive Discipline, 2005. E-book available at www.positivediscipline.com.

Nelsen, Jane, Riki Intner, and Lynn Lott. *Positive Discipline for Parents in Recovery*. Lehi, UT: Empowering People, 2005. E-book available at www.positivediscipline.com.

Nelsen, Jane, and Lisa Larson. *Positive Discipline for Working Parents*. New York: Three Rivers Press, 2003.

Nelsen, Jane, and Lynn Lott. *Positive Discipline for Teenagers,* revised 3rd edition. New York: Three Rivers Press, 2012.

———. *Positive Discipline in the Classroom: A Teacher's Guide*. Lehi, UT: Empowering People (www.empoweringpeople.com).

Nelsen, Jane, Lynn Lott, and H. S. Glenn. *Positive Discipline A–Z,* 3rd edition. New York: Three Rivers Press, 2007.

———. *Positive Discipline in the Classroom,* 3rd edition. New York: Three Rivers Press, 2000.

Nelsen, Jane, Ashlee Wilkinson, and Bill Schorr. *Jared's Cool-Out Space*. Available at www.positivediscipline.com.

Pelo, Ann. *The Goodness of Rain*. Redmond, WA: Exchange Press, 2013.

Piaget, Jean. *The Origins of Intelligence in Children*. New York: International Universities Press, 1952.

Sammons, William, and T. Berry Brazelton. *The Self-Calmed Baby*. New York: St. Martin's Press, 1991.

Schiller, Pam. "Early Brain Development Research Review and Update," in *Exchange* magazine, Nov./Dec. 2010 (www.childcareexchange.com/library).

Shore, Rima. *Rethinking the Brain: Research and Implications of Brain Development in Young Children*. New York: Families and Work Institute, 1997.

Siegel, Daniel J., M.D., and Tina Payne Bryson, Ph.D. *The Whole-Brain Child: 12 Revolutionary Strategies to Nurture Your Child's Developing Mind*. New York: Delacorte Press, 2011.

Siegel, Daniel J., M.D., and Mary Hartzell, M.Ed. *Parenting from the Inside Out: How a Deeper Self-Understanding Can Help You Raise Children Who Thrive*. New York: Tarcher Putnam, 2003.

Singer, Dorothy G., and Tracey A. Revenson. *A Piaget Primer: How a Child Thinks*. New York: Plume, 1996.

Summers, Susan Janko, and Rachel Chazan-Cohen, eds. *Understanding Early Childhood Mental Health: A Practical Guide for Professionals*. Baltimore: Brookes Publishing, 2012.

Zentner, Marcel, and John E. Bates. "Child Temperament: An Integrative Review of Research, Programs, and Concepts," in *European Journal of Developmental Science*, vol. 2, no. 1/2, 2008.

ADDITIONAL RESOURCES

CCFC: *Campaign for a Commercial-Free Childhood*, c/o Judge Baker Children's Center, 53 Parker Hill Avenue, Boston, MA 02120–3225. Ongoing information available at www.commercialfreechildhood.org.

For free downloadable, month-by-month or annual milestone checklists, go to: www.cdc.gov/ncbddd/actearly/milestones. These checklists also include warning signs of behaviors that should be assessed.

Circle of Security. www.circleofsecurity.net.

Duffy, Roslyn Ann. "From a Parent's Perspective," bimonthly column in *Exchange* magazine (Exchange Press, Redmond, WA 98073-3249, 800-221-2864).

Information for parents and childcare programs at www.childcareexchange
.com.

Early Moments Matter: Small Steps, Long-Lasting Effects, a handbook and DVD
produced in collaboration with the PBS television series *This Emotional Life*
(www.pbs.org/thisemotionallife).

Frieden, Wayne S., and Marie Hartwell Walker. *Family Songs.* Available as
downloadable MP3 files at www.positivediscipline.com.

Guys Read. www.guysread.com

La Leche League. 1400 N. Meacham Road, Schaumburg, IL 60173-4808, 847-519-
7730. www.lalecheleague.org.

Mothers of Preschoolers. www.mops.org.

Parents Action for Children. www.parentsaction.org.

PEPS: Program for Early Parent Support. www.pepsgroup.org.

Positive Discipline information:
www.positivediscipline.org (for information about the nonprofit Positive
Discipline Association and its workshops and training)
www.positivediscipline.com (for books, other products, and helpful information)
www.positivediscipline.ning.com (a free online community of parents, teachers,
and professionals who are using Positive Discipline)

Sensory Processing Disorder Foundation: www.spdfoundation.net.

TRUCE: Teachers Resisting Unhealthy Children's Entertainment. P.O. Box 441261,
West Somerville, MA 02144. More information at www.truceteachers.org.

Zero to Three: National Center for Infants, Toddlers, and Families. www.zerotothree
.org.

INDEX

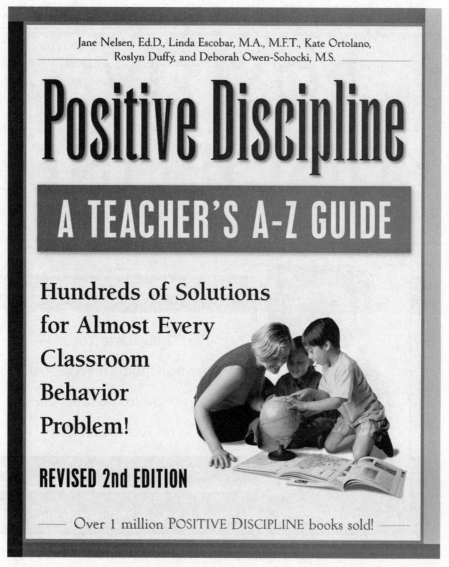

Completely Revised and Expanded 3rd Edition

POSITIVE DISCIPLINE

FOR PRESCHOOLERS

For Their Early Years—
Raising Children Who Are
Responsible, Respectful,
and Resourceful

JANE NELSEN, ED.D., CHERYL ERWIN, M.A., AND ROSLYN ANN DUFFY

Positive Discipline for Preschoolers
Proven methods to raise children who are responsible, respectful, and resourceful.

Now Available Wherever Books Are Sold

HARMONY
BOOKS · NEW YORK

Jane Nelsen, Ed.D., and Cheryl Erwin, M.A.

Positive Discipline

FOR CHILDCARE PROVIDERS

A Practical and
Effective Plan for
Every Preschool
and Daycare
Program

Over 1 million POSITIVE DISCIPLINE books sold!

Positive Discipline for Childcare Providers
A thorough, practical program that is easily adaptable to
any childcare or preschool situation and setting.

Now Available Wherever Books Are Sold

HARMONY
BOOKS · NEW YORK

Revised 3rd Edition

POSITIVE DISCIPLINE

FOR TEENAGERS

Empowering Your
Teens and Yourself
Through Kind and
Firm Parenting

JANE NELSEN, ED.D., AND LYNN LOTT, M.A., M.F.T.

Positive Discipline for Teenagers
Break the destructive cycle of guilt and blame, and work toward greater
understanding and communication with the adolescents in your life.

Now Available Wherever Books Are Sold

HARMONY

BOOKS • NEW YORK

POSITIVE DISCIPLINE

FOR CHILDREN WITH SPECIAL NEEDS

Raising and Teaching
All Children to Become
Resilient, Responsible,
and Respectful

JANE NELSEN, ED.D., STEVEN FOSTER, AND ARLENE RAPHAEL

Positive Discipline for Children with Special Needs
A positive approach to helping children with special needs realize their potential.

Now Available Wherever Books Are Sold

HARMONY
BOOKS · NEW YORK

Revised and Expanded 4th Edition

POSITIVE
DISCIPLINE
IN THE CLASSROOM

Developing Mutual
Respect, Cooperation,
and Responsibility
in Your Classroom

JANE NELSEN, ED.D., AND LYNN LOTT, M.A.

Positive Discipline in the Classroom
Tools for developing mutual respect, cooperation, and
responsibility in your classroom.

Now Available Wherever Books Are Sold

HARMONY
BOOKS · NEW YORK